EQUITABLE SCHOOL SCHEDULING

CHERYL HIBBELN

LORI RHODES

CORWIN

CORWIN
A Sage Company

For information:

Corwin
A Sage Company
2455 Teller Road
Thousand Oaks, California 91320
(800) 233-9936
www.corwin.com

Sage Publications Ltd.
1 Oliver's Yard
55 City Road
London EC1Y 1SP
United Kingdom

Sage Publications India Pvt. Ltd.
Unit No 323-333, Third Floor, F-Block
International Trade Tower Nehru Place
New Delhi 110 019
India

Sage Publications Asia-Pacific Pte. Ltd.
18 Cross Street #10-10/11/12
China Square Central
Singapore 048423

Vice President and Editorial Director: Monica Eckman
Acquisitions Editor: Megan Bedell
Content Development Editor: Mia Rodriguez
Senior Editorial Assistant: Natalie Delpino
Production Editor: Vijaykumar
Copy Editor: Taryn Bigelow
Typesetter: TNQ Tech Pvt. Ltd.
Proofreader: Girish Sharma
Indexer: TNQ Tech Pvt. Ltd.
Cover Designer: Scott Van Atta
Marketing Manager: Melissa Duclos

Copyright © 2025 by Corwin Press, Inc.

All rights reserved. Except as permitted by U.S. copyright law, no part of this work may be reproduced or distributed in any form or by any means, or stored in a database or retrieval system, without permission in writing from the publisher.

When forms and sample documents appearing in this work are intended for reproduction, they will be marked as such. Reproduction of their use is authorized for educational use by educators, local school sites, and/or noncommercial or nonprofit entities that have purchased the book.

All third-party trademarks referenced or depicted herein are included solely for the purpose of illustration and are the property of their respective owners. Reference to these trademarks in no way indicates any relationship with, or endorsement by, the trademark owner.

Printed in the United States of America

Paperback ISBN 978-1-0719-2828-8

This book is printed on acid-free paper.

SUSTAINABLE FORESTRY INITIATIVE
Certified Sourcing
www.sfiprogram.org
SFI-01028

24 25 26 27 28 10 9 8 7 6 5 4 3 2 1

DISCLAIMER: This book may direct you to access third-party content via web links, QR codes, or other scannable technologies, which are provided for your reference by the author(s). Corwin makes no guarantee that such third-party content will be available for your use and encourages you to review the terms and conditions of such third-party content. Corwin takes no responsibility and assumes no liability for your use of any third-party content, nor does Corwin approve, sponsor, endorse, verify, or certify such third-party content.

CONTENTS

Acknowledgments — vii
About the Authors — ix
Introduction — xi

Chapter 1 The Invisible Hand of Equity — 1
    Why Scheduling Mindsets Matter — 1
    The Problem — 2
    Designing Scheduling Teams That Are Architects of Equity — 6
    Flipping the Script: Logistical Scheduling Versus Strategic Scheduling — 8
    Maintaining Focus — 10

Chapter 2 Status Quo Is Waiting Around the Corner — 13
    Shifting Traditional Scheduling Mindsets — 15
    Confronting the Status QUO — 16
    Challenging the Team MindSET — 22
    Transforming Strategically Rather Than Logistically — 25
    Working Technically and Adaptively — 26
    Looking Forward and Changing Practice — 29

Chapter 3 The Scheduling Whisperer — 33
    Using Equity Self-Assessments to Determine Gaps Between Intention and Action — 33
    Good Intentions, Inequitable Outcomes — 34
    The Four A's for Self-Assessment — 36
    Final Thoughts — 57

Chapter 4 Designing the Equitable Core as a Road Map to Potential — 59
    Using Courses to Support Talent, Not Sort It — 59
    Sorting Talent Rather Than Supporting It — 60
    Traditional Sequencing — 63

    Four Commitments for Equitable Scheduling   72
    Four Strategies for Designing Systems That Support Course Equity   74
    Proactive Monitoring to Ensure Access to the Equitable Core   77
    Final Thoughts   78

Chapter 5 Scheduling the Margins   81

    Scheduling the Margins   82
    Mindset and the Margins   83
    Dual Enrollment Staffing in the Schedule   96
    Bell Schedules and Mindset   96
    Strategies for Scheduling the Margins   99
    Barriers to Scheduling the Margins   99
    Final Thoughts   104

Chapter 6 Strategic Structures   105

    Pathways, Teams, and Cohorts, Oh My!   105
    The Effects of Being Known Well in School   107
    Making the Math Work   118
    Nine Enabling Conditions for Pathway Design   123
    Using Cohorting as a Schedule-Building Tool   126
    Additional Pathway-Building Considerations   134
    Final Thoughts   134

Chapter 7 Resource Equity   137

    The Costs of Inequitable Scheduling Practices   137
    Resource Equity   138
    Enabling Condition #1: Understanding the Relationship Between Graduation Requirements, Student Enrollment, and Site Funding   139
    Using an Allocational Tool   143
    Adjusted Teacher Minimums With Math, Science, and Pathway Strategies   151
    The Importance of Aligning Allocations Connected to Mandates   152
    Enabling Condition #2: Understanding the Alignment Between Selecting Courses, Building Sections, and Staffing the Schedule   153
    Avoiding Misaligned Course Selection Processes   154
    Avoiding Singleton Madness   156
    The Importance of the Course Tally Process   158
    Building Sections   164
    Assigning Teachers   164

Enabling Condition #3: Understanding the Impacts of Bell Schedules, Schedule Balance, and Scheduling Experience on Resource Equity	165
Bell Schedule Selection	165
Balancing the Schedule	168
How to Balance a Schedule	169
Avoiding a Bad Build	170
Additional Tools to Monitor Resource Equity	170
Final Thoughts	174

Chapter 8 Equity by Design — 175

Establishing Guiding Structures for Scheduling Teams	175
The Intentional Structuring of Time	176
Overall District and Site Scheduling Timelines	177
The Risks of Operating Without Timelines	183
The Importance of Input During Timelines	184
Final Thoughts	187

Epilogue	189
Appendix	191
Glossary	217
References	219
Index	225

Visit the companion website at
https://companion.corwin.com/courses/equitableschoolscheduling
for downloadable resources.

ACKNOWLEDGMENTS

CHERYL'S ACKNOWLEDGMENTS

Amazing women have always surrounded, protected, and inspired me. My road to scheduling equity is paved with the genius of these mentors: Dr. Janet Allen was my first teacher. Her coaching built the literacy foundation that I would transfer from teacher to principal; Cheryl Seelos (Big Cheryl) was my first mentor. Watching Cheryl navigate the adaptive and technical challenges associated with leading high school reform gave me the courage to lead with equity; Ana Diaz-Booz was my first educational ally (and loyal friend). We built a shared purpose across multiple schools that reinforced the idea that all students could learn if the school conditions were designed for that outcome. I believe that it was our willingness to argue about excellence and hold each other accountable to the highest of standards that allowed us to support the amazing staff at the Kearny Educational Complex; Dr. Suzette Lovely is my business partner and champion. She taught me the importance of building networks *before you need them*—a lesson that I will never forget; and Dr. Lori Rhodes is my coauthor and scheduling thought partner. From the moment we were connected, it was clear I had met the perfect partner for this labor of love.

I would also like to extend a special thank you to the inspiring and exceptional team of educators within the Kearny Educational Complex and the San Diego Unified School District (SDUSD) Office of School Innovation and Integrated Youth Services—I know how lucky I was to collaborate with all of you.

And to my constant companions over the years, Chili, Roxie, Avery, and Sasharoo, your unconditional love has been so appreciated.

LORI'S ACKNOWLEDGMENTS

When I started searching for a consultant to assist with scheduling in my new school district, I had no idea how fortunate I would be to be put in contact with Cheryl. From our initial conversation, we were aligned in our approach to creating equitable schedules for all students. A couple of years later, here we are with a book that started as an idea in Cheryl's mind. Throughout our time working together, I have been consistently impressed with her thoughtfulness, focus, and passion.

I have spent my entire career in the field of education, and I have benefited greatly from my experiences working alongside school teams looking to create schedules that serve all students. I am indebted to these incredible educators who are committed to deeply reflective practices and dedicated to creating a sense of belonging for all students.

I am incredibly grateful for the team at Corwin, especially Dan Alpert and Megan Bedell, for your assistance and guidance throughout this project.

I would especially like to thank my husband for being my rock. Your encouragement and support have allowed me to keep pushing myself and achieve what I only dreamed possible.

FROM LORI AND CHERYL:

Thank you to Dr. Delores Lindsey for seeing the value in this topic and making the critical introduction that propelled the work forward.

PUBLISHER'S ACKNOWLEDGMENTS

Corwin gratefully acknowledges the contributions of the following reviewers:

Brenda Fletcher
K–12 School Administrator
Jeffco Public Schools
Golden, CO

Dr. Jerry Jailall
Educational Consultant
Assistant Chief Education Officer (Inspectorate), Ministry of Education, Guyana
Georgetown, Guyana

Laura Ray
Secondary English Teacher
Jefferson County Public Schools
Arvada, CO

ABOUT THE AUTHORS

Cheryl Hibbeln is the Founder and President of IlluminatED Collective, a group of transformative educational consultants who partner with businesses, nonprofits, institutions of higher education, and school districts to support strategic planning and change management in service of equitable outcomes for all. Cheryl spent over 20 years in the San Diego Unified School District, where as a principal she was part of the successful transformation of a large urban high school into four award-winning small schools, and as an executive director who designed efforts to align the district graduation requirements to the University of California entry course requirements, expanded the dual enrollment program with the colleges, and redesigned secondary site schedule efforts. Cheryl knows what it takes to lead diverse district teams to achieve challenging systemic efforts in service of equity. In addition, Cheryl built impactful partnerships with business/industry, philanthropic, higher education, nonprofit, and cross-district leaders to design transformative experiences for students across the city of San Diego.

Cheryl's contributions to the work in San Diego Unified has been highlighted in several recent reports, including the Local Control Funding Formula Case Study, *Giving Learning & Graduation New Meaning: One Student at a Time* (University of California, Los Angeles, Center for Transformation of Schools); the *San Diego Unified School District: Positive Outliers Case Study* (Learning Policy Institute); Education Resource Strategies' Districts at Work series, *San Diego Unified School District: Building Paths to Graduation for Every Student*; and the SDUSD's *Board Select Committee on Graduation Standards and Strategies*. Cheryl holds an MA in Education from Chapman University; a BA in Literature and Writing Studies from California State University, San Marcos; and Professional Clear Administrative and Teaching Credentials from the California Commission on Teacher Credentialing. Learn more about bringing Cheryl Hibbeln to your school or district at illuminatedcollective.org.

Dr. Lori Rhodes is currently an Associate Superintendent with Stamford Public Schools in Connecticut. In her current work as a district administrator, she focuses on family and community engagement, innovative educational opportunities to provide access and opportunity for each student, principal supervision and support, and student discipline. Prior to this, Lori was an Assistant Professor of Educational Leadership, a secondary school site administrator, founding principal of a charter high school, and a bilingual (Spanish) teacher. Lori started her career almost three decades ago with the Teach for America program in Los Angeles. Her areas of expertise include scheduling, teaching English learners, using data and assessments to increase student achievement, improving school culture, and developing leaders in schools. Lori is committed to providing equitable and inclusive educational opportunities by creating a rigorous and supportive culture that results in a sense of belonging for all students.

INTRODUCTION

In *Dare to Lead*, Brene Brown (2018) states that to be unclear is to be unkind. In the field of education, this mantra is often invoked when discussing how difficult conversations must be held to create accountability and true understanding of the work that must be done to improve schools. This same principle can be applied to the process of scheduling students at the secondary level—the purpose and practice of scheduling must be clearly communicated to cultivate a shared purpose around why certain shifts must be made in traditional practices in the service of equity.

Having served as school site and district leaders as well as education consultants in a variety of contexts, we have witnessed how murky and unclear scheduling routines have led to practices that have left many students on the margins of our educational system. Writing this book allowed us to offer a clear path to creating an equitable approach to scheduling. Over the course of the following eight chapters, we hope to illustrate that the schedule should not be static and restrictive, tracking students into prescriptive pathways, but rather it should be flexible and sensitive to the learning needs of all students. Effective scheduling can and should serve as a strategy to eliminate the isolation that too often permeates our educational systems.

SCHEDULING AS A TOOL FOR EQUITY

Too often scheduling at the secondary level is the responsibility of one or two counselors and administrators who work in isolation from the central office. These staff are doing double-duty of their daily jobs and creating a complicated system where all students are scheduled, and staff have their assignments before they leave for summer break. The pressure can be enormous, and accuracy and student need may not always be the top priority. The framework and tools provided in this book will put administration and teams in control of the process to create equitable, efficient, and sustainable cycles of scheduling.

The schedule must be aligned to the values and vision of a school system that is inclusive and equitable with the aim of supporting the learning and achievement of all students. The schedule doesn't just divide the day so people know where they are supposed to be at any given time, but rather it reflects the philosophy of the leadership of a school. If a school has the goal of student-focused success outcomes, this will be evident in a strategically created schedule. The structuring of time and sequences of courses must be done with intentionality as they ultimately influence everything from how teachers collaborate, to how students move throughout the day, to what options students have following graduation. When the schedule is only viewed logistically, those for whom less is expected or provided—students of color, students with disabilities, multi-language learners, and students living below the poverty line—consistently face barriers that prevent opportunities for greater access to what they need to succeed.

MAKING EQUITABLE SCHEDULING PRACTICES ACCESSIBLE

Over the past several decades, the process of creating schedules has stayed relatively consistent, despite the availability of expansive technological platforms. This could be because policy mandates regarding graduation and university entrance requirements, teacher credential requirements, and instructional minutes have all expanded, thus complicating the nature of scheduling in large, comprehensive secondary schools. However, it is not only requirements that have increased, but also the needs of many of our students—from those with disabilities to English learners and from students with advanced academic status to those who have needs outside of the traditional academic programming—where we are falling short with our scheduling practices.

This book will provide secondary school and system leaders with tools and techniques for building transformative schedules within an individual school site or a large school system. It will support school and district teams to leverage the power of scheduling within 10-month rather than 10-year cycles. By taking stock of learning inequities and using scheduling to close equity gaps, necessary changes can be sustained over long periods of time, leading to greater academic achievement for all students.

THE INTENTION OF THE BOOK

This book is a guide to rethinking and restructuring the practice of scheduling at your secondary school and district. The goal is to provide structured opportunity for teams to do the work of considering the "why" of their scheduling practices. Using reflective questions and activities, teams can shift their mindsets and deeply consider why they do what they do and what must change for equitable scheduling practices for all students.

By considering the values, beliefs, and practices in place, teams will

- Think about the perceptions and values that define the scheduling process and reinforce the status quo.
- Think differently about what's possible in designing schedules.

- Ask the right questions and use supportive tools.
- Shift from adult-centered to student-driven scheduling design.

The vignettes we tell are based on the decades of experience we have had in real districts with real students, teachers, and administrators. Throughout our experiences, we have witnessed a large portion of scheduling teams emphatically making decisions based on what is referred to as "student need," but the needs and the metrics for success have not been clearly defined. Success could mean enjoyment of course topics, meeting graduation requirements, preparation for college, and/or preparing for the workforce, but how is this guaranteed for all students?

Understanding how the schedule can truly be a vehicle for altering how students are assigned teachers and grouped and whether or not they graduate high school prepared for their postsecondary lives, will put scheduling teams in the driver's seat when it comes to creating an equitable space for each student.

WHAT THIS BOOK IS AND HOW IT WILL HELP

Over the years, we have seen that by using schedule assessments with a focus on equity and access, schools and districts have been able to successfully shift their practices. The work does not necessarily have to be incremental or take years to see the benefits. Indeed, by thoughtfully engaging in a cycle of improvement that seeks feedback, reflection, and joint decision making, the schedule can be personalized to meet the vision and goals of every school.

Using an inclusive, collaborative, and thoughtful process to create such a schedule for all students, schools and districts will make gains by addressing the leaky pipeline and bringing students through to graduation. The opposite holds true as well: By maintaining the traditional scheduling process with the acceptance of the results of the leaky pipeline, schools and districts will continue to reinforce inequities, something we cannot afford as a society. This does not necessarily mean that creating a schedule that best meets the needs of students, equity, and equitable practices is achieved immediately. This book reinforces the idea that the schedule is a tool for equity, one that must be partnered with the work toward best instructional and truly student-centered practices.

The topics covered and strategies provided will equip readers with the confidence and know-how to dismantle the systemic inequities that exist in the intentional or unintentional structures we build within school systems. If you are a secondary school leader trying to build a schedule aligned to your vision for learning or a district leader trying to think systematically about efforts toward meaningful graduation for all, this book is for you. Over the course of eight chapters, we will examine current scheduling constraints, highlight schools and districts attempting to address these constraints, and offer concrete tools and artifacts that support teams in illuminating and addressing constraints in their unique contexts.

Each chapter begins with a vignette that will lift a scheduling issue and its impact on students. Chapters 3 through 8 focus specifically on developing the following changes in practice:

Changing Practice 1: Scheduling Teams Must Know the System to Change the System

Changing Practice 2: Scheduling Teams Must Design Core Sequences That Impact Equity

Changing Practice 3: Scheduling Teams Must Prioritize the Historically Marginalized

Changing Practice 4: Scheduling Teams Must Organize Strategically and Intentionally

Changing Practice 5: Scheduling Teams Must Understand How to Use Resources Strategically

Changing Practice 6: Scheduling Teams Must Structure Time and Input Intentionally

The following table illustrates the problems and consequences associated with scheduling that will be unpacked in each chapter.

	PROBLEM	**CONSEQUENCES**
Chapter 1	Students are not programmed consistently toward graduation.	Some students graduate with a transcript/diploma that leads to a postsecondary future and others do not.
Chapter 2	Despite scheduling data that reflect inequities, schedules continue to be built the same way each year.	Equity continues to be grounded in talk rather than action.
Chapter 3	Intentions, actions, and outcomes are not aligned and monitored in the schedule.	Despite good intentions, student group achievement gaps do not close.
Chapter 4	Access to course work is determined by perceptions about ability, prior course-taking patterns, tests, grades, and prerequisites.	Graduation outcomes continue to reflect privilege for students living above the poverty line, and White and Asian students.
Chapter 5	Scheduling decisions do not prioritize historically marginalized students.	Doing the same thing each year and expecting different outcomes is insanity. Result is continued gaps in achievement by student groups.

	PROBLEM	**CONSEQUENCES**
Chapter 6	Supportive environments are the exception not the rule.	The mindset of each school determines the scheduling "treatment" students will receive.
Chapter 7	Resource equity is not monitored in many schedules.	Classes are under-enrolled and overstaffed. The neediest students are in the largest classes with the least experienced teachers.
Chapter 8	Scheduling teams do not operate within clearly outlined timelines/roles.	Scheduling is a siloed and secretive process and/or a process delegated without oversight.

The chapters in this book tackle difficult topics to change practices around traditional scheduling processes and procedures.

Chapter 1 establishes the schedule as the invisible hand of equity, outlining the theory of action from shifting mindsets to changing practices to improving actions. Scheduling teams are introduced as Architects of Equity as practice is moved from not merely logistical but to intentionally strategic.

Chapter 2 unpacks the scheduling theory of action as it guides teams to tackle the status quo and addresses personal mindsets as a prerequisite to successfully challenging current practices. The focus shifts to the idea of addressing both the technical and adaptive needs to successfully change practices.

Chapter 3 introduces the idea that scheduling teams must know the system to change the system. The power of equity assessments as a strategy for school and system transformation is revealed by showing the gaps between current reality and the ideal state.

Chapter 4 outlines the importance of establishing an Equitable Core to most impactfully bring about equity. Revision of the course of study, articulation processes, bell schedule selection, and access to advanced studies are highlighted.

Chapter 5 teaches that by shifting practices to schedule the margins first—students most often on the edges of the scheduling process, such as English learners and students with disabilities—schools can both prioritize student needs as well as produce more efficient and effective schedules.

Chapter 6 highlights the use of pathways and cohorting for strategically and intentionally organizing the schedule to maximize resources and best practices. Learning to leverage the scheduling of teachers, counselors, and support staff is a crucial skill for transformative leaders and their scheduling teams. This chapter will share tools and techniques for organizing and supporting teaching teams.

Chapter 7 examines the costs of inequitable scheduling practices and how to use resources strategically through a system of checks and balances to ensure fiscal responsibility in scheduling.

Chapter 8 provides timelines and checklists as teams begin their 10-month cycle of equitable practices using data, goals, and assessment to shift outcomes.

Finally, the epilogue emphasizes that scheduling for equity is the beginning of the work ahead toward more equitable and inclusive practices.

GETTING THE MOST OUT OF THIS BOOK

If you want to understand a school's values and priorities, look at its schedule. Like sedimentary rocks, schedules can reveal where—and even why—gaps between student potential and opportunity emerge and where they begin to calcify. The purpose of this book is to provide site and school leaders with strategies to rethink the design of schedules in their schools and larger systems. This is crucial because every secondary school uses a schedule to enact their vision for learning each school year, yet they rarely alter the structure and simply roll schedules over year-to-year, too often reinforcing inequities. Interrupting schedule design with an equity focus is a moral imperative.

It is understood that not all books are to be read chronologically, sticking to the table of contents from first chapter to last. As tempting as it might be to rush to the end, we recommend going through each chapter in the order we have chosen. We believe that using the tools provided, both in the book and on the accompanying website as well as answering the reflective and self-assessment questions at the end of each chapter, your teams will be supported as you move to more equitable and sustainable scheduling processes.

CHAPTER 1

THE INVISIBLE HAND OF EQUITY

WHY SCHEDULING MINDSETS MATTER

The schedule should make possible the best educational program for each individual pupil.

—*Wilbur Devilbiss*

It was years after he graduated from high school, and after he became an engineer, before Terrence was finally able to articulate that something wasn't right with his math placement in high school. In ninth grade, he was assigned to a Pre-Algebra class. He didn't know why, and his parents certainly didn't have time to find out. His parents were first-generation immigrants from Haiti living in a mid-sized urban area in the Northeast, were busy holding down multiple jobs to keep food on the table, and they trusted the school to schedule their son in the classes he needed to graduate on time and with options.

Terrence was a bright student, but he often found himself bored and not particularly engaged in his classes. The work was easy for him in the Pre-Algebra class, and he was earning good grades. Over the next two years, Terrence took Algebra 1 and Geometry, both of which he passed with ease, fulfilling his state's graduation requirement.

It was his senior year when Terrence suspected he was not on a four-year college track. His college-bound friends were all in Pre-Calculus, the minimum course needed to enroll in a business program in the type of four-year college he envisioned for himself. But his counselor hadn't even recommended he take math, since he was already done with his requirements. Because Terrence's transcript courses limited his options, he gave up on what he thought was a silly fantasy anyway.

For the next couple of years, Terrence bounced around through community college and a series of minimum-wage jobs. He eventually completed his basic courses and transferred to a state school. It was a few years later when he completed his MBA that he really started to understand how deeply scheduling had affected his life. He wondered, "How could a student who was able to major in business and earn an MBA in finance be tracked into the lowest levels of math in high school?"

It's a good question, and it's why scheduling mindsets matter.

THE PROBLEM

In 1991, Asa Hilliard asked, "Do we have the *will* to educate all children?" Consider how this would be answered today. Are all students being educated with the goal of high achievement levels to be successful in today's global economy? Are schools meeting the social and emotional needs of all students considering how they experience pandemics, climate change, school shootings, racial unrest, social justice movements, social media, and so on?

To create a system in which all students achieve at high levels, learners must have access to highly qualified educators who hold high expectations. Educators must believe that each student can learn when provided an appropriate and relevant learning environment. Because this is not the current reality for all students, school leadership at all levels must take the necessary steps to reach a more ideal state. This book takes the approach that the first steps to achieve these goals can be implemented through highly structured and tightly held secondary school schedules. By confronting the status quo of how schedules are typically implemented at the secondary level and shifting scheduling team mindsets to make change, best practices in curriculum, instruction, and assessment can be implemented to produce equitable student outcomes.

Traditional conversations about high school reform have focused on the importance of shifts in instructional practices as the greatest lever for more equitable student results (Bondie et al., 2019; Chetty et al., 2014). Yet, for over one hundred years, long-held practices in education have demonstrated that a focus on curriculum, instruction, and assessment in the absence of structure does not serve all students equally (Bae, 2017; Buczala, 2010; Chenoweth, 2016; Clay et al., 2021; Pisoni & Conti, 2019). Instructional changes in the absence of structural support put in place to protect the way teachers, students, and content interact are slow at best and futile at worst. This book is grounded in the belief that powerful instructional changes must be supported by effective structures that change the way students and teachers interact meaningfully with content (City et al., 2009). The by-product of a system that has aligned structural and instructional efforts is a school-going culture focused on postsecondary success for all, as shown in Figure 1.1.

Reimagining a tightly structured schedule that prioritizes providing supports for all students is a strategy to avoid what has been described as the "Leaky Pipeline to Graduation" (see Figure 1.2). When schedules do not meet the needs of students, whether that be through targeted intervention, language

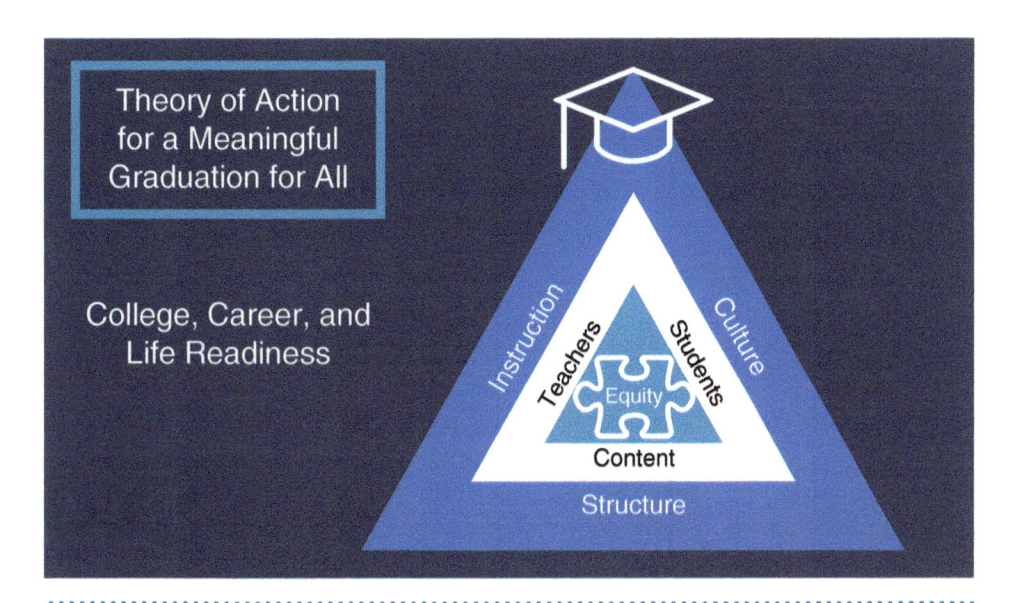

FIGURE 1.1 THEORY OF ACTION

This is a theory of action for schools that prioritize equity at the core. The triangle reflects the important balance among structure, instruction, and culture at a school site. When school leaders build structures that protect instructional strategies and allow students, teachers, and content to interact in meaningful ways, the result is a school culture where all students see themselves having a postsecondary future. School schedules act as powerful structures in this culture.

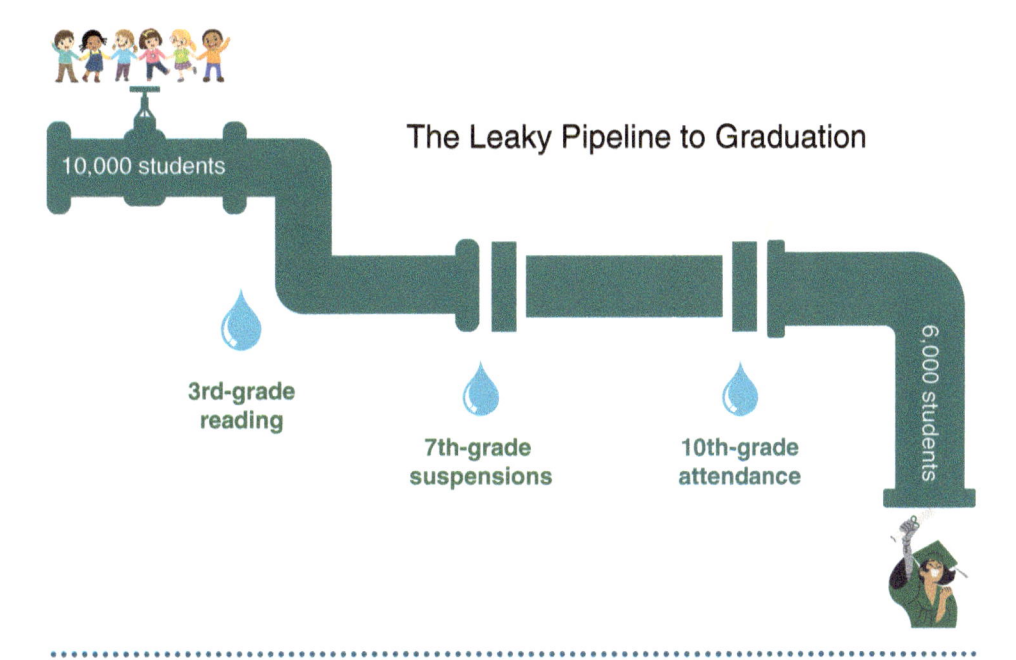

FIGURE 1.2 THE LEAKY PIPELINE

The leaky pipeline to graduation that prohibits many students from achieving their goals.

support, specialized programming, or advanced course work, the result is a pipeline from PK–12 that leaks students. The students lost are typically either not programmed to graduate on time or are denied access to the tier 1 mainstream environment through push-out strategies, and both actions are grounded deeply in mindsets about who can and can't learn.

Once students are pushed out of the tier 1 mainstream (general education) environment, it is very hard to re-enter, and historically push-out structures meet compliance regulations but don't regularly result in meeting grade-level mastery goals (Education Commission of the States, 2005; Kelly & Carbonaro, 2012; TNTP, 2018; Yonezawa et al., 2002). The result is a pipeline where students are lost and/or don't experience a meaningful graduation that leads to postsecondary success, and unfortunately these outcomes are disproportionately experienced by students of color and other marginalized student groups. Because of this, scheduling mindset shifts that lead to changing practices and improved outcomes are a moral and ethical imperative.

Why Does This Problem Exist?

Secondary school schedules dictate how students and educators move through time and space, serving as powerful levers to help school and district leaders actualize their vision for student learning. Schedules are at their best when they intentionally align physical space, personnel, and curriculum toward equitable graduation and postsecondary outcomes. According to the National Association of Secondary School Principals (2011),

> *The [Site] Schedule is to a school what grading policies are to teachers and classrooms. It reveals the true beliefs, attitudes, values, and priorities of the school. The school's [Site] Schedule is like looking at an MRI of the inner workings of a school. It is the window to the soul of the school. (p. 1)*

For over a century, scheduling in schools has been used as a sorting mechanism—a way to move students from one classroom to another, typically in isolation from each other and too often based on student age and (perceived) ability (Callahan, 1964; Education Commission of the States, 2005; Meyer, 1977; Spring, 2019). Jeannie Oakes (2005, 2008) defined student tracking as the process whereby students are divided into categories based on their perceived ability level so they can be assigned to groups. Whether this is intentional or incidental, students often find themselves placed in learning environments based on how others perceive their capabilities. Often entire demographic or socioeconomic groups are tracked whether they are college bound or not (Braddock & Slavin, 1992; Burris & Garrity, 2008; Domina et al., 2016; Grissom et al., 2015; Kettler & Hurst, 2017; Yonezawa, 2000).

Even though the goal may be to provide all students in a school with the same learning experiences, research shows that tracking is harmful to students who need more support and personalization (Domina et al., 2016; Kalogrides & Loeb, 2013; Nord et al., 2011; TNTP, 2018). These practices perpetuate the sorting of students and inequities that have existed in education for over a century. Schedules are seen as a logistical process and are routinely static from year-to-year, rolled over in a student information system or in online scheduling software with new courses pigeonholed into an already-existing structure.

Far from being an insignificant way to measure time throughout the day, school schedules matter because they represent the values and priorities of classrooms, schools, and systems. Whether it is the way a teacher organizes the daily flow of instruction, the way a high school principal organizes staff, students, courses, and periods over the school day, or the way a district-level director sequences the course of study, the policies and decisions around scheduling impact outcomes for underestimated students[1] in profound ways (Braddock & Slavin, 1992; Chetty et al., 2014; Grissom et al., 2015; Kalogrides et al., 2013; Kalogrides & Loeb, 2013; Kettler & Hurst, 2017).

Schedules have traditionally been approached logistically and in secrecy. Hidden from view, a few select staff solve a complex puzzle with the goal of balancing student "butts in seats" and providing teaching assignments that meet the "druthers" of staff. The result is that secondary schedules do the job they were designed to do—sort students toward the same predictable outcomes each year. Too often this sorting is the result of gatekeeping, which can happen at many levels and can affect students at so many points in their academic careers. The gatekeepers create sections, set prerequisites, and assign teachers—all of which can preclude and exclude certain students from classes they need to set them up for success (Clay et al., 2021).

The policies and decisions around scheduling impact outcomes for underestimated students in profound ways.

It is through the schedule that students gain access to course work, teachers, and opportunities that define the difference between graduation and a meaningful graduation. Viewed in this light, the school schedule is the invisible hand of equity. Scheduling teams that operate *without* a growth mindset are the greatest barriers to achieving educational equity. Thus, the question facing the school system at its very core is, **"How does a shift in scheduling team mindsets result in scheduling practices that produce equitable student outcomes?"**

---

[1] "Underestimated students" refers to those students who have the potential to do great things, but may not be given the opportunity to achieve to their potential for many reasons, among those being stereotypes, place of birth or residence, lack of resources, unchallenged paradigms, they don't know what they don't know, and so on (Sammy Ortiz, published in *Micro is the New Macro*, March 13, 2020).

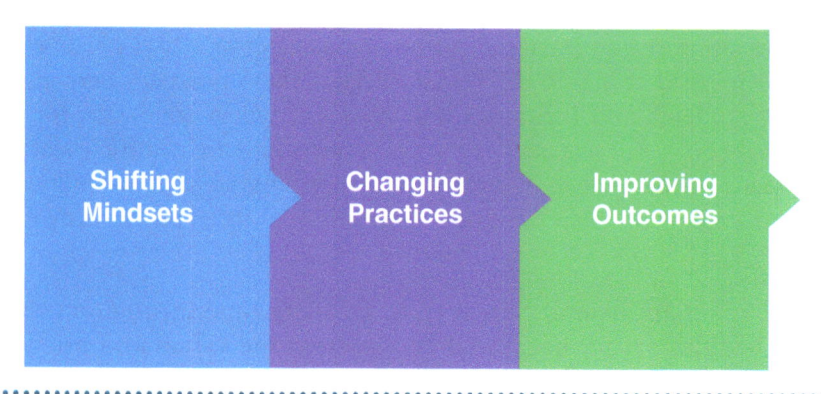

FIGURE 1.3 SCHEDULING THEORY OF ACTION
The steps of the theory of action to create a schedule with equity at its core.

Turning this essential question into a theory of action (see Figure 1.3 and chapter 2), the focus of this book is on shifting scheduling team mindsets, which leads to changed practices, and ultimately improves outcomes for all students. This book will not teach the reader the technical and logistical aspects of scheduling. There are websites and resources available for this more detailed and specialized work within the student information system (College & Career Alliance Support Network, 2018). Rather, this book will lead scheduling teams through the process of confronting the status quo to shift mindsets to employ strategic scheduling design that leads to improved outcomes for students. These scheduling teams will become the **Architects of Equity**.

DESIGNING SCHEDULING TEAMS THAT ARE ARCHITECTS OF EQUITY

> *Sometimes administrators construct schedules as if schools were created for the convenience of teachers rather than the instruction of pupils.*
>
> —*Wilbur Devilbiss*

Leithwood et al. (2004) state that leadership is second only to classroom instruction in terms of impact on student learning. Leaders must use their positions to right the wrongs of past practice with the school schedule, first by bringing together an equity-focused team with a student-centered mindset. Scheduling teams composed of a diverse cross-section of stakeholders from a school site or district can use their positions to view the schedule holistically and in support of access and opportunity for all students. These teams must prioritize equitable practices focused on eliminating tracking and sorting that typically benefit only students who are recognized as motivated, and college bound. Traditional scheduling team practices have created "agents of

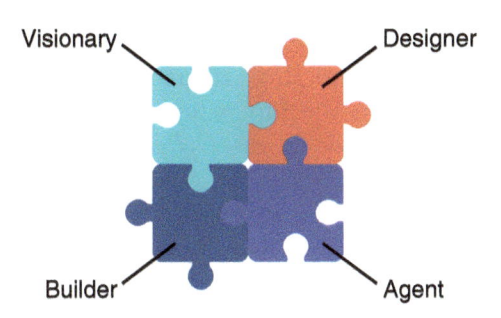

FIGURE 1.4 ARCHITECTS OF EQUITY
The four major roles involved in creating an equitable schedule.

compliance" (Clay et al., 2021), whereas scheduling teams operating with a growth mindset can be Architects of Equity.

Scheduling teams that act as Architects of Equity are composed of four important roles (see Figure 1.4). This does not mean teams are necessarily composed of only four people or that one person cannot assume more than one role, but rather that these four positions must be filled for balanced and successful collaborative scheduling practices. The work described below includes technical aspects of scheduling, but the focus is on the relational work that must be done to enact a truly inclusive and collaborative process. Ultimately, neither the technical nor the relational can occur successfully without a strategy.

The first role is that of the **visionary**, or the school leader. The schedule of a school is the site leader's road map to excellence. It is a map that is not static but is rather adjusted each year as student populations and needs ebb and flow with each new group of students. The visionary supports the scheduling team to see the connections between how fiscal and human resources for the upcoming year will support intentional structural and instructional strategies that will lead to desired student outcomes over the next 10 months. The visionary must communicate clearly and strategically how students and staff exist within the schedule to meet these goals.

The next role belongs to the **designer**. This person deeply understands the vision and knows which resources are necessary and available to enact what the school leader has communicated. The designer works with staff and community members to ensure that all students have access to the courses they need for postsecondary success. The designer is not afraid to collaborate with a broad coalition of stakeholders to create a scheduling blueprint consistent with the school's vision and desired outcomes. The designer does not see boxes, easy rollovers, or barriers, but rather manifests what the leader envisions for all students.

The **builder** is responsible for exporting the designer's blueprint into the student information system (SIS). The builder is an expert on finding creative (and legal) ways to ensure that the SIS does not become a barrier to implementing desired life-changing strategies for students. Once the builder completes a draft of the blueprint, the entire scheduling team is invited into a cycle of review to discuss any potential barriers and/or challenges that may arise due to changing factors like attendance, grades, compliance, and so forth.

Finally, the **agent** is a critical member of the scheduling team because he or she is an ongoing advocate who ensures that each student has the appropriate courses needed for a meaningful graduation. Typically, agents are the counselors in this ecosystem. They are adept at relational work, as they navigate the world between students and teachers regularly.

Architects of Equity do not work in isolation. Scheduling is a highly collaborative and interactive process between members of the scheduling team, as well as with internal and external stakeholders. It is an iterative and fluid process that includes new ideas, revisions, and epiphanies. To achieve scheduling goals focused on equitable outcomes, these four scheduling roles must develop a cadence of team accountability that is grounded in a growth mindset.

FLIPPING THE SCRIPT: LOGISTICAL SCHEDULING VERSUS STRATEGIC SCHEDULING

As students advance to secondary schools, student placement in courses becomes progressively more complex and tracked, creating intricate schedules often separating entire groups of students in large schools. These tracks are seen across such groups as English learners, students with disabilities, and advanced placement students, resulting in isolation along racial, ethnic, linguistic, and economic lines (McFarland et al., 2018; Oakes, 2005, 2008; TNTP, 2018; U.S. Department of Education, 2014). Continuing these practices and rolling over schedules are exactly the shortcuts that must be avoided if students' needs are going to be met.

Too often, schedules are determined for teacher convenience, teacher seniority, and teacher requests. Many times, excellent teachers are not equitably distributed among students and classes (Bruno et al., 2019; Chetty et al., 2014; Darling-Hammond, 2002; Goldhaber, 2023; Kalogrides et al., 2013; Levitan et al., 2022). Teachers with the most experience are typically in leadership positions and can secure the sections of courses with higher-achieving and/or older students. Luschei and Jeong (2019) found that inequitable teacher sorting and assignment patterns emerged most often with veteran teachers less likely to teach at-risk students. In lower-income and more transient neighborhoods, students are often in schools with higher teacher vacancy rates and are placed in low-track courses (Oakes, 2005, 2008). These students too often receive lower-quality instruction and have lower graduation rates (Alhadabi & Li, 2020; Chetty et al., 2014).

Logistical Scheduling (in absence of strategy)	Intentionally Strategic Scheduling
The schedule is delegated to a specific person/role.	The scheduling team is identified and developed as Architects of Equity.
The schedule is used to protect the prior year's teaching lines and courses with little analysis of the schedule's impact on outcomes.	The schedule is used to prioritize the instructional strategies and fiscal resources needed to achieve student learning goals based upon analysis of prior year impacts on student outcomes.
Enrollment projections are used to identify teachers and courses.	Enrollment projections are used to create a strategic scheduling frame grounded in desired outcomes.
The purpose of the articulation process is to choose from a menu of courses. Prerequisites exist for some courses.	The purpose of the articulation process is to ensure that students provide input in co-constructing schedules that meet meaningful graduation goals for all. Increasing course access is the vision.
Course tallies are used to build schedule sections based on numbers.	Course tallies are verified and used as input for constructing equity-achieving course enrollment patterns within the schedule.
Students/families and staff participation is passive.	Students/families and staff are actively engaged during the process.

FIGURE 1.5 LOGISTICAL VERSUS STRATEGIC SCHEDULING

What happens when logistics are prioritized over strategy when scheduling.[2]

To better serve all students, site and district leaders must consciously decide to disrupt the reality of schools upholding and participating in the structural inequalities so well documented in education. This can be done by creating schedules grounded in equitable practices. Figure 1.5 demonstrates flipping the script on traditional scheduling by prioritizing being intentionally strategic over merely being logistical.

High levels of educational attainment, including the minimum high school diploma, are correlated strongly with positive results in life, such as better overall health, higher earnings, family stability (Hahn et al., 2015; Wilson & Tanner-Smith, 2013; Zajacova & Lawrence, 2018). The schedule can be used by scheduling teams to expose students to excellent teachers and increase

---

[2]One of the authors of the book was interviewed for *About Time: Master Scheduling and Equity*, a report published by the Center for Public Research and Leadership at Columbia Law School (Clay et al., 2021). The report frames scheduling work as logistical and strategic for much of the discussion. We credit the report for contributing to our work.

academic gains through targeted sequencing of courses and student placement. By intentionally disrupting past logistical practices and strategically scheduling students to increase high school graduation rates and create a strong foundation for postsecondary college and career readiness, equity-driven schedule design creates access and opportunity for each student.

Addressing Change: The Elephant in the Room

The word *change* can mean to alter or modify, to make different in form, and to replace or exchange with something else. School site leaders are often called on to lead change while being sensitive to the many reasons why change in programs or procedures are needed and becoming more urgent. Despite the difficulties often encountered when attempting significant change in education, change seems to have become or is at least perceived to be a way of life in schools and districts, especially in a post–COVID-19 world.

In *The Principal*, Michael Fullan (2014) writes about resistance to change in schools. The fear of the unknown is not something new to humans. It is much easier to maintain the status quo since the outcome (like it or not) is known, which is more comfortable for most than what might be lost with the unknown. Often those who are most against change are the loudest in the room, and those who might be in favor of change are reluctant to express their support because they are timid or fear it will upset their colleagues. Yet, we also know that schools are not serving all students and the only way to change the outcome is to change the narrative, which means disrupting the status quo. As Fullan (2014) states, this is where it takes real courage as a leader to be a proponent of change and help others through the process.

Strong scheduling teams are needed when a school or district is considering a new schedule. The school schedule gives many people the structure and comfort needed to plan their lives, commutes, breaks, and so forth. For some, the schedule provides identity, purpose, and belonging. Acknowledging that disrupting inequity can be very scary for some people, even when it is understood that the schedule is not meeting the needs of every student in the school. This is an important step in the process, but should not be a barrier to change.

> *The only way to change the outcome is to change the narrative, which means disrupting the status quo.*

MAINTAINING FOCUS

Aligning a school's vision and mission within the schedule is the key to equity. School leadership must be supportive and creative, allowing time and space for the staff to grow into their own with the school schedule. By maintaining this focus, teacher time and assignments, and student time and course work can be arranged to serve the learning and developmental needs of all students (Bae, 2017).

The schedule is a road map that reveals the connection between a vision for learning and the human and fiscal priorities committed to those strategies (Clay et al., 2021). If some students benefit from co-requisite support, then funds must be allocated for those classes. If personalization and interdisciplinary work are critical to the mission and goals, then courses and collaborative planning must be provided. If the administration believes in equity, then the schedule and the allocation of resources will reflect the equitable distribution of resources and access.

> *The schedule is a road map that reveals the connection between a vision for learning and the human and fiscal priorities committed to those strategies.*

The way schools organize the schedule has a significant effect on how students progress through schools, what expectations have been established for different groups of students, and how much time teachers spend interacting directly with students. The collaborative, equitable scheduling process helps leadership teams avoid the typical tracking and sorting model by providing an excellent experience for each student. The traditional system has failed to provide access and opportunity for all students. Those who have been served by the traditional way of scheduling are those for whom it was designed—college-bound students who are tracked to take college preparatory courses. Only by implementing an intentional, strategic, equitable system can those historically underserved be given access to the same opportunities including career readiness courses.

The next chapter will unpack the theory of action. It will explore how the status quo serves to maintain systemic and institutional barriers to equity in educational practices, specifically through the schedule in secondary schools. A framework will be offered to support scheduling teams as they confront the status quo and get their mindsets ready to refine their personal equity lens prior to attempting technical scheduling changes.

Chapter 1 Self-Reflective Questions

Chapter 1 Individual Reflective Questions

- How does scheduling currently take place at your district/school?
- What is your role in the scheduling process?

(Continued)

(Continued)

- What is your mindset when it comes to creating the schedule?
- In what ways might you assess your values, beliefs, and assumptions about constructing the schedule?

Chapter 1 Team Reflective Questions

- How does scheduling currently take place at your district/school?
- How are responsibilities divided among the team in the scheduling process?
- What is the timeline for scheduling at your district/school?
- In what ways might you assess the team's values, beliefs, and assumptions about constructing the schedule?
- How would the team answer the following question: Is the schedule equitable for all students?

CHAPTER 2

STATUS QUO IS WAITING AROUND THE CORNER

Be brave enough to start a conversation that matters.
—Margaret Wheatley (2006)

Let us introduce you to Status Quo. If you look over the shoulder of any individual or team of individuals working to achieve equity in a traditional school system, you will find Status Quo waiting patiently for an opportunity to interrupt progress. Status Quo is a consistent figure in most efforts to dismantle inequities in the traditional school system because he exploits our fear of change and provides us the comfort of a familiart friend. To forge a new path and let Status Quo go, scheduling teams acting as Architects of Equity must refine their own mindsets before beginning the strategic work. They must ask themselves, "Have we done the inner work? Have we self-assessed our team scheduling mindset?"

Teams must examine how their current perspectives have created practices that don't produce equitable results.

Scheduling team mindsets matter because people bring who they are to the design process—their own values, beliefs, and assumptions—and these perspectives influence what the team produces (Anaissie et al., 2024). To disrupt inequities and move from being Agents of Compliance to becoming Architects of Equity, teams must examine how their current perspectives have created practices that don't produce equitable results.

There exists in education a strong pull to the status quo or what Tyack and Cuban (1995) refer to as the routines of schooling or the "grammar of schooling." Many have experienced that moment when a new idea is introduced, and someone immediately says either "We've already tried that" or

"That's not the way we do that here." While there may be many sociological reasons for this initial reaction to change, this is the perfect time to move beyond what has always been "normal" and challenge systems that perpetuate the status quo. Dismantling inequitable systems like secondary schedules requires a personal willingness to examine beliefs that lead to practices that influence system designs.

Maintaining the status quo in schools today has been framed as a desire to return to the normal of a pre-pandemic world, often for the sake of students who do not need any additional upheaval. The result is that the post-pandemic status quo has become a continuation of what has always been done—including the construction of schedules that continue to produce inequitable student outcomes.

Consider the commercials for Allstate Insurance, in which "Mayhem" is personified as a recurring character. Each of the ads follows a very similar formula. Mayhem appears wearing a suit but looking a little beaten up. He identifies the risk he is portraying before creating a disaster for an unwitting driver or homeowner. Mayhem in education is the Status Quo. He lurks around the corner, poking his head into progressive efforts to make sure traditional factory models keep moving along. Mayhem is every person who says, "That can't be done, that won't work, that's not going to change anything anyway."

This chapter provides a framework to achieve the theory of action laid out in chapter 1: To improve student outcomes, changes must be made in scheduling practices. This process begins by shifting scheduling team mindsets (see Figure 2.1).

Mayhem is every person who says, "That can't be done, that won't work, that's not going to change anything anyway."

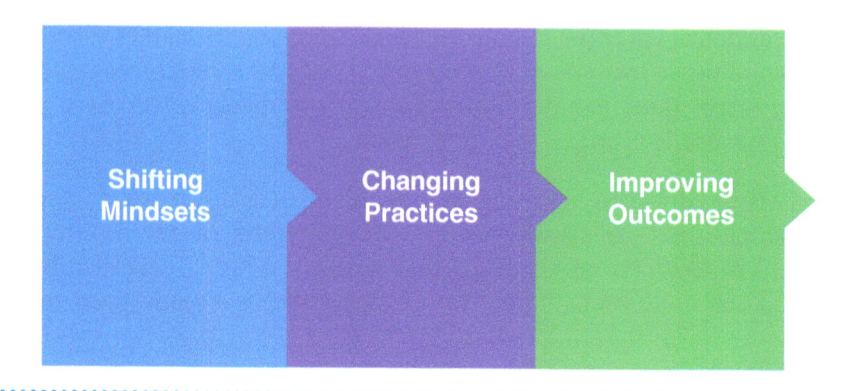

FIGURE 2.1 SCHEDULING THEORY OF ACTION
The steps of the theory of action to create a schedule with equity at its core.

SHIFTING TRADITIONAL SCHEDULING MINDSETS

Historically, policymakers as well as county and district leaders have given little focus to developing best practices for designing and implementing schedules (Bryk et al., 2006; Devilbiss, 1947; Education Commission of the States, 2005; Linderman, 1975; Sparacio, 1973). As a result, scheduling is not taught in many educational leadership programs. And yet, innovative and equitable scheduling may hold the key to higher student achievement and greater engagement with core content, arts, civics, and career pathways.

A typical scheduling cycle is driven by students selecting courses on an articulation card. Numbers are tallied, sections created, teachers' instructional lines in the schedule emerge, and finally, students are assigned their classes as they are available. Often, courses are offered based on teachers' credentials and seniority levels, and what the school can offer based on their allotted FTE (full-time equivalent) from the district.[1] Additional constraints that can impact a schedule are physical space, teacher recommendations, prerequisites, the desire for smaller class sizes in advanced placement (AP), international baccalaureate (IB), and dual enrollment classes; English learner (EL) and special education sections; and specialized programming, such as pathways and remedial classes. These factors often create a schedule that is most appealing to faculty and most supportive of students who have already been identified as college ready.

Despite the best intentions of staff, many schedules reflect resource inequalities, and too often gatekeeping results in imbalanced classes and disproportionate opportunities for all students. Socioeconomically disadvantaged and historically marginalized students are often not provided access to AP, IB, honors, and other college-level courses (Goldhaber, 2023; Kettler & Hurst, 2017; McFarland et al., 2018; Pisoni & Conti, 2019; TNTP, 2018; U.S. Department of Education, 2014). Many schools track students into remedial and low-level courses due to perceptions about readiness for more rigorous work. To make matters worse, course sections that are intended to remediate literacy and numeracy competencies are often assigned to the least experienced teachers (Bruno et al., 2019; Grissom et al., 2015; Kalogrides et al., 2013; Levitan et al., 2022; TNTP, 2018). These decisions make it difficult for students who are underestimated to graduate high school or prepare for careers. The imperative for change is immediate.

In contrast to the traditional model, schedules must be fluid documents subject to change based on students' needs and flexible enough to

---

[1] In education lingo, an FTE means one full-time teacher. Saying a person is a .4 FTE, for example, means they teach 40 percent of a full schedule. A teacher who is 1.0 FTE teaches the full contractual schedule.

accommodate new learning pathways for college and career-bound students. All of which must also support co-requisite programs for learners who may need targeted programming. Schedules should allow for a wide variety of learning levels within each classroom, so all students receive equal opportunities for achieving success. Ultimately, when done strategically, collaboratively, and equitably, scheduling should place students in the most appropriate courses with the most experienced and effective teachers who give them the most constructive support (deGregory & Sommer, 2021; Goldhaber et al., 2023; Kalogrides et al., 2013).

An equity-driven schedule is deeply grounded in the idea that inequity must be addressed at the systemic level. This is done by answering the essential question: **How do scheduling teams move from being Agents of Compliance to Architects of Equity?**

CONFRONTING THE STATUS QUO

This book will outline the steps scheduling teams must take to embark on this journey together as they seek to change past practices at their schools and districts. The first step is to confront the status QUO (see Figure 2.2). After that, teams must ensure they have the correct mindSET to accomplish the work. Finally, as Architects of Equity, teams will continually work to simultaneously address the technical and relational work of creating equitable schedules for their schools.

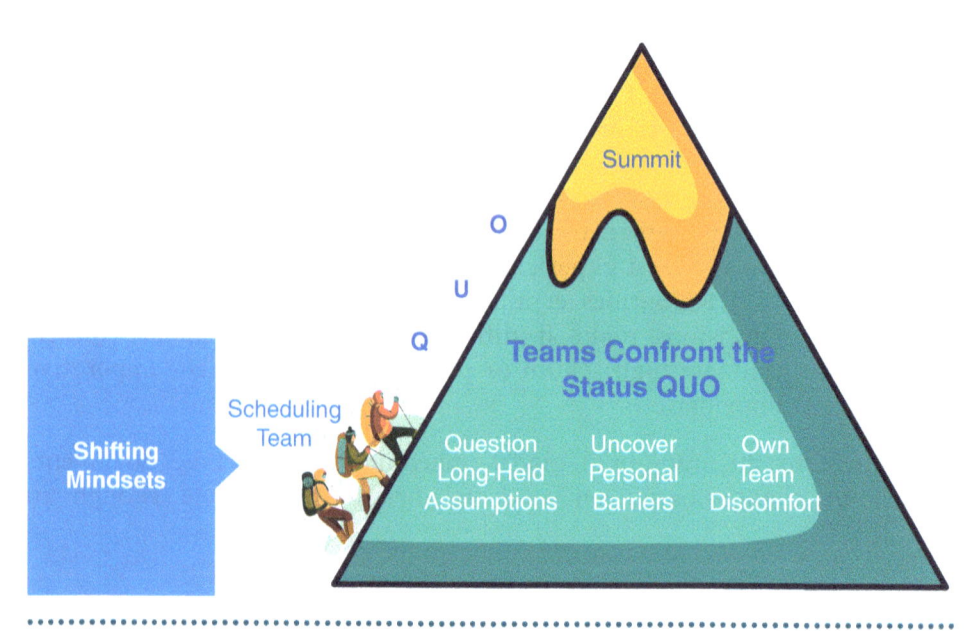

FIGURE 2.2 CONFRONTING THE STATUS QUO
Mindsets must shift to confront the status QUO in scheduling practices.

For schools to chart a new course for student success, scheduling teams must move from acting as Agents of Compliance (logistical) to Architects of Equity (strategic). Truly equity-focused teams begin by looking inward and refining their mindset prior to engaging strategically with the scheduling process. This work can be done individually, as a team, or preferably both, so that teams have time to grow and reflect on their own experiences and perspectives. Scheduling teams can start refining their mindset by cultivating a willingness to confront the status quo, with QUO defined as follows:

- Question Long-Held Assumptions
- Uncover Personal Barriers
- Own Team Discomfort

> *For schools to chart a new course for student success, scheduling teams must move from acting as Agents of Compliance (logistical) to Architects of Equity (strategic).*

Question Long-Held Assumptions

The first step toward becoming an Architect of Equity is to begin the inner work of questioning one's long-held assumptions regarding student achievement and the traditional structures in secondary schools. Since personal practices influence system designs, it is imperative for individuals on collaborative teams to assess their own impacts on the scheduling process (deGregory & Sommer, 2021; Fullan, 2001; Grissom et al., 2015; Yavuz, 2016). This impact is typically determined by one's own experiences and biases.

An assessment like the one in Figure 2.3 can help individuals and teams assess, connect, and reflect before, during, and after the design process.

REFLECTIVE QUESTIONS

- What did I learn about myself from this assessment?
- What did I learn about myself that could impact the way I design?
- What did I learn about my team from this assessment?
- What did I learn about others that could impact the way they design?
- How will individual and/or team identities be considered in our design process?

Scale: 1 (Significantly Disagree), 2 (Disagree), 3 (Neutral), 4 (Agree), 5 (Significantly Agree)

Item	Rank 1–5	How the Item Connects to Scheduling Design	Actions That Ensure Accountability for Our Scheduling Team
I believe with appropriate support and resource equity, all students can meet grade-level expectations and graduation requirements.			
I am aware that my identity impacts my practices through my perspectives.			
I am aware of how my culture and ethnicity impact my decision making.			
I recognize systemic and institutional barriers to student growth and achievement when I see them.			
I recognize that structures, policies, processes, and practices can intentionally or unintentionally produce inequities.			
I recognize that current scheduling norms do not serve students equitably.			
I anticipate how stakeholders will interact with, conflict with, and enhance one another.			
I understand that authentic collaboration is messy.			
I am comfortable managing fear and discomfort.			
I am willing to have courageous conversations when needed.			
I work to develop skills to manage conflict in productive ways.			
I check myself to see if an assumption I am making about a person or an idea is based upon facts or upon stereotypes about a group and how this in turn will affect student learning.			
I realize that to cultivate an equity lens, I will most likely need to change and grow as a leader.			
I speak up if I notice that a policy or practice unintentionally discriminates against or causes an unnecessary hardship for a particular group of students, educators, or families.			
I recognize that equity is a belief that requires action.			

FIGURE 2.3 SELF-ASSESSMENT: BECOMING AN ARCHITECT OF EQUITY
Self-assessment is critical to shifting the team approach to scheduling.

Uncover Personal Barriers

The second step in confronting the status QUO is to uncover the personal barriers that can complicate one's ability to lead or collaborate with a scheduling team. The ability to manage personal fears and establish credibility as a leader and collaborator is critical to the development of an equity mindset (Fullan, 2001; Kezar et al., 2021; Ravitch & Herzog, 2024; Yavuz, 2016). Managing personal fears begins with the inner work of refining mindset and building relationships that are deeply rooted in the context of the work ahead.

Part of building powerful equity-achieving relationships is making sure that the leader establishes his or her credibility as the lead learner and instructional leader (Fullan, 2014). Effective leaders don't delegate what they don't know. Effective leaders understand that vulnerability and productive conflict are necessary to the change process. Fear and lack of credibility are two obstacles that must be overcome by leaders for the scheduling process to successfully move forward (see Figure 2.4).

REFLECTIVE QUESTIONS

- What fears do I bring to the scheduling process? Why?
- What factors concern me when I think about addressing inequities in the schedule?
- What can I do to overcome any fears I have about leading change?
- What are my own strengths and limitations as a scheduling team member?
- What are the strengths and limitations of the members of our scheduling team?
- What do I need to do to lead the scheduling process?
- What strategies can I use to ensure that school stakeholder relationships are built in the context of our equity work?

Own Team Discomfort

The third step to confronting the status QUO as an Architect of Equity is to be willing to own any team discomfort that may arise during the change process. Discomfort for scheduling teams has many root causes, with most grounded in the personal fears described in the previous step: Uncover Personal Barriers. Sometimes, however, discomfort comes from professionals being conflict averse or not being trained in having difficult conversations.

Managing Fear	Manages fear of not being liked/well received by staff.
	Manages fear of causing attention that could compromise future promotion.
	Manages fear of union relationships.
	Manages fear of leading change.
	Manages a desire to be all things to all people.
	Manages the temptation to delegate work you don't know how to do.
	Manages nostalgia for personal high school experience.

Establishing Credibility	Understands how schedules are built.
	Understands current policies, procedures, regulations, rules, mandates, and contracts.
	Understands how to communicate authentically, frequently, and transparently.
	Understands how to use resources strategically and equitably.
	Willing to remove barriers to access.
	Understands how to use data to change student outcomes.
	Recognizes competing priorities, gatekeeping, and inclusive practices.
	Understands how to cast a vision for change and establish a shared purpose.

FIGURE 2.4 CLEARING THE PATH FOR THE SCHEDULING PROCESS
Acknowledging and confronting personal barriers and fears is critical to clearing the path for a scheduling process that prioritizes students and equity.

For scheduling teams to overcome this discomfort, they must acknowledge that conflict is a natural part of change, and it does not have to be a negative experience (Fullan, 2001). Conflict in and of itself is not the problem, but rather how people react and deal with the conflict is what most often perpetuates problems. Conflict can impede the process when it causes people to shut down and be afraid to offer ideas. Conversely, conflict can be harnessed for constructive good when it leads to better decisions, innovative solutions, and organizational growth.

The U.S. Navy SEALs are known for saying, "Get comfortable being uncomfortable" to help team members grow and achieve the impossible (Sof, 2018). Once it is acknowledged that healthy conflict and discomfort can advance the work of scheduling successfully, Architects of Equity can indeed own the discomfort and use it to their advantage. They do this by taking the necessary time to enact strategic processes that include considering factors that might be triggers for conflict. They proactively respond to these triggers by appropriating time for conversations, establishing a cooperative environment structured with team norms, practicing active listening, using brainstorming strategies to encourage full participation, and identifying problems as they arise.

By working together to anticipate where there might be conflict in the process and owning the discomfort this might create, members of highly effective scheduling teams support one another, all in service to the greater good of the equitable and accessible schedule. In owning discomfort and creating space to grapple with difficult topics and face inequities, true Architects of Equity can stretch beyond the impossible, challenge traditional beliefs and ideas, and embrace divergent thinking (see Figure 2.5).

Stretch beyond the impossible.	**TEAMS THAT STRETCH** ★ The schedule is newly created each year. ★ Courses are offered based on a vision for student achievement. ★ Courses are assigned to teachers based on student needs. ★ The student information system does not limit possibilities. ★ The priorities of the school and district are reflected in the schedule.
Challenge traditional beliefs and ideas.	**TEAMS THAT CHALLENGE** ★ All students are provided access and opportunity through the schedule. ★ Students receive co-requisite support rather than intervention and/or remediation. ★ Course prerequisites are removed. ★ The schedule ensures high expectations for all students.
Embrace divergent thinking.	**TEAMS THAT EMBRACE** ★ New ideas are brought forth and discussed. ★ The schedule is viewed as flexible and can be manipulated to serve all students. ★ The team thinks creatively to generate ideas and multiple solutions to problems. ★ The team seeks different viewpoints to arrive at solutions.

FIGURE 2.5 ACTIONS OF TRUE ARCHITECTS OF EQUITY
Challenging traditional mindsets around scheduling is a critical role for architects of equity.

REFLECTIVE QUESTIONS

- Does our current scheduling process reflect a reinforcement of what has always been done?
- Am I willing to point out inequities that currently exist in scheduling practices and outcomes?
- Am I willing to challenge traditional thinking on the team when it creates a barrier to equity?
- Do I feel comfortable challenging other team members' ideas constructively?
- Do I feel comfortable admitting when my own thinking is creating barriers?
- Do I feel comfortable admitting when I am wrong about something?
- Do I feel comfortable when others constructively challenge my thinking?
- Do I consider other perspectives, especially those that are not in line with my thinking, as part of the design process?

CHALLENGING THE TEAM MINDSET

Once teams have done the inner work of confronting the status QUO, the next step is to work on the scheduling team's mindSET. This is a crucial step in the process as most scheduling barriers are not simply the result of poor technical design. Many schedules are designed as they are intended and are the result of adult mindsets that design systems that sort the "capable" and/or college-bound students from the underestimated students. The result is a cyclical process of redesigning the same schedule with the same inequities each year. And to make matters worse, these inequities are not shrouded in secrecy.

Most educators, especially school administrators, are aware that these inequities exist as they are asked to examine student outcome data year after year. To break these patterns, scheduling teams must shift from assessing and acknowledging their role in reinforcing the status quo, to designing scheduling teams that are highly collaborative, intentionally strategic, and operate from a growth mindset. Applying the work of Carol Dweck (2006) to scheduling teams, there must exist a growth mindset among all members of the Architects of Equity. Leaving behind deficit thinking, the schedule must be viewed as a lever for change in a system in which all assets—including the unique assets of each student—are used.

Shifting the team's mindSET involves three components that are not necessarily sequential, but occur simultaneously as the planning process continues into more concrete phases (see Figure 2.6).

Start Supporting Rather Than Sorting

Obvious gaps exist in the ways students experience scheduling and course work in secondary schools. The connection between the schedule and postsecondary success cannot be underscored enough. Students who have been sorted out of college-track pathways and career readiness courses are left behind, illuminating biased practices that have existed since the beginning of the comprehensive high school model. In 2008, researcher John Hattie reviewed more than 300 studies on tracking and concluded that whereas tracking has minimal effects on learning outcomes, it does have profound negative effects on equity outcomes.

Sorting (or tracking) students refers to the practice of enrolling students in particular classes, curricula, and courses of study based on perceived ability. Schools sort students into different classes or sets of classes, often with differentiated, usually sequential, curriculum. Rather than achieving its often-accepted goal—to tailor instruction to the diverse needs of students—"

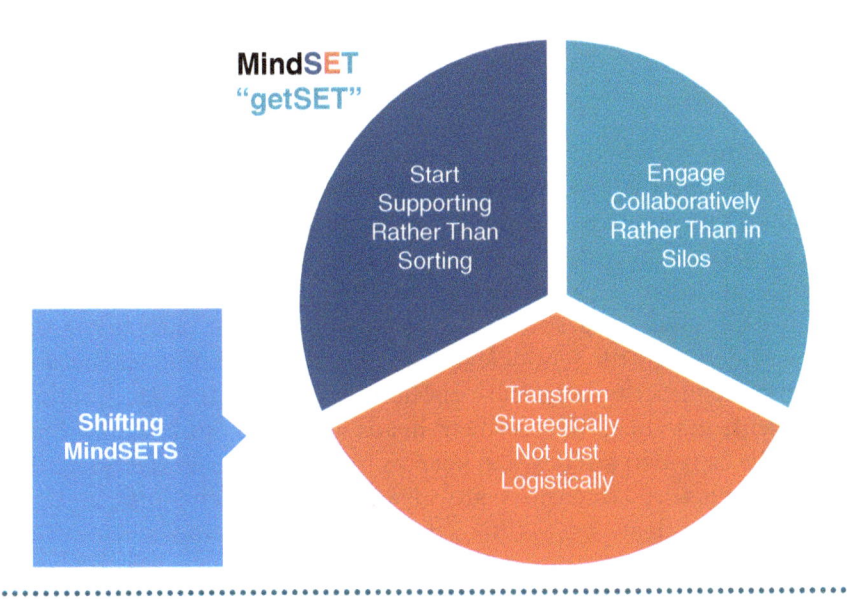

FIGURE 2.6 SHIFTING MINDSETS
Developing the right mindSET for scheduling is a pathway to equity.

tracking has, over decades of extensive research, been repeatedly found to be harmful to students enrolled in lower tracks and to provide no significant advantages for higher-tracked students," writes William Mathis (2013).

These practices sometimes begin as early as kindergarten, where pre-first-day screenings sort students into different classes (Higgins, 2019). By the time they are juniors or seniors in high school, students' access to college-preparation courses may be determined by whether they have taken honors classes and maintained a certain grade average. "Whether known as sorting, streaming or ability grouping, an expansive body of literature conclusively shows tracking is harmful and inequitable and remains an unsupportable practice," Mathis (2013, para. 4) explains. If it is believed there are students who might struggle academically in classes that are necessary for graduation and college and career readiness, rather than track the students, schools can build in supports to encourage student success and guide them through the necessary course work.

Sorting as a strategy is connected to a scheduling mindset and is deeply rooted in beliefs about differentiation. Architects of Equity establish an equitable core set of courses for all students—a guaranteed viable curriculum for each student who enters the school. Strategies to differentiate are focused on pushing students into the tier 1 mainstream environment over pushing students out of the core. Architects of Equity recognize that students have many needs—acceleration, intervention, and/or remediation—but rather than address those needs through course segregation, fiscal priorities are allotted to supplement the equitable core experience. This concept will be developed further in chapter 4.

Engage Collaboratively Rather Than in Silos

When it is time to schedule, it can often appear as though there are several different tracks running parallel and never crossing during the process. At the district level, the Human Resources and Business Services offices may be examining FTE allotments and what will be granted for the upcoming year. Teaching and Learning or the Academic Office may be examining the programs of study and what should be offered to provide pathways to graduation for students. At the school level, schedulers are creating teacher lines for teaching, sometimes thinking more about what staff want to teach rather than what students may need. Department heads are given options, and they may see their role as one to advocate to keep as many sections in their departments as possible. Finally, counselors are given stacks of schedules and told to ensure that all students have a full schedule, regardless.

These scheduling processes cannot continue to occur independent of one another. The scheduling process from start to finish (and as it continues almost seamlessly into the next year) must engage teams and be inclusive of school site and district personnel. Scheduling is an iterative process that needs many eyes to ensure that students are at the center of the work, and no one is falling through the cracks. Architects of Equity work within carefully structured district and site scheduling timelines and processes that have been crafted with intention. This concept will be developed further in chapter 8.

TRANSFORMING STRATEGICALLY RATHER THAN LOGISTICALLY

Logistical scheduling is the act of moving through a technical set of scheduling steps in the absence of thinking strategically and urgently about student needs and resource priorities. Logistical scheduling is a typical way of operating in traditional systems. The scheduling process is grounded in numbers: How many course sections and content area teachers can we afford based on the site-allocated budget? As a result, sometimes fiscal and human resource decisions in these systems are based solely on how to maintain the current number of sections and teachers in the schedule. Logistical scheduling is a critical component of strategic scheduling but can have devastating consequences when enacted in isolation.

> *Logistical scheduling is a critical component of strategic scheduling but can have devastating consequences when enacted in isolation.*

Architects of Equity enact strategic scheduling processes. Strategic scheduling is the act of prioritizing fiscal and human resources around specific structural strategies that protect instructional practices targeted for the upcoming year. Strategic schedulers do not simply roll over the prior year's schedule for the convenience of minimizing the build time for the upcoming year. Decisions about the schedule are grounded in what worked and did not work in the prior schedule, and what is currently needed for incoming/returning students to master desired expectations over the next 10 months.

The real challenge is to understand how school leaders can reconceptualize and improve the schedule and do so every year for every student. Ultimately, improving the schedule doesn't just change where and when students attend class, but when created with intentionality and with a lens toward equity, the schedule can change how students see their experience as personalized, supportive, and equitable. School schedulers face the same choices today as they did in the pre-coronavirus world. They can take the same one-size-fits-all approach to structuring the schedule, or they can shore up the cracks in the foundation and align the schools' calendars, instructional days, and resources with their mission statements (Hibbeln, 2020).

As Pisoni and Conti (2019) explain,

> *It's time to embrace not only the potential, but the essential role of operations in furthering the pursuit of educational equity. When overlooked or underestimated, school-level processes can inhibit access to rigorous, high-quality teaching and learning. But when harnessed correctly with equity at the core, school operations have the*

power to improve every student's experience—and to catalyze all other efforts to enhance pedagogy, rigor, and engagement. (para. 13)

Through the schedule, students should be exposed to excellent teachers, rigorous curriculum, high expectations, supportive environments, and a large cross-section of their peers—all of which can contribute to greater rates of success and efficacy for students. Reimagining the schedule and what it can do for students is the key to disrupting inequity, which is not done accidentally.

WORKING TECHNICALLY AND ADAPTIVELY

Once the Architects of Equity confront the status QUO, and get their mindSET, these teams must tend to technical changes and adaptive (human) changes simultaneously, or meaningful change will not occur. In 1983, Margaret Wheatley and Tim Dalmau created the Six Circle Model, placing three circles above and three below a green line. The circles above the green line represent the technical aspects of change: patterns (strategies), structures (organization), and processes (operations). The authors make the case that these technical areas implemented in isolation will fail to bring about substantial and sustainable change. Even as work is conducted above the green line, which has been referred to as the logistical work of scheduling, attention must also be paid to the human and/or relational aspects of change: relationships, information, and identity. Humans cannot move forward if they do not feel valued, connected, and as a vital part of the process. Figure 2.7 outlines the connections between this research and scheduling.

Architects of Equity put year-long scheduling processes in place to support the technical build of the schedule. At the same time, the visionary and designer must attend to the relational aspects of scheduling by taking steps to understand how changes to the scheduling may affect staff identity, how the flow of information about the schedule may impact perceptions about scheduling intentions, and how the relationships between teams and programs might be affected positively and/or negatively by the changes. Scheduling teams that work in secrecy and focus only on technical aspects of scheduling (in the absence of considering the human impacts) are likely to fail. Architects of Equity leave nothing to chance. Discussions focused on potential impacts happen strategically, not after something unforeseen has "blown up" and must be addressed.

To ensure that technical and relational considerations are part of the work of changing practices in the upcoming chapters, each chapter will provide reflective questions that attend to the work being done at the technical and relational/adaptive levels.

Through the schedule, students should be exposed to excellent teachers, rigorous curriculum, high expectations, supportive environments, and a large cross-section of their peers.

	National Equity Project Definition	**How It Might Look In Scheduling**	**Where It Goes Awry**
Technical Changes			
Structure	The way a system organizes itself to conduct its work.	The responsibility for building the site schedule is within the role of the principal.	The schedule is delegated to one staff member at the school site with little oversight.
Pattern	The systematic ways in which a system focuses its key strategies to accomplish its mission and goals.	Co-requisite supports are prioritized to keep students in the tier I classroom with highly qualified teachers.	Staff does not share a common understanding and/or embraces misconceptions of what co-requisite support means to implement.
Process	The standard processes (operations) that are used to build consistency and efficiency.	Creating a site and district scheduling timeline.	Site and district scheduling timelines have not been co-created and aligned.
Adaptive Changes			
Relationships	This has to do with how a team or organization values its people—their emotional, physical, and spiritual well-being; the level of connectivity among people across the system; the value placed upon collaboration and high functioning teams; and the level of connectivity of and the type of relationship between key teams, programs, and operational systems.	Building trust through highly collaborative scheduling practices that include ongoing stakeholder feedback loops.	Failing to consider the impacts that a technical change can make to a preexisting staff scheduling relationship (i.e., team teaching, co-teaching, or pathway relationship) can have negative unintended consequences.
Identity	Human beings are meaning-seekers. Our actions are completely driven by our own set of values, beliefs, and sense of identity. Therefore, shared purposes and principles of people in teams motivate individuals to work together in organizations.	Building and cultivating a shared purpose around the scheduling WHY.	Failing to consider the impacts that a technical change in the schedule can make to a staff member's identity (i.e., department chair, AP teacher, EL lead, etc.) can have negative unintended consequences.

(Continued)

(Continued)

Information	Information is like oxygen in a system. In its absence, people will "make it up" to keep moving forward. Access to information greatly minimizes the negative rumors. When information is abundant, people focus on what is important and have greater security in knowing what is going on in the organization.	Implementing ongoing, open, and transparent communication about the schedule.	Failing to design and implement an ongoing and transparent flow of information during the scheduling process can result in suspicion and/or inaccurate information being discussed to fill the void.

FIGURE 2.7 TECHNICAL AND ADAPTIVE CHANGES AS THEY RELATE TO SCHEDULING PRACTICES

Note: The National Equity Project translated Margaret Wheatley and Tim Dalmau's (1983) work into specific definitions used in this graphic (https://www.nationalequityproject.org/resources/frameworks).

NAVIGATING HESITANT LEADERSHIP IN THE FACE OF INEQUITIES

In response to difficult decision making around scheduling and resource equity, hesitant leaders may offer loosely unstructured opportunities for collaboration and distributed leadership in lieu of structuring a clear path toward helping staff develop a shared purpose around equity.

Managing working environments with hesitant leaders is difficult. That's because hesitant leaders

- Are reluctant to tackle assumptions.
- Are reluctant to change.
- Adhere to inequitable and outdated practices.
- Seek spaces where they feel confident.
- Stay in their comfort zones.
- Are afraid of personal consequences when acting on equity.
- Are reluctant to question the status quo.

Possible ways to engage hesitant leaders include the following:

- Find low stakes opportunities for the principal to consider as an entry to equity. (For example, offer to teach an AP class filled with students who don't meet standard criteria to demonstrate that success is possible under supportive conditions.)
- Offer to participate on and/or lead a scheduling team. Help create collaborative scheduling norms, expectations, and so on to keep the focus on equity.
- Identify equity-minded staff members with social capital to help raise concerns, questions, and ideas about equitable changes.
- Offer to conduct a schedule audit with a team. First, bring the data about the cost of under-enrolled sections and the enrollment numbers by demographics in AP, IB, and regular course work. Point out what could be done with surplus funds if the schedule was more efficient and equitable. Second, bring design trends forward for discussion about the rationale behind patterns of scheduling decisions that haven't led to shifts in achievement over time.
- Engage students (including clubs and student government groups) about scheduling inequities through ties to the curriculum. Ask them to share ideas about how to make the scheduling practices more equitable. Have them present at staff meetings.

LOOKING FORWARD AND CHANGING PRACTICE

The first two chapters of this book ask two essential questions of the reader:

- How does a shift in scheduling team mindsets result in scheduling practices that produce equitable student outcomes?
- How do scheduling teams move from acting as Agents of Compliance to becoming Architects of Equity?

These questions formed the foundation for a theory of action (see Figure 2.8) grounded in the belief that if scheduling team mindsets shift, scheduling practices will change, and outcomes will improve.

To achieve the first step in shifting mindsets, it has been established that the status QUO must be upended through the deeply reflective and at times uncomfortable work of questioning assumptions, uncovering barriers, and owning discomfort. It is only through these processes that the team can be prepared to get their minds SET and start creating schedules that are grounded in equity and access for all students. To get SET, the team—which has been created collaboratively with much stakeholder input—will start to create a schedule that supports all students and is strategic on all fronts,

Shifting Mindsets › Changing Practices › Improving Outcomes

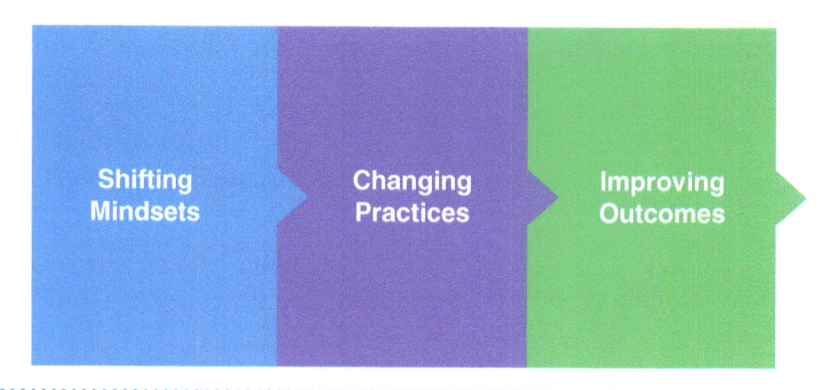

FIGURE 2.8 SCHEDULING THEORY OF ACTION
The steps of the theory of action to create a schedule with equity at its core.

including maximizing academic, fiscal, and human resources. The team members will now be Architects of Equity.

This chapter opened describing the pitfalls of the mayhem that awaits around the corner. School leaders can remove the mayhem and make change a positive experience, using an equity lens to envision new systems and new outcomes as a result. If equity is giving students what they need, when they need it, and in the way they need it, it is a moral imperative for schools to acknowledge and act to dismantle inequities in scheduling. For real change to occur to bring about equity, old ideas and practices must be left behind. It is the only way forward. As Richardson and Tavangar from the Big Questions Institute remind us, "Status quo is around the corner, and it has a strong pull. It will take discipline, community, courage, strong arguments, and a healthy dose of optimism and wonder to resist that pull" (2021, p. 16).

Chapter 2 Self-Reflective and Team Reflective Questions

To achieve substantive and sustainable change in the schedules of schools, scheduling teams must understand that asking difficult questions may bring about discomfort. The questions below are offered to create an environment in which teams can grapple with the scheduling process. These questions aim directly at the heart of which students are being best served and how a schedule can be created for all students—topics that can create discomfort for some.[2]

---

[2] We credit the Big Questions Institute for providing the basis of these questions we present.

- What is so sacred about the school experience that I/we would fight to keep it in the schedule?
- Is the schedule coherent for all students? Is there a continuum of learning?
- Where is the power in our schedule?

    Who has input into creating the schedule?

    To what extent are students able to pursue learning on their own terms and make decisions regarding their experiences?

- Why do we schedule as we do?

    Are students at the center of planning and decision making?

    Is our schedule effective for student learning?

    Are our practices publicly defensible?

- Who is unheard in our scheduling process?

    What systems have we created to limit the voices heard in the creation of the schedule?

    What are the demographics of our classes and tracks? Do they represent the population we serve?

CHAPTER 3

THE SCHEDULING WHISPERER

USING EQUITY SELF-ASSESSMENTS TO DETERMINE GAPS BETWEEN INTENTION AND ACTION

> *Changing Practice 1: Scheduling Teams Must Know the System to Change the System*

The trouble is that once you see it, you can't unsee it. And once you've seen it, keeping quiet, saying nothing, becomes as political an act as speaking out.

—*Arundhati Roy*

The superintendent of Cedar Valley School District was excited about entering year three of his five-year strategic plan. To support a focus on college and career readiness, the district adopted a pathway strategy that integrated career technical education courses with core academic course work in the hope of increasing literacy and certification rates. Upon examination of two years of summative state data, the student group literacy and certification gaps targeted for change were static.

In response to this data, the superintendent decided to examine the enrollment trends within site schedules to try to identify factors that might be impeding implementation. Surprisingly, despite providing site leaders with scheduling expectations in writing, many student groups, including those receiving special education and English learners, did not have access to the pathway strategy due to conflicting course mandates coming from multiple departments at the district office.

To support a shift, the superintendent worked with his executive team to pull all the written communications that sites were receiving about student scheduling. This data revealed that while the assistant superintendent of

Educational Services was messaging scheduling expectations in line with the district vision, the English learner and special education directors were messaging additional directions that were forcing students into courses that made pathway access difficult.

In response, the superintendent met with the general education, special education, and English learner teams to examine the current site schedules and collaboratively design scheduling models that would allow all students access to pathway courses while meeting all compliance requirements outlined by the state. The new expectations and models were codified in one clear written communication and unpacked in scheduling team professional learning. Within a year, the number of students accessing the pathway model increased by 80%.

Equity lives in the alignment of intention, action, and outcomes. To accomplish this and as demonstrated in the story told above, equity self-assessments are the key to knowing the system well enough to change it.

GOOD INTENTIONS, INEQUITABLE OUTCOMES

Well-intended actions and ideas are only as good as the student outcomes they produce. Too often, good ideas in school districts are acted upon without sufficient systems in place to measure the desired impacts and without a plan that ensures fidelity of implementation (Chenoweth, 2016; Daly, 2009). The purpose of this chapter is to support district and site scheduling teams, the Architects of Equity, to assess and impact the alignment between intention, action, and outcomes. This is done through a system of equity self-assessments (see Figure 3.1). By using strategic self-assessment that is focused on understanding how systems and structures reinforce inequities, action steps can be designed to address current equity issues and prevent new ones from reemerging.

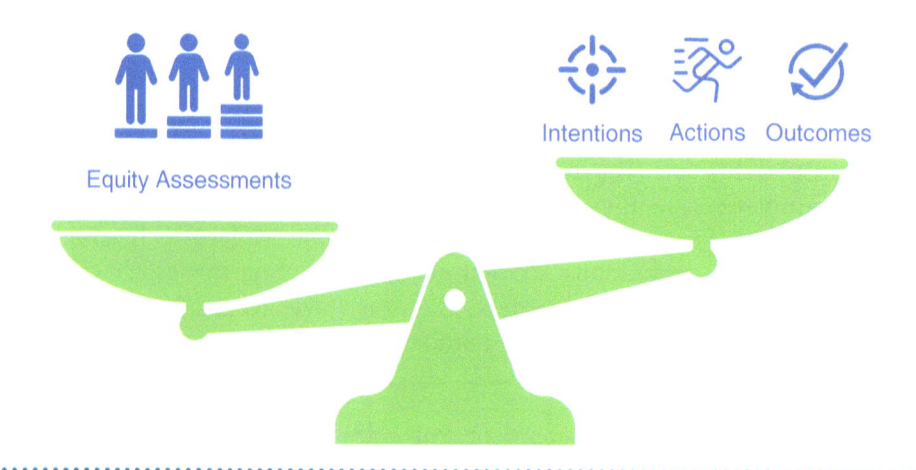

FIGURE 3.1 EQUITY ASSESSMENTS SUPPORT PATHS TO EQUITABLE OUTCOMES

Speaking the language of equity has emerged as a trend as schools attempt to return to "normal" after the global pandemic of COVID-19. As a result, district leaders are more frequently contracting services for equity assessments and diversity training in response to the current health and social crises (Annie E. Casey Foundation, 2014; Lovely, 2020). Yet, professional learning and data analysis are not new to education. Many educators have been examining data for decades and are acutely aware that the current system is one that produces inequality by design—whether intentional or unintentional (Alhadabi & Li, 2020; Coleman, 1966; Hammond, 2015; TNTP, 2018).

The disparities in academic outcomes between minoritized students and their White and Asian counterparts as well as across economic and linguistic divides tell the story. And let us be clear: Such disparities are the product of deep-rooted opportunity and funding gaps in society that have been replicated and reinforced in our educational system (Carter et al., 2013; Coleman, 1966). Clearly, there is a cost to addressing inequity in the U.S. public school system. The question remains, will the steps necessary to shift from a scheduling culture of sorting to a culture of supporting be made?

Why the Shift Matters

The educational system is not built to produce fearless leaders. In fact, the way leaders are promoted up the system may not have anything to do with a leader's ability to impact student outcomes. Many times, promotion is based on the ability of a leader to avoid controversy rather than a willingness to respectfully confront inequities in the system that threaten the status quo (Bastian & Henry, 2015; Béteille et al., 2012). To make matters worse, school districts struggle to find principals who are not already overloaded and near burnout (DeMatthews, 2021).

Often, the school principal delegates to the vice/assistant principal, and they do as they are told. This, in turn, creates a system in which leading isn't learned, rather it is assigned. In many cases, discipline, supervision, scheduling, parent/community meetings, special education individualized educational plans (IEPs), and other operational tasks are assigned to vice/assistant principals. While teacher and department evaluations may be a part of these assignments, the deep work of instructional leadership is difficult to learn while managing most of the daily operations and discipline problems that arise. Unfortunately, the result may be that a loyal, hard-working, vice/assistant principal is promoted without a clear understanding of how to build a respectful and urgent culture focused on educational equity. Often, the only safeguard to this kind of promotion is professional learning for the masses and a supervisor who must support dozens of leaders simultaneously. Each time a new principal is selected under these conditions, the timeline for effecting change restarts, and the inequities in the system remain unaddressed.

Intentional, purposeful, well-focused leadership is key to all aspects of school and district transformation (Fullan, 2001; Grissom et al., 2021; Leithwood et al., 2004; Lovely, 2020). To dismantle and reimagine a public school system that adapts to the learner, instead of asking the learner to adapt to the system, leaders at all levels must be willing to ask difficult questions. These questions emerge from a careful examination of trend data that reveal underlying inequities in school policies and practices. One important step school and site leaders can take is to build self-assessment systems that frequently provide feedback on whether intentions, actions, and outcomes are aligned with high expectations to produce the postsecondary readiness outcomes expected for all students in the building. An effective self-assessment system identifies gatekeepers that maintain the advantages for a select few and the disadvantages for the marginalized many. Equity is action.

THE FOUR A'S FOR SELF-ASSESSMENT

There should be an alignment between intention, action, and outcomes within site and district courses, schedules, transcripts, and the K–12 pipeline. Through self-assessments, Architects of Equity must first examine the perceptions, values, and beliefs scheduling teams bring to their work. These self-assessments are implemented in four stages (see Figure 3.2).

1. **Actualize equity:** During this stage, leaders are casting a vision to define the desired state for student learning, the Equitable Core. High-impact equity levers are identified as priorities for the schedule.

2. **Assess equity:** During this stage, student outcome trend data are examined to determine the distance between the current reality and the desired state. This is done through course of study, transcript, schedule, and/or pipeline self-assessments.

3. **Act on equity:** During this stage, the data from the self-assessments are used to establish equity-driven scheduling expectations. Considering district context, leaders also determine the order and timing of required adaptive and technical shifts to move the current reality closer to the ideal state.

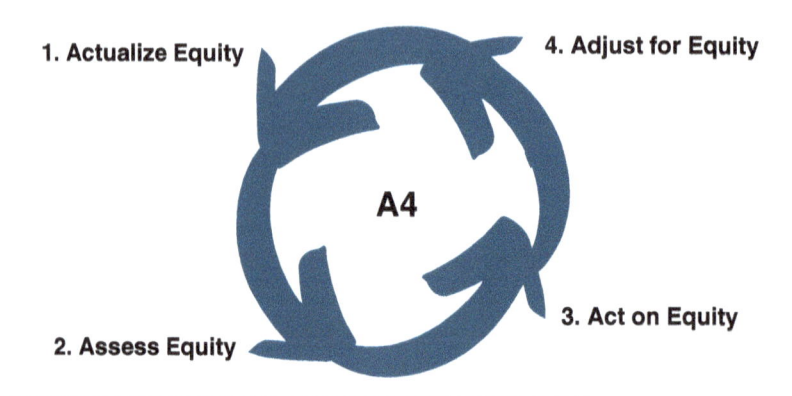

FIGURE 3.2 THE FOUR A'S OF SELF-ASSESSMENT

4. **Adjust for equity:** Throughout the school year, checks and balances are in place to continuously monitor the effectiveness of actions being taken.

Actualize Equity

The first step in this self-assessment process is to actualize equity by establishing meaningful graduation standards that are communicated through district policy and procedure. Many districts have a graduation policy, but most do not translate that policy into clear procedures for site implementation. That is why programming variants begin to emerge. There is no clear guidance in writing, so well-intentioned adults begin to implement the policy based on their own interpretation of it. In addition, when there is little or no oversight over courses, this can be a recipe for inequities across the system.

To actualize equity requires that the graduation policy is translated into an Equitable Core—the standard set of courses that any student can take to qualify for university. This does not mean that the district expects all students to enter a four-year college. Instead, it sends a clear message to the system that access to these courses cannot be denied, and the only variants authorized for use are those listed under the Alternative Means to Graduation Procedure, which in practice is school board–approved guidance for what can and cannot be altered in the meaningful graduation sequencing.

In Figure 3.3, only world language and visual and performing arts might occur in different grade levels, depending on the bell schedule of each school. In many cases, there would be a corresponding advanced version of each English, math, science, and social science course, but any opportunity to use layering, differentiated syllabi, and/or identify opportunity youth would be encouraged before creating ability tracks. An example of this is running Biology and Honors Biology concurrently, in the same period. Students who seek honors credit must submit additional work or projects or take additional assessments to demonstrate honors-level mastery of standards. This way, all students have access to honors-level course work, and they have agency to choose their level. (See the differentiated syllabi option in the appendices.) If layering course work is not a desired option, consider identifying opportunity youth for advanced sections. Opportunity youth are students who have been performing well in regular course work over multiple years. These students show an aptitude for acceleration with appropriate support.

Regardless, all students are expected to be supported to successfully complete the Equitable Core. The Equitable Core does not include every class a student will take in high school, but rather every class the students must take to meet meaningful graduation standards. The Equitable Core is a road map to excellence for each student—the guaranteed access to a meaningful graduation that the district has promised. Sites are expected to offer these options without discrimination. This chapter will provide additional support for building an Equitable Core. Blank templates of the Equitable Core pathway and standard versions (the latter shown in Figure 3.3) are available in the appendices and online.

Academic Core Classes	Grade 9	Grade 10	Grade 11	Grade 12
ELA	English Language Arts 9	English Language Arts 10	English Language Arts 11	English Language Arts 12
Math	Algebra I or Integrated Math I	Geometry or Integrated Math II	Algebra II or Integrated Math III	
Science	Biology	Chemistry	Physics	
Social Science	Global Studies	World History	U.S. History	Government/ Economics
World Language	Year 1 Language	Year 2 Language		
VAPA			Visual and Performing Arts 1–2	
Physical Education	Physical Education 9	Physical Education 10		
Mandates (EL, SpEd)				
Electives				

Board-Approved Graduation Requirements:
English: 4 years required
Mathematics: 3 years required
Science: 3 years required
Social Studies: 4 years required
Physical Education: 2 years required
World Language: 2 years or LOTE required
Fine Art: 1 year required
Two Additional Elective Courses

Note: All students must maintain an overall 2.0 grade point average.

Student: _____

Parent: _____

Counselor: _____

Date: _____

FIGURE 3.3 COURSE REQUIREMENTS THAT ILLUSTRATE AN EQUITABLE CORE

Note: EL is English learner; SpEd is special education; LOTE is language other than English.

online resources Available for download at https://companion.corwin.com/courses/equitableschoolscheduling

Assess Equity

The second step in this self-assessment process is assessing equity, which requires scheduling teams to determine the distance between the current reality and desired state as defined by meaningful graduation standards codified in the Equitable Core. An Equitable Core that exists as a list of courses is just that. What must accompany a vision for learning that is grounded in equity is an alignment of appropriate actions that facilitate intention. This stage is focused on dismantling systemic, structural inequities by self-assessing the alignment between intention, action, and outcomes. If outcomes in the school and/or district are not equitable by student groups, structures like the course of study or the schedule can help perpetuate what isn't working, or in the best-case scenario act as a lever for change. Structures that are powerfully reimagined can help school and district leaders make impactful instructional and cultural changes. Rather than conduct external audits, Architects of Equity lead educational equity self-assessments using highly structured frameworks to guide each focused process.

According to the Intercultural Development Research Association (2020), equity audits (assessments) keep six educational equity goals in mind:

- Goal 1: **Comparably high academic achievement and other student outcomes** for all learners, as evidenced by disaggregated data.

- Goal 2: **Equitable access and inclusion** that affords all learners unobstructed entrance and participation in academic and extracurricular activities.

- Goal 3: **Equitable treatment** in a welcoming and inclusive learning environment.

- Goal 4: **Equitable opportunity to learn** in an academic setting with high standards that offers a strong system of supports.

- Goal 5: **Equitable resources** that include fair allocation of funding, staffing, facilities, instructional materials, and equipment.

- Goal 6: **Accountability** that assures all stakeholders hold themselves and each other responsible for the success of every student.

All six of these goals can be examined through the analysis of transcripts, schedules, the course of study, and overall student group outcomes from transitional kindergarten through twelfth grade, or said another way, from cradle to career.

Equity self-assessments at the structural level can be done through many forms:

- **Course of study assessments:** Assessing the ideal and actual grouping of students.
- **Schedule assessments:** Assessing a site leader's strategic use of course sequencing, student cohorting, and teacher assignments to increase desired outcomes.
- **Transcript assessments:** Assessing the reality of student progress in course work.
- **Leaky pipeline assessments:** Assessing how one graduation cohort (K–12) progresses.

Course of Study Assessments

To design equity-achieving schedules, site and central office leaders must define an Equitable Core set of courses in which each student is guaranteed access. This is critical because courses are the vehicle by which students access teachers, strategies, and pathways that lead to postsecondary possibilities. There is no element in scheduling more tied to tracking than course assignment. For example, most schools do not simply offer English 11 to all the juniors. Many schedules include layered ability diploma-bound tracks as offerings, such as English 11, English 11 Co-Taught, English 11 Sheltered, Honors English 11, and/or AP English Language and Composition. These courses appear on course request sheets as a variety of student options, but they typically end up acting as sorting mechanisms creating barriers to access and opportunity for underestimated student groups. The result of this type of course tracking is the reinforcement of the factory model, which continues to perpetuate inequitable outcomes for historically underserved groups (Bowles & Gintis, 1976; Callahan, 1964; Darling-Hammond et al., 2007; Education Commission of the States, 2005). For this reason, courses and course sequencing must be assessed at all levels to ensure equity.

> *Courses are the vehicle by which students access teachers, strategies, and pathways that lead to postsecondary possibilities.*

Course of study self-assessments can be conducted at the district and site levels. Figure 3.4 reflects the process as it is aligned to the Course of Study Framework for Self-Assessment. Additionally, Figure 3.5 provides questions that should be considered when conducting a course of study self-assessment.

Course of Study Framework for Self-Assessment

At the district level, a course of study self-assessment examines all available district course offerings alongside the Equitable Core. At the site level, the site four-year course sequencing plan is examined against the Equitable Core. The Equitable Core is the standard course sequence that any college-bound student would progress through toward graduation.

Course of Study Framework for Self-Assessment Checklist

Step 1: Actualize Equity

- ☐ **District:** Define the ideal state through establishing a graduation policy, graduation procedure, and an alternative means to graduation procedure that give clear guidance on options for providing access to the Equitable Core. Ensure that the course of study reflects an offering of courses in alignment with these policies and procedures.
- ☐ **Site:** Define the ideal state through establishing a four-year course sequencing plan that ensures access to the Equitable Core.

Step 2: Assess Equity

- ☐ **District:** Determine the distance between the current reality and the ideal state as defined by how closely district course work aligns to the district's Equitable Core.
- ☐ **Site:** Determine the distance between the current reality and the ideal state as defined by how closely site course taking processes align to the district's Equitable Core.

Policies	☐ Examine the current board-approved Graduation Policy.
Procedures	☐ Examine the current Graduation Policy and Alternative Means to Graduation Procedures for guidance on Equitable Core. At the site, examine the Equitable Core through the four-year plan articulation card.
Tracking	☐ Examine courses by core content area, grade level, and "tracks."
English	☐ Analyze English courses available/active, expected course sequences, and course enrollment by student group.
Math	☐ Analyze math courses available/active, expected course sequences, and course enrollment by student group.
Science	☐ Analyze science courses available/active, expected course sequences, and course enrollment by student group.
Social Science	☐ Analyze social Science courses available/active, expected course sequences, and course enrollment by student group.
World Language	☐ Analyze world Language courses available/active, expected course sequences, and course enrollment by student group.
Middle School	☐ Analyze the alignment between middle school and high school world language, mathematics, and career technical education (CTE) offerings.
Middle School	☐ Analyze the alignment between middle school and high school world language offerings by students' home languages.
CTE	☐ Analyze CTE courses available/active, expected course sequences, and course enrollment by student group.

(Continued)

(Continued)

VAPA	☐ Analyze visual and performing arts (VAPA) courses available/active, expected course sequences, and course enrollment by student group.
PE	☐ Analyze physical education courses available/active, expected course sequences, and course enrollment by student group.
Electives	☐ Analyze elective courses available/active, expected course sequences, and course enrollment by student group.
Advanced Studies	☐ Analyze advanced studies (AP, IB, CTE, dual articulated, and college) courses available/active, expected course sequences, and course enrollment by student group.
Weighted	☐ Analyze weighted courses available/active, expected course sequences, and course enrollment by student group.
Prerequisites	☐ Analyze the impacts of course prerequisites by student group.
Testing	☐ Analyze the impacts of any tests or measurements used to determine course access by student groups.
Alternative Means	☐ Examine the use of course equivalents and/or alternative means by student group.
Articulation	☐ Examine articulation/course selection materials for Equitable Core alignment.
Step 3: Act on Equity ☐ **District:** Considering district context, determine the order and timing of required adaptive and technical shifts to move the current reality closer to the ideal state. ☐ **Site:** Considering each site's context, identify what the order and timing of required adaptive and technical shifts should be to move the current reality closer to the ideal state.	
Step 4: Adjust for Equity ☐ Continuously monitor and address the effectiveness of actions being taken.	

FIGURE 3.4 CHECKLIST ASSESSING THE EQUITY OF THE COURSE OF STUDY

Note: AP is Advanced Placement; IB is International Baccalaureate.

- ☑ How many course variants are offered to meet grade level graduation requirements in each subject area?

- ☑ Do any course variants appear to be associated with ability tracking, courses that are perceived to be easier, mindset about capabilities, and/or gatekeeping?

- ☑ Are any of the course variants resulting in student group tracks and/or silos? How are advanced, AP, IB, and college classes being offered and accessed?

- ☑ Are any course variants created by district mandates? Do these variants remove students from the highly qualified core course teachers?

- ☑ Are any course variants created by prerequisites? What is the rationale for each prerequisite? Are the results of prerequisites sorting the highest achieving students into higher levels of courses?

- ☑ Do some students get additional access to core coursework (i.e., taking Adv. World and/or AP Human Geography) in 9th grade so they can take AP World in 10th grade? What is the student group enrollment in these classes? Are any student groups overrepresented? Are any student groups underrepresented? If so, why?

- ☑ Are the same languages being offered at the middle and high schools in each feeder? If not, why are languages offered at the middle school that are not offered at the feeder high school?

- ☑ How many languages are offered? How many levels of languages are offered? Are these classes filled to capacity?

- ☑ Are students who have a different home language other than English placed in a third language because their home language is not offered at the school? Do students have access to a Language other than English exam (university approved for admission) to meet graduation and university requirements at the year 2 level?

FIGURE 3.5 QUESTIONS TO CONSIDER WHEN CONDUCTING A COURSE OF STUDY SELF-ASSESSMENT

STEPS TO CONDUCT AT DISTRICT- OR SITE-LEVEL COURSE OF STUDY SELF-ASSESSMENT

Request and review reports by student group to determine if access to specific items in the Course of Study Framework for Self-Assessment Checklist is equitable or segregated. Consider the following:

- What patterns did you observe?
- Reflect on why these patterns might exist.
- What concrete actions might you (or your team) take to disrupt the patterns that stand in the way of equitable outcomes?

Schedule Assessments

To design equity-achieving schedules, site and central office leaders must examine how courses, staffing, and strategy are used in schedule design and implementation. The site schedule can be a vehicle for leveraging powerful structures to support transformative instruction or a restrictive system that provides access and opportunity to a small number of students who are perceived to be ready for college. A school's schedule is a map that reveals priorities and values about what matters most. A critical design flaw in scheduling is a school's reliance on the course selection process to determine course offerings. Course selection processes that are focused on organizing students by perceived ability reinforce scheduling processes that result in sorting over supporting. Because of this, site schedule assessments must happen at critical points throughout the year to be effective.

Site schedule self-assessments can be conducted at the district and site levels. The template in Figure 3.6 reflects the process as it is aligned to the Schedule Framework for Self-Assessment. Additionally, Figure 3.7 provides questions that should be considered when conducting a schedule self-assessment.

Schedule Framework for Self-Assessment

At the district level the schedule assessment compares schools against scheduling expectations. If schedule expectations have not been established at the district level, guidance provided in the Graduation Procedure can be used to define the desired state. At the site level, the site assesses its own alignment to the schedule expectations. In the absence of schedule expectations, guidance provided in the Graduation Procedure can be used to define the desired state.

Schedule Framework for Self-Assessment Checklist

Step 1: Actualize Equity
- ☐ **District:** Define the ideal state through establishing schedule expectations that are aligned to desired graduation outcomes.
- ☐ **Site:** Use the schedule expectations to message and implement a schedule consistent with district expectations for equity.

Step 2: Assess Equity
- ☐ **District:** Determine the distance between the current reality and the ideal state as defined by how closely each school's schedule reflects the intended schedule expectations.
- ☐ **Site**: Determine the distance between the current reality and the ideal state as defined by how closely the site's schedule reflects the intended schedule expectations.

Sequencing	☐ Analyze the sequencing of core course work, the Equitable Core.
Placement	☐ Analyze course work placement in the schedule by student group.
Course Access	☐ Analyze enrollment by student group in courses by classroom.
Class Size	☐ Analyze class size by course, teacher, and student group.
Teacher Assignments	☐ Analyze teacher assignments by course and student group.
Teacher Loads	☐ Analyze teacher loads by course and student group.
Collaboration	☐ Analyze the strategic use of common planning time.
Unfilled Seats	☐ Analyze the financial impacts of unfilled seats by course.

Step 3: Act on Equity
- ☐ **District:** Considering district context, determine the order and timing of required adaptive and technical shifts to move the current reality closer to the ideal state.
- ☐ **Site:** Considering each site's context, identify what the order and timing of required adaptive and technical shifts to move the current reality closer to the ideal state.

Step 4: Adjust for Equity
- ☐ Continuously monitor the effectiveness of actions being taken.

FIGURE 3.6 CHECKLIST ASSESSING THE EQUITY OF THE PROPOSED SCHEDULE

- ☑ What are the student group trends in classes?
  - Are the course enrollments evidence of any student group isolation? If so, why?
  - Are all courses enrolled at the same levels? If not, why?
  - What are the enrollment trends in advanced studies?
  - Are any Equitable Core variants present? What is the student group enrollment in these classes?

- ☑ Are prerequisites and/or mandates affecting course access for any student groups? If so, which classes?

- ☑ Are any courses being used as "interventions"? What is the student group enrollment in these classes? How many students meet grade level standards with this support and move onto the next course successfully? How often do students in these courses graduate meeting four-year college entrance standards?

- ☑ What do teacher assignments reflect? How are teacher assignments constructed? Are teacher caseloads balanced? Are teachers organized with limited preps?

- ☑ Are special education, English learner, and/or students who need additional supports scheduled strategically in core coursework early in the day and with the most successful teachers?

- ☑ Is there any evidence of teacher and/or student collaboration in the schedule? If so, what is available?

- ☑ Are enrollments in electives lower than core course enrollments in ELA, math, science, and social science? Are sections with higher max loads (i.e., PE) enrolled to the max?

- ☑ Are English learners, students with disabilities and other students who need additional support strategically scheduled within the day? Are mandated support classes directly connected to core coursework? How?

- ☑ Are research-based strategies being implemented to fidelity? (i.e., are pathway students cohorted within student teams anchored by common preps?)

- ☑ Is the bell schedule equitable? Can all students accelerate, remediate, and take co-requisities within the school day and without losing elective options?

FIGURE 3.7 QUESTIONS TO CONSIDER WHEN CONDUCTING A SCHEDULE SELF-ASSESSMENT

STEPS TO CONDUCT A DISTRICT- OR SITE-LEVEL SCHEDULE SELF-ASSESSMENT

Request and review reports by student group to determine if access to specific items in the Schedule Framework for Self-Assessment Checklist is equitable or segregated.

Consider the following:

- What patterns did you observe?
- Reflect on why these patterns might exist.
- What concrete actions might you (or your team) take to disrupt the patterns that stand in the way of equitable outcomes?

Transcript Assessments

To design equity-achieving schedules, site and central office leaders must examine the types of courses that are offered and the ways in which these courses are used in schedules. Transcript assessments are a great way for school leaders to examine the distance between intention, action, and outcomes because at each grading period the site leader can examine whether students are experiencing school as initially intended. This gives leaders the data needed to have constructive discussions that support making the necessary adjustments to scheduling and programming throughout the school year, rather than year to year. Transcript self-assessments are usually conducted in conjunction with graduation credit check forms and grading reports.

Transcript self-assessments can be conducted at the district and site levels. The template in Figure 3.8 reflects the district process as it is aligned to the Transcript Framework for Self-Assessment.

Additionally, Figure 3.9 provides questions that should be considered when conducting a transcript self-assessment.

Transcript Framework for Self-Assessment

At the district level the assessment compares **schools** against desired graduation outcomes. At the site level the assessment measures the **school** against desired graduation outcomes. This type of assessment is best done in combination with a grade analysis report review. Transcript assessments are also beneficial when they occur right after formal grade reporting periods.

Transcript Framework for Self-Assessment Checklist

Step 1: Actualize Equity
- ☐ **District:** Define the ideal state through board policy and procedure.
- ☐ **Site:** Use board policy and procedure to implement scheduling strategies to achieve the ideal state.

Step 2: Assess Equity
- ☐ **District:** Determine the distance between the current reality and the ideal state as defined by graduation expectations and/or outcomes at each school by grade level and student group.
- ☐ **Site:** Determine the distance between the current reality and ideal state at the school site as defined by graduation expectations and/or outcomes by grade level and student group.

Nongraduates	☐ Examine the transcript trends of nongraduates for three or more years.
IEPs	☐ Analyze the impacts of special education/IEP scheduling mandates, for example, push out support classes taught by a special educator.
English Learners	☐ Analyze the impacts of English learner scheduling mandates, for example, newcomer centers, English Language Development, Academic Language Development, push out supports, and so on.
Mandates	☐ Analyze the impacts of additional local, state, and federal mandates.
Summer School	☐ Analyze the impacts of summer school.
Grading	☐ Analyze the impacts of course failure.
MS Math	☐ Analyze the impacts of middle school math on course placement.
MS Language	☐ Analyze the impacts of middle school world language on course placement.
Course Sequences	☐ Analyze intended versus actual Equitable Core course sequencing and access by student group.
Transcriptions	☐ Analyze transcription errors.
Waivers	☐ Analyze requests for graduation waivers due to site error.

Step 3: Act on Equity
- ☐ Considering district context, determine the order and timing of required adaptive and technical shifts to move the current reality closer to the ideal state.

Step 4: Adjust for Equity
- ☐ Continuously monitor the effectiveness of actions being taken.

FIGURE 3.8 CHECKLIST ASSESSING THE EQUITY ACROSS TRANSCRIPTS

- ✓ Which student groups are not graduating on time each year? Are they programmed to graduate on time? Are there particular courses that act as gatekeepers due to continued failure?

- ✓ Are mandated course work for special education and English learners positively impacting student outcomes? Are mandated interventions and remedial courses positively impacting outcomes?

- ✓ Which students are passing and failing by student group? Which teachers, content areas, and/or courses have the highest and lowest failure rates? Which periods of the day experience the highest failure rates?

- ✓ Is summer school working? Who is successfully recovering credits?

- ✓ Are students being enrolled in the Equitable Core and appropriate alternative means course sequences? If not, what trends exist?

- ✓ Are visual and performing arts courses scheduled as pathways not electives and/or courses to place students who have holes in their schedules?

- ✓ Are the middle schools supporting kids to reach Algebra/Integrated Math I and language course competition? At what rate? Which middle schools?

- ✓ Do transcripts contain errors? If so, what trends are in the errors? Which sites are writing transcript waivers? What are the trends in these errors?

- ✓ Is the bell schedule equitable? Are all students accelerating, remediating, and taking co-requisities within the school day without losing elective options?

- ✓ Are students accessing dual college course work and other advanced studies opportunities equitably?

FIGURE 3.9 QUESTIONS TO CONSIDER WHEN CONDUCTING A TRANSCRIPT SELF-ASSESSMENT

STEPS TO CONDUCT A DISTRICT- OR SITE-LEVEL TRANSCRIPT SELF-ASSESSMENT

Request and review reports by student groups to determine if access to specific items in the Transcript Framework for Self-Assessment Checklist is equitable or segregated.

Consider the following:

- What patterns did you observe?
- Reflect on why these patterns might exist.
- What concrete actions might you (or your team) take to disrupt the patterns that stand in the way of equitable outcomes?

Leaky Pipeline Assessments

To design equity-achieving schedules, site leaders must be able to use data to prioritize what is important from what is **most** important. They must be able to work with other site leaders in their clusters to align these priorities. Districts must use this data to examine the system as a pipeline and identify the "leaks" (i.e., dropouts, etc.) that exist in the entire school system. Pipeline audits allow school systems to focus on triage and systems change simultaneously. Pipeline audits allow school districts to disrupt systemic inequities.

> *To design equity-achieving schedules, site leaders must be able to use data to prioritize what is important from what is most important.*

Leaky pipeline self-assessments can be conducted at the district level. The template in Figure 3.10 reflects the district process as it is aligned to the Leaky Pipeline Framework for Self-Assessment. Additionally, Figure 3.11 provides questions that should be considered when conducting a leaky pipeline self-assessment.

Leaky Pipeline Framework for Self-Assessment

This is a district-level assessment that examines one graduation cohort from K–12 against desired graduation outcomes.

Leaky Pipeline Framework for Self-Assessment Checklist	
Step 1: Actualize Equity ☐ Define the ideal state through board policy and procedure.	
Step 2: Assess Equity ☐ Determine the distance between the current reality and the ideal state as defined by graduation expectations and/or outcomes at each grade level.	
Nongraduates	☐ Examine the nongraduates or students who did not graduate high school in four years.
Retention	☐ Examine which students left, why they left, and when they left.
Behavior	☐ Examine which students exhibit behavior, which behaviors, and when these behaviors occur.
IEP Referrals	☐ Examine special education referrals by school, grade, and classroom.
English Learners	☐ Examine reclassification and long-term English learners trends by school and grade.
Access	☐ Examine student group access to the Equitable Core.
Readiness	☐ Examine the relationship between elementary outcomes and graduation outcomes, for example, third-grade reading levels.
Alternative Means	☐ Examine alternative means to the Equitable Core in middle school.
Step 3: Act on Equity ☐ Considering district context, determine the order and timing of required adaptive and technical shifts to move the current reality closer to the ideal state.	
Step 4: Adjust for Equity ☐ Continuously monitor the effectiveness of actions being taken.	

FIGURE 3.10 CHECKLIST ASSESSING THE LEAKY PIPELINE TO GRADUATION

- ☑ Which student groups didn't graduate on time? Were these students programmed to graduate on time? Are there particular courses that acted as gatekeepers due to continued failure?

- ☑ When did students leave the district (i.e., grade levels)? Which students left the district (i.e., student groups)? Why did students leave the district (i.e., moving from area, transferring to charter schools, military transfer, dropouts, and so on)?

- ☑ Are there patterns connected to students who didn't graduate on time and/or who left the district for alternatives like charter schools?
  - Were there any academic and/or behavioral trends in elementary and/or middle school? Were any trends specific to classrooms and/or schools?
  - Were any students pushed out of the tier I environment for mandates in elementary and/or middle school? Were any trends specific to classrooms and/or schools?
  - How many students were referred for special education services in elementary and/or middle school? When were they referred (i.e., grade)? Who referred them (i.e., are there any classroom trends)? Did any of these students ever exit special education? Were any trends specific to classrooms and/or schools?
  - Were diploma-bound special education students scheduled in regular courses (not a separate track with special education teachers) in middle school? Were any trends specific to classrooms and/or schools?
  - How many students were identified as English Learners in elementary school? How many students were reclassified? When were they reclassified? Did any of these students leave elementary and/or middle school as long-term English learners? Were any trends specific to classrooms and/or schools?

- ☑ Is there any relationship between academic outcomes, behavioral trends (as measured by suspensions and expulsions), and attendance rates from TK–12?

- ☑ When students earned D or F grades, was anything significant done to address gaps? Were these strategies successful?

- ☑ What do grading trends look like in classrooms and schools over multiple years? Are there patterns like a bell curve? What are the implications?

- ☑ Are bell schedules equitable? Do some bell schedules support more positive outcomes?

- ☑ Are there any examples of classrooms and/or schools where all student groups experience success? Where are they? Are there particular strategies and/or mindsets present?

- ☑ How can pipeline data be used to disrupt graduation trends in the future? Does your system currently reflect an understanding that graduation begins in elementary school?

FIGURE 3.11 QUESTIONS TO CONSIDER WHEN CONDUCTING A LEAKY PIPELINE SELF-ASSESSMENT

Note: TK is transitional kindergarten.

STEPS TO CONDUCT A DISTRICT- OR SITE-LEVEL LEAKY PIPELINE SELF-ASSESSMENT

Request and review reports by student groups to determine if access to specific items in the Leaky Pipeline Framework for Self-Assessment Checklist is equitable or segregated.

Consider the following:

- What patterns did you observe?
- Reflect on why these patterns might exist.
- What concrete actions might you (or your team) take to disrupt the patterns that stand in the way of equitable outcomes?

Whether your self-assessment includes an examination of the course of study, schedules, transcripts, and/or the K–12 pipeline, knowing the distance between intention, action, and outcomes within a system is a powerful tool for identifying the most effective levers for change. Once data are collected, it is important that the information be used to norm teams around equity-driven scheduling behaviors. Self-assessments conducted through the lens of cultural proficiency require both technical and adaptive considerations in response to findings.

Act on Equity

The third step in this self-assessment process is acting on equity. The data collected from equity self-assessments reveal the distance between the desired state and the current reality, so data from these assessments can be used to establish context-specific guidelines for scheduling teams focused on equitable outcomes. Establishing equity-driven schedule expectations helps scheduling teams ask the right questions before making important decisions about schedule design. Consider the following example of how a schedule and transcript self-assessment set of data findings was translated into schedule expectations.

HIGH SCHOOL SCHEDULING EXPECTATIONS: *STUDENT CENTERED AND EQUITY DRIVEN*

Establishing an Equitable Core

- The scheduling team in partnership with stakeholders have approved a sequencing of courses that eliminates the possibility of tracking students, and limits the number of stratifying courses within the same subject area, to maintain overall school demographic heterogeneities within each course offering.

Postsecondary Access

- All students are scheduled into the courses needed for graduation and college-ready requirements, that is, the Equitable Core.

Maximizing Instructional Time

- The bell schedule is leveraged to support the instructional program by providing time for monitoring student learning. Alternative bell schedules such as a 4×4 block or a seven-period day provide students the opportunity to accelerate course work, recover credits, and engage in co-requisite support within the school day. Schedules that include strong advisory and/or AVID (advancement via individual determination) programs provide opportunities for student goal setting, monitoring, and mentoring, and the reinforcement and alignment of college/career readiness skills.

AP, IB, and College Course Work

- School staff are acutely aware of the diversity gap in advanced placement or international baccalaureate courses offered on site, and the scheduling team has established goals and targeted scheduling strategies to increase the diversity of students accessing AP/IB courses offered.
- College course work opportunities are strategically built into the schedule to expand offerings each year with the same awareness toward diversity gaps in student placement.

Embedded Supports

- Student performance and diagnostic data are reviewed and used to determine which students need co-requisite support.
- Schoolwide diagnostic assessments for student reading comprehension levels and algebra readiness levels are used to identify all student needs beyond student labels such as ELs and IEPs.

Common Planning Time Within the School Day

- Preparation periods are strategically assigned to provide opportunities for teachers to collaborate during the school day. Common prep periods may be assigned by departments or grade-level interdisciplinary teams.

English Learners and Students With IEPs

- Diploma-bound priority consideration of course offerings are given to ensure on-time graduation requirements are met.
- Students are grouped strategically and placed with expert teachers certified to support English learners.
- Support and services are pushed into the general education environment so that students can access tier 1 instruction.

Least Number of Teacher Preps as Possible

- Taking into consideration that strong instruction begins with thorough lesson planning and preparation, limiting the number of classes teachers need to prep for facilitates better planning and instruction.

Maximizing Enrollment in Elective and Physical Education Courses

- Scheduling ensures the adequate number of elective and physical education course offerings based on student enrollment and class size.
- Student choice and the variety within elective offerings does not supersede a student's academic needs.
- The scheduling team in partnership with the instructional leadership has a clear vision of which courses will be offered to all students prior to course requests being collected.

Middle-School Course Completions

- Student scheduling in ninth grade aligns to the course completions in eighth grade, for example, world language, math, music, college career and technical education courses, AVID, and so forth, to properly schedule incoming students.

Strategic Science Sequencing

- Sequencing of science courses in grades nine through eleven include Biology, Chemistry, and Physics.
- Science course work is not selected to track based on mathematics performance.

(Continued)

(Continued)

Strategic Sequencing of CTE and VAPA Courses

- CTE and VAPA courses are an integral part of the instructional program and the students enrolled in these courses are interested in pursuing a multiple-year sequence that includes foundational, intermediate, and advanced courses.

Recovering Credits

- A thoughtful and strategic credit recovery plan that offers students a variety of methods for making up courses is developed and implemented. This plan includes viable and rigorous offerings within the school day, during extended days, online opportunities, and summer school offerings.

Strategic Staffing

- The placement of teachers within the schedule ensures that the neediest students have access to the most effective teachers.

Physical Classroom Assignments

- Classroom assignments should support the site's instructional program, structure, and teacher collaboration. A multiyear plan should be developed and implemented to ensure that classroom assignments are purposeful.

[online resources] Middle school, high school, and Linked Learning versions of the scheduling expectations are available online.

Adjust for Equity

The final step in this self-assessment process is to adjust for equity. Because scheduling teams evolve, self-assessments cannot be one-time events. Adjusting and reevaluating plans cannot be done with finality. One way that leaders can build a system of checks and balances throughout the school year, is to turn their schedule expectations into reportable analytics. At the district level, these analytics should be aligned to ongoing board of education reporting. At the site level, these analytics are part of an ongoing timeline aligned to grade reporting and the tracking of student progress. If scheduling expectations are attached to summative data outcomes, there will need to be additional formative monitoring systems in place. Adjusting for equity is not something done at the end of each year. It's something done all year. Schedules that aren't working for students shouldn't be "dealt with next year." They need to be addressed at the quarter or semester.

Adjusting for equity also means recognizing that one size does not fit all. There is no one strategy that works in all situations. School leaders who can cast a vision for change and support staff to identify the high-impact lever strategies for achieving that vision can build schedules that support students in their unique contexts. For this reason, the practice of copying the schedule over for the convenience of the builder must not be the first step of scheduling. It removes the strategic thinking needed to address the unique needs of any new group of students being served by the school. In addition, the course selection process must be reformed and updated yearly to align to the schedule expectations—a process that will be explored more fully in the next chapter. Schedules are the embodiment of the best thinking about what will meet students where they are as well as accelerate learning for all students. Self-assessing the effectiveness of that thinking is a critical step in achieving educational equity.

> *Adjusting for equity is not something done at the end of each year. It's something done all year.*

FINAL THOUGHTS

Architects of Equity know that to change the system they must understand the system. They use self-assessment to support their analysis of the alignment between action, intentions, and outcomes, doing so by always maintaining a focus on the four A's model–actualize, assess, act, and adjust. Whether beginning a self-assessment or using the results of an assessment to act, the adaptive and technical considerations that are needed within each unique context are critically important and must be carefully considered. Many change efforts fail when technical changes are not accompanied by adaptive considerations. Status Quo is always waiting around the corner, so carefully thinking through what to do with the data uncovered and who might need to be engaged prior to enacting change is an essential part of the self-assessment process. Reflecting on the following questions is one way to prepare for the self-assessment.

TECHNICAL SELF-ASSESSMENT QUESTIONS (above the green line)	ADAPTIVE SELF-ASSESSMENT QUESTIONS (below the green line)
1. Do districtwide administrative regulations currently exist for Graduation Procedures and Alternative Means to Graduation? If not, how will our team help facilitate this process? 2. What high-impact levers and/or strategies do you see surfacing from the self-assessment? How do you know they are high impact? What actions are attached to those levers? 3. What timeline have you established for the change process? How will you organize people and resources to engage your context with appropriate urgency? 4. What will ongoing monitoring of the self-assessment findings and responses look like? How will you structure efforts to build consistency and efficiency?	1. Will this self-assessment cause anxiety and/or concern for any stakeholders? Why? How will you message the "why" in a way that is nonthreatening? 2. How will you build a shared purpose for the self-assessment? How will stakeholders feel connected to the self-assessment in positive ways? 3. How will you select members of the self-assessment team? (It is as important to consider those **you** think should be at the table as those who think **they** should be at the table.) 4. How will information be messaged frequently, transparently, and authentically throughout the process? (In the absence of information, people will fill the space.) 5. Are any of the proposed changes going to challenge stakeholder values, beliefs, and sense of identity? How will you predict potential impacts and address them prior to impact?

CHAPTER 4

DESIGNING THE EQUITABLE CORE AS A ROAD MAP TO POTENTIAL

USING COURSES TO SUPPORT TALENT, NOT SORT IT

> *Changing Practice 2: Scheduling Teams Must Design Core Sequences That Impact Equity*

> *There is no heavier burden than an unfulfilled potential.*
> —Charles Schulz

Griselda was excited for the new school year. She had successfully completed two years of high school earning all A's and B's in her courses, and she felt she was ready for a challenge during her junior year. Griselda visited her counselor to request access to advanced placement (AP) English Language and Composition, which would be the first advanced course she would take in high school.

During the meeting with her counselor, Griselda found out that requesting an AP class was not as easy as it sounded. Since she didn't take advanced English in tenth grade, she would have to take a written test to qualify for access to the AP section. She was also told that she could access Honors American Literature instead of the AP class, a course that also earned a weighted credit. Griselda was confused. If Honors American Literature and AP English Language and Composition were both weighted courses, why could she easily access one but not the other?

Griselda decided to take the test for the AP class. She asked if there was a test prep class or any guidance for what would be expected on the writing exam.

There wasn't. She took the writing test and received word that she did not qualify for the AP class. Griselda enrolled in the Honors American Literature class where she noticed that many of the students looked like her, Latinx. This contrasted with the AP class where many of her White and Asian peers were scheduled.

Something about this did not sit right with Griselda, but she trusted that the school was acting in her best interest. It was only when she applied for colleges two years later that she learned to get into her dream college, they expected applicants to challenge themselves by taking the most rigorous course work available at the school. Griselda had not done this as she was denied access to several AP classes, which were the gold standard at her high school. While Griselda was still accepted to a state college, she was keenly aware that the course access provided to students at her high school was a gateway or an obstacle to postsecondary opportunities.

Griselda's story is an example of schedule design grounded in the belief that course access should be determined based on perceptions of readiness. Gatekeeping structures like prerequisites, tests, prior course-taking patterns, and so on were used before anyone took the time to examine her transcript, recognize her strengths, and offer her co-requisite support that might be necessary to take on the challenge of advanced placement courses. Instead, she was enrolled into a class that matched her perceived ability. Griselda was sorted rather than supported.

SORTING TALENT RATHER THAN SUPPORTING IT

As discussed in chapter 3, most educators build schedules with the wrong purpose in mind: sorting talent rather than developing it. Nowhere is this more apparent than in course sequencing—the order in which students progress through course work in various subject areas, most notably in math and science. Sequencing has been a part of our educational system since time immemorial (Education Commission of the States, 2005). It operates under the belief that in some subjects, knowledge builds sequentially—that students can't be exposed to Statistics until they complete Algebra II, or they can't understand Physics until they've learned Physical Science.

> *Most educators build schedules with the wrong purpose in mind: sorting talent rather than developing it.*

The problems with sequencing are the same as those with traditional scheduling in general. Students who are perceived as advanced receive access to rigorous course sequences, since schedulers assume they're on a pathway to college. Meanwhile, students who plan on entering the workforce, who haven't reached proficiency, or who are not behaviorally compliant are shunted into less demanding classes, severely limiting their options after graduation.

The assumption that varying levels of tracked courses will expose all students to the same knowledge and expectations for rigorous instruction throughout four years of school does not hold true across the educational system. Research shows low- and high-track classes are provided with vastly different content and markedly different learning opportunities (Argys et al., 1996; Domina et al., 2016; Kettler & Hurst, 2017; Oakes, 2005, 2008). Thus, a system exists in which well-meaning, intelligent, hard-working students are not provided equal access to excellent teachers, and the widely held belief that education is the great equalizer becomes a myth.

There's a reason why course sequencing continues despite all that educators know about the disparities it creates: It's easy and it's safe. Educators don't have to spend time carefully determining a student's academic needs or providing challenging course materials regardless of their academic abilities and future plans. Instead, they can herd students through a predetermined sequence of classes based on subjective (and too often culturally biased) beliefs about their intelligence and ability to succeed in the future (Alhadabi & Li, 2020; Darling-Hammond et al., 2007; Grissom et al., 2015). The process has profound implications for academic achievement, since the students scheduled away from college-ready sequences generally don't have access to the most capable teachers, as well (Sampson, 2019).

But there's a more insidious rationale behind this pervasive practice of sequencing. It's a way to keep students "in their place." Course sequencing, which is a form of tracking, was intentionally designed at the turn of the 19th century to deal with the rise of immigrant children enrolled in public schools (Futrell & Gomez, 2008). Over the next half century, it became a means through which students were segregated not just by race, but by income, class, and religion. As Futrell and Gomez (2008) write,

> *Students in the higher-level track are often taught enriched, challenging content, whereas those in the lower track are often given rote lessons characterized by filling in the blanks on a worksheet. Students in the first group may be taught a curriculum that reinforces how to learn and how to apply what is learned, whereas students in the second group may receive a more watered-down curriculum that emphasizes memorization. (para. 8)*

Decisions about student placement and course sequences, therefore, become institutional tracks, creating paths of benefit and paths of oppression. As a result, students absorb the qualities of the sequence in which they're tracked as they move through school, believing that they're "advanced," "average," or "below average" (Burić & Kim, 2020; Hammond, 2015; Kanno & Kangas, 2014). The most vulnerable populations—special education students, English learners, students who have historically failed course work, and other underestimated populations—are affected most profoundly.

Unfortunately, many public education systems operate within a self-fulfilling frame, a system where adult expectations of students become the students' realities. Some adults who design schedules hold deficit mindsets about learners that are deeply embedded in their decision-making processes. Consequently, students encounter unimaginable hurdles that lead to disengagement, passivity, and a feeling of invisibility in plain sight. Encountering these barriers is especially true for many students living in poverty who traditionally have less access to early childhood education, more access to segregated schools with low test scores and graduation rates, and less exposure to experienced and effective teachers (Levitan et al., 2022; McFarland et al., 2018; TNTP, 2018; U.S. Department of Education, 2014).

It's not surprising, then, that minoritized students often come up on the losing end of these sequencing decisions, particularly in math. As Ngo and Velasquez (2020) write, those Black and Latinx students who are directed into low-stakes courses not only miss out on opportunities afforded to their White and Asian peers, but also receive "a harmful message that advanced courses are not for them, or worse, that they are not smart enough to participate. It's a dangerous perception that fuels the persistent gaps in opportunities that exist in schools across the country" (p. 4).

Like scheduling in general, sequencing is a moral issue.

Additionally, a significant barrier to scheduling students on the margins is connected to resource equity. Because supporting these students might require a shift in how resources are assigned and used, conversations about making these changes are sometimes met with a scarcity mindset—the fear that if resources are allocated to one group of students they will be taken away from another group of students. This fear is often associated with the positions of privilege that have been established as precedent in many schedules. For example, to provide a support class for reclassified English learners in an advanced section of English, might compromise an under-enrolled section of AP Research with 10 students in it.

There are ways, however, that Architects of Equity can create subject matter sequences that support more equitable outcomes and maximize opportunities for all students. The purpose of this chapter is to demonstrate the importance of scheduling teams intentionally and purposefully constructing course sequencing within the Equitable Core, so that all students have access to the same rigorous courses taught by content area experts. This chapter supports a shift from traditional sequencing patterns to a strong Equitable Core; explains the four commitments educators need to create more equitable sequencing; offers four strategies to build equitable course management systems; and recommends ways to monitor course scheduling with an eye toward providing a rigorous Equitable Core for all students.

TRADITIONAL SEQUENCING

Think of traditional sequencing in a K–12 school system as a triangle. All students enter at the base and a selected few leave at the top as college and career ready. Traditional sequencing takes on different forms depending on the grade level. In elementary schools, where students have one primary teacher for an entire school year, access to core subjects is directly correlated to the approximately six-hour lesson map designed by the teacher. These maps are focused primarily on tested subjects like math and English language arts, and subjects like science and social studies are attended to at varying levels.

Where equitable scheduling becomes a challenge is in how schools and districts choose to provide support and services for English learners, special education students, and students reading below grade level. Some elementary schools push the support and services into the general education environment so that these students can access tier 1 instruction. Other schools push the support and services out of the general education environment to "fill in the gaps," which many times widens the gaps. These elementary school scheduling decisions have serious consequences for graduation from high school and postsecondary access.

In most middle schools, students experience education through a series of siloed courses throughout the day. Unfortunately, much of what has occurred in elementary school has a direct impact on what is done with students in the middle school schedule (Irizarry, 2021). Students who are perceived as being proficient are placed in accelerated math and advanced sections of classes and often have access to a variety of electives. Many times, diploma-bound students who were pulled out of tier 1 mainstream instruction for intervention in elementary school, are further isolated in courses like Reading Intervention, Math Intervention, or in parallel core course work that is taught by special education staff. Due to traditional bell schedules that accompany these scheduling decisions, these students lose access to electives to make room for these interventions, which further isolates them from the ability to connect to a strength, interest, or passion like the arts or career pathways.

High school is where traditional sequencing patterns are applied most consistently. Ability grouping, often denied as a practice by administrators today, but extremely prevalent, provides layers of choices within grade levels, which create tracks of benefit and tracks of oppression. Educators who serve underestimated students—and operate with a deficit mindset—are more likely to counsel them to pursue easier sequences. Underestimated students are more likely to receive intervention, remediation, and reading support, and less likely to have access to college prep courses, advanced studies, and algebra. Some student groups can't even get all the courses they need to graduate on time.

Figure 4.1 represents course variants that may emerge from the Equitable Core referenced in chapter 3. These core courses are typically offered as "choices," but end up tracking students by ability. In many districts, the variants expand by including separate sections for sheltered instruction and co-taught special education sections.

English 9
English 9 Advanced
English 9 Co-Taught
English 9 Sheltered

English 10
English 10 Advanced
English 10 Co-Taught
English 10 Sheltered

English 11
Honors English 11
English 11 Co-Taught
English 11 Sheltered
AP Language & Composition

English 12
English 12 Co-Taught
English 12 Sheltered
AP Literature & Composition
College Course

Unpacking a Course Sequence

- The titles of the courses in this sequence are not a factor. Any course that qualifies as college prep and meets 4-year college requirements is acceptable.
- The number of courses offered in each grade level are only an issue if they result in tracking student groups by race or ability. More course options, while well-intended, are not always utilized equitably. If proactive monitoring at the start of scheduling does not accompany good intentions, the results may not be equitable.
- The 11th grade course sequence might raise questions. If Honors English 11 and AP Language & Composition both earn weighted credits, why is there a need for both? If a student doesn't want to take the AP exam there is no reason he or she can't take the AP course and not the exam. Many school boards approve earning the weight without the exam. Students can also take AP exams without taking the course.
- Course sequences that exist beyond one course for all, must be accompanied by proactive enrollment monitoring.

FIGURE 4.1 TRACKED COURSE SEQUENCE
This is a tracked scope and sequence of courses in the English subject area. Some states separate course work for special education and English learners through parallel course work and other states do not.

Architects of Equity must ensure that a shift from traditional to equitable sequencing is made to eliminate decision making that results in student group isolation and segregation. Typical sorting mechanisms include grades, tests/test scores, prerequisite course work, special population designations (gifted and talented, English learner, special education), and so forth. One frequent by-product of these sorting mechanisms is that students identified for advanced tracks typically engage with teachers who have more experience, smaller class sizes, and lower loads overall.

These sorting practices lead to a troubling homeostasis: Those who make sequencing decisions for ninth graders hold the power to guarantee or prevent access to rigorous course work opportunities for these students for the rest of their high school career. Students in honors or advanced classes in middle school move into honors or advanced classes in ninth grade. This often sets students on a path of no return—one that leads toward graduation, the other a "road to nowhere," with no timeline and no certainty.

To ensure that course selection processes are crafted to support equitable outcomes, Architects of Equity must commit to building an Equitable Core that meets the following criteria (summarized in Figure 4.2):

1. **Course Choice Is Simple:** Offer standard course offerings that are amazing for all students.

2. **Course Choice Provides Advanced Access for All:** Rather than offer one regular and one advanced option in a grade level, offer two advanced options. One traditional and one grounded in a differentiated syllabus that allows students to earn advanced credits through competencies. (Refer to the Honors Biology/Biology example in chapter 3.)

3. **Course Sequencing Includes Proactive Co-Requisite Supports:** Students who are identified as needing additional support to master grade-level course competencies are provided co-requisite course sequencing support taught by the core teacher.

4. **Course Sequencing Prioritizes Push In Versus Push Out Strategies:** Course sequencing decisions protect access to the tier 1 environment by pushing supports and services in rather than out.

5. **Course Prerequisites Are Removed:** No course prerequisites, including prior course taking (i.e., completing Algebra to take Engineering, or taking Honors Chemistry to take AP Chemistry), test taking, grades, and so on are used to determine course access.

6. **Course Sequencing Decisions Include Proactive Monitoring Systems:** Course sequences must not become segregated ability tracks. Schools that

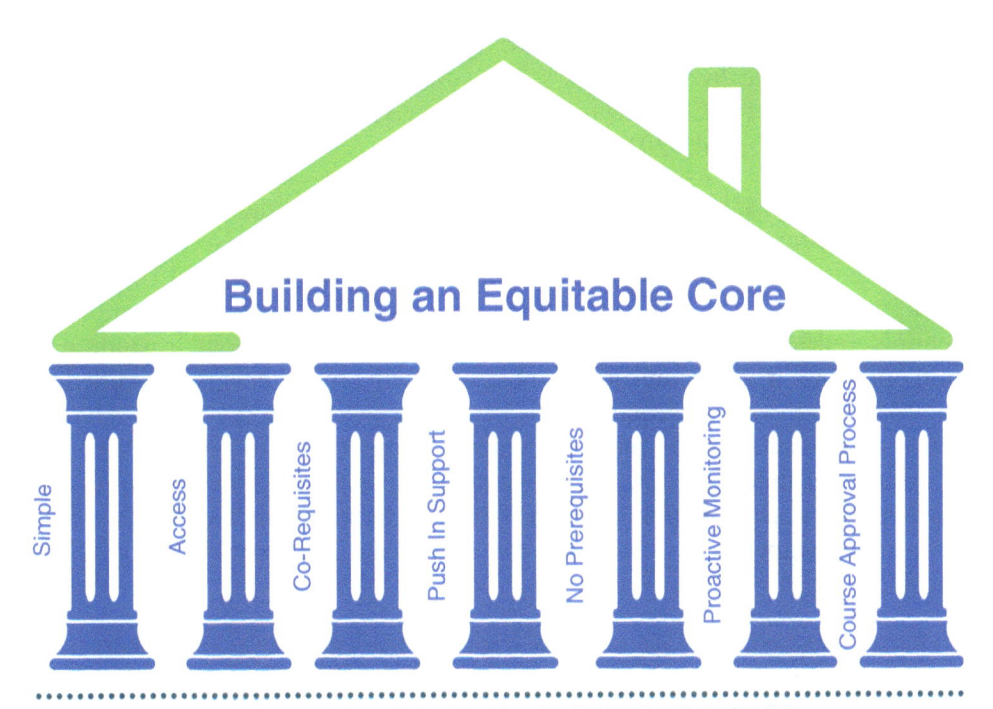

FIGURE 4.2 CRITERIA FOR BUILDING AN EQUITABLE CORE

adopt a stance that students should have "choices and options" that translate directly as courses, must design proactive monitoring systems that prevent choices from becoming a means to segregate student groups by race and/or ability.

7. **Course Selection and Approval Processes Exist:** The district ensures that the course of study, course approval process, and course approval committee are aligned to site selection of the Equitable Core.

While the criteria for establishing the Equitable Core in any context should be consistent, the actual courses established in varying local and state contexts may vary due to unique standards associated with graduating from high school. The bottom line is that the standard that is expected of the students perceived to be advanced is the standard for all students regardless of academic perceptions. Keeping the bar high but providing students appropriate supports to meet that bar is where equity lives.

Scheduling Mathematics: Moving Toward the Equitable Core

As the Asia Society (2023) states on its website, to understand the world through math means that we can understand patterns, quantify relationships, and predict the future. This idea underscores the belief that math helps us see the interconnectivity of the world through recognizing connections and possibilities. Math is the ultimate "opportunity sequence," write Federick Ngo and David Velasquez (2020), since it has the most obvious linear trajectory, with one course a prerequisite for the next. The sequence moves accordingly from Pre-Algebra (typically in middle school), Algebra 1, Geometry, Algebra 2, Trigonometry or Pre-Calculus to the ultimate goal for high-achieving students: Calculus (Schiller et al., 2010).

Of all the subjects, traditional (and inequitable) sequencing is most profound in math, because beliefs about mathematical ability and mindset are so deeply ingrained in our system. According to math scholar Jo Boaler (2013), "Ability grouping as a practice rests upon fixed mindset beliefs—it is implemented by schools and teachers who themselves have fixed beliefs about learning and potential and it communicates damaging fixed ability beliefs to students" (p. 149). Math course sequencing is crucial to improving equity in schools, but it's unfortunately the most challenging content area to reform. Whereas it's clear that understanding math is a critical competency for a future-ready learner, the structures that exist in many secondary schedules don't reflect that it's a competency all students can access and master (Schiller & Hunt, 2011).

Typically, secondary math systems organize in one of two sequences: integrated (a three-year sequence of Integrated Math) or traditional (a three-year sequence of Algebra–Geometry–Algebra 2). In addition, many districts offer advanced courses that don't go deeper into content, but rather accelerate students forward into higher grade-level content (see Figure 4.3). This

	6th	7th	8th	9th	10th	11th	12th
Integrated Math (IM) Sequence	Advanced 6	Advanced 7	Advanced IM I	Advanced IM II	Advanced IM III	Honors Pre-Calculus	AP Calculus
	Regular 6	Regular 7	Regular 8	IM I	IM II	IM III	Pre-Calculus
Traditional Course Sequence	Advanced 6	Advanced 7	Advanced Algebra	Advanced Geometry	Advanced Algebra II	Honors Pre-Calculus	AP Calculus
	Regular 6	Regular 7	Regular 8	Algebra I	Geometry I	Algebra II	Pre-Calculus

FIGURE 4.3 TYPICAL MATH SEQUENCES IN SECONDARY SCHOOLS, FEATURING AN ADVANCED TRACK AND A REGULAR TRACK

decision prevents movement for students from regular to advanced course work from grades six through eight, which is why the tests that allow access into sixth- and ninth-grade math are so coveted and are a finite sorting mechanism.

But multiple studies have shown that educators put significantly less emphasis on math sequences designed for non–college-bound learners. In a study published in 2010 in the journal *Equity & Excellence in Education*, researchers found that "lower track students were not only lagging behind in the mathematics course sequence, but also getting fewer opportunities to learn the material being covered in the courses in which they did enroll" (Schiller et al., 2010, Discussion and Conclusions, para. 1).

Math experts nationally discourage the use of accelerated math in middle school (Boaler, 2016; Steenbergen-Hu et al., 2016). But school districts still implement accelerated courses in middle school because there's a strong belief among parents and communities that there's a "race to Calculus" for college admission, and that the key to getting ahead is getting in the gifted or advanced math track. Several systems have attempted to remove accelerated courses in middle school but have been met with significant opposition from parents despite resounding support from national experts (Berwick, 2019; Boaler et al., 2018).

Unfortunately, this gateway-to-advancement stance continues to reinforce inequitable math outcomes and a need for remediation in math for many students who enter college. Access to the Equitable Core must mean access to a standard set of courses that support the mastery of competencies for graduation. Because ability tracking in middle school math has been a precedent for so long, some districts are piloting innovative options for mathematics as an alternative. One example is the San Diego Unified School District's (2023) Enhanced Mathematics (see Figure 4.4). While parents may still opt to place their students in the traditional advanced sections of math

	6th	7th	8th	9th	10th	11th	12th
Enhanced Algebra Options (SDUSD)	Advanced 6	Advanced 7	Advanced IM I	Advanced IM II	Advanced IM III	Pre-Calculus	AP Calculus
	Regular 6	Regular 7	Regular 8	IM I	IM II	IM III	Pre-Calculus
	SDEM 6	SDEM 7	SDEM 8	SDEM 9	SDEM 10	SDEM 11	AP Calculus

FIGURE 4.4 SAN DIEGO ENHANCED MATHEMATICS (SDEM) IN GRADES SIX THROUGH ELEVEN

Note: SDUSD is the San Diego Unified School District.

6 and 7, other parents have the option of placing their students in an alternative advanced course that teaches the same content and competencies but through a multidimensional approach to math. Students are not tested into this course and all students can opt in. This rigorous course requires students to go deeper, not faster, into content through project-based and hands-on learning. The hope is that eventually Enhanced Mathematics will be the core course offering for all students.

Course access to mathematics has profound racial and cultural implications, as revealed in a 2002 study by the National Center for Education Statistics:

> *In accord with previous research on coursetaking patterns, the most advanced course sequences—precalculus–calculus and precalculus–Advanced Placement/International Baccalaureate calculus—were more likely to be followed by Asian and White students, high SES [socioeconomic status] students, students who live with both parents in the family, students who attended Catholic schools, and students who expected to earn a bachelor's degree.*
> (Bozick & Ingels, 2008, p. iv)

If systems want to stop sorting students and start supporting them, Architects of Equity must recognize that adult expectations become student expectations of themselves. There is no single course sequence that is the "right" one, and no one-size-fits-all approach exists—or would be advisable to adopt even if it did. However, sometimes the intent of a course can be lost by the mindset of the user. Figure 4.5 examines the complexities and potential inequities of tracked math courses over a four-year period.

There is no one right way to build the Equitable Core in mathematics. However, once a district designs and adopts an Equitable Core, this act cannot be met with exceptions based on categorical presumptions about who can and cannot master the Equitable Core. If an Equitable Core is adopted, but then staff decides the Equitable Core is only for some students, the district hasn't adopted an Equitable Core.

Algebra I
Algebra I Advanced
Algebra I Co-Taught
Algebra I Sheltered
Geometry I
Geometry I Advanced
Geometry I Co-Taught
Geometry I Sheltered

Geometry I
Geometry I Advanced
Geometry I Co-Taught
Geometry I Sheltered
Algebra II
Algebra II Advanced
Algebra II Co-Taught
Algebra II Sheltered

Algebra II
Algebra II Advanced
Algebra II Co-Taught
Algebra II Sheltered
Data Science I
Data Science I Advanced
Pre-Calculus
Honors Pre-Calculus
Statistics
AP Statistics

Data Science I
Data Science I Advanced
Pre-Calculus
Honors Pre-Calculus
Statistics
AP Statistics
AP Calculus A/B
AP Calculus B/C
Business Math
Financial Math

Unpacking a Course Sequence

- The titles of the courses in this sequence are a factor. Most students who enter high school needing Geometry and/or Algebra II are a small group of students who took accelerated math in middle school. Many times this small group of students becomes the most under-enrolled and powerful singleton in the schedule.
- The number of courses offered in each grade level is only an issue if it results in tracking student groups by race or ability.
- Co-requisite supports must be prioritized to accelerate grade level math mastery for students in the "lower" track.
- The smaller a school's enrollment, the more financially impactful ability sequencing becomes.
- Course sequences that exist beyond one course for all must be accompanied by proactive enrollment monitoring.
- Many school districts do not require a third year of math even though it is a 4-year college requirement. This decision can promote inequities as the parents of college-bound students will follow a higher standard sequence.
- Specialty courses like Data Science, Business Math, and Financial Math must be carefully monitored if they are offered in the 3rd year against the standard high-quality Algebra II graduation requirement. These courses must be equitably enrolled, receive the same weight as Algebra II, and meet the same level of college entry requirements. All students should be required to meet the Equitable Core. If Algebra II is the high-quality option for students on the advanced track, resources must be in place to support all students to master this course. High-quality alternative means to graduation courses, including college courses and integrated career pathway themed courses, should be available if proactive monitoring is in place.

FIGURE 4.5 SCOPE AND SEQUENCE OF COURSES IN MATH SUBJECT AREA

Using Co-Requisites Versus Prerequisites

One solution to increasing equitable access in math is allowing all students open access to what have traditionally been considered "advanced" math classes — but with proactive support. This might mean enrolling students in co-requisite math courses, ideally those taught by their core content teacher.

Unlike prerequisites, which are courses taken before the core class, co-requisites are horizontal supports that provide immediate access to the Equitable Core at the same time students are mainstreamed into it. Students can work on what they don't understand with the same teacher who determined that they don't understand it. Assuming core classes have approximately thirty students enrolled, the co-requisite classes would be capped at sixteen, which would give the teacher more time for individual instruction. In Figure 4.6, three highly qualified teachers have been assigned co-requisite classes connected to their core math classes, providing over one-third of their students additional support.

Occasionally, arguments are made that co-requisite supports are too expensive. It is an interesting argument given that when AP classes have low enrollments, they are still offered. Many people believe students have the right to access AP classes and they should be offered despite the cost. On the other hand, when students struggle—especially English learners and special education students—arguments are made that additional support classes are not possible because the district did not allocate funding for them. The district did not allocate funding for AP classes to run at ten students and below either—but for some reason there is a belief that access to AP is a right but access to co-requisite support is a luxury. This is not equity-driven thinking.

In addition, many secondary schedules include math sequences that include a variety of math support courses, math intervention courses, and double blocks of math that reinforce the idea that time is the solution for accessing math content. Rarely are these interventions connected to the tier 1 math class in support of first-time math course taking mastery. Unlike interventions, co-requisite supports are proactive structures that assume students will

	P1	P2	P3	P4	P5	P6
Math Teacher 1	Algebra I 30 students	Algebra I 30 students	Algebra I 30 students	Co-requisite 16 students	Co-requisite 16 students	PREP
Math Teacher 2	Co-requisite 16 students	Co-requisite 16 students	Algebra I 30 students	Algebra I 30 students	Algebra I 30 students	PREP
Math Teacher 3	Algebra I 30 students	Co-requisite 16 students	Co-requisite 16 students	Algebra I 30 students	Algebra I 30 students	PREP

FIGURE 4.6 SCHEDULES FOR CORE/CO-REQUISITE MATH TEACHERS
Notice that teachers share a common prep, which allows them to collaborate on designing, implementing, and refining the core content and co-requisite class.
Note: This model could also be used to design English learner support in ELA with the designated English language development (ELD) course acting as the co-requisite.

success when provided the appropriate support. These courses should be taught by the most successful tier 1 math teachers.

Scheduling Science: Moving Toward the Equitable Core

Science can be an engaging and hands-on medium for learning by doing—but only if the experiences are designed with an asset mindset. The Next Generation Science Standards (NGSS) are giving schools permission to think more strategically about how science instruction can help accelerate learning in other content areas. But like math, scheduling science as a subject area has been plagued by traditional gatekeeping for access and opportunity.

Sequencing in science varies due to two philosophies about the order in which content should be taught. One school of thought argues that the sequence should be physics, chemistry, then biology so the student moves from the cell to the mammal. The other claims that biology, chemistry, then physics is the best sequence, since it moves students from the least to the most math-heavy course. Another challenge in science sequencing is the use of prerequisites, a staple for accessing advanced or AP course work. Prerequisites make it difficult, if not impossible, for underestimated students to move to a more advanced science track that leads to high-wage, high-skill professions in science, technology, engineering, or math (STEM). It also makes some courses redundant, especially for advanced students taking AP courses, who are often required to pass the advanced or regular versions of the same course first or are required to pass a math class at a certain level prior to acceptance. Advanced placement, international baccalaureate, and college options should be open to all students, with the appropriate support to ensure student learning and success.

In many districts, only one life science and one physical science course are required for graduation; however, standards for four-year colleges often require a three-course sequence. This leaves many students only taking the minimum of an integrated science and biology, leaving them without the opportunity to enroll in chemistry and physics, classes that are typically required for STEM majors. Indeed, too often, physics is not even offered in urban schools largely attended by minoritized students (Kelly, 2013). This inequity in access to physics needs to be addressed in a comprehensive district and school site plan to improve science education for students in urban locales if the goal of "science for all" is to be attained.

Too often minoritized students are underrepresented in math-heavy courses like calculus, physics, engineering, and computer science under the guise of being unprepared or not having taken the appropriate prerequisite math class. Lack of access creates barriers to possibility. If students do not have opportunities to engage in calculus, physics, engineering, and computer science course work, how will they know of the opportunities to pursue career pathways in these highly lucrative fields? Figure 4.7 examines the complexities and potential inequities of tracked science courses over a four-year period.

Unpacking a Course Sequence

Physics I
Honors Physics I
Physical Science I
Earth Science I

Chemistry I
Honors Chemistry

Biology I
Biology I Advanced

AP Physics
AP Chemistry
AP Biology
AP Environmental Science

1. The titles of the courses in this sequence are a factor. Science courses should not be used to track students by perceived math ability. Many schools place math savvy students in one course and less math savvy in another.
2. The number of courses offered in each grade level are only an issue if they result in tracking student groups by race or ability.
3. Co-requisite supports must be prioritized to accelerate grade level math mastery for students in the "lower" track.
4. Course sequences that exist beyond one course for all, must be accompanied by proactive enrollment monitoring.
5. Many school districts do not require a third year of science desipte the fact that it is a 4-year college requirement. this decision can promote inequities as the parents of college bound students will follow a higher standard sequence.
6. Many AP courses in science occur after the typical physics, chemistry, and biology sequence, but they earn the same graduation credit so it is not necessary.

FIGURE 4.7 SCOPE AND SEQUENCE OF COURSES IN SCIENCE SUBJECT AREA

Alternative Means and the Equitable Core

Most states include alternative means to graduation as part of their Graduation Policy. Usually, the alternative means regulations are used to qualify conditions by which special populations (military, homeless, foster, English learners, etc.) can meet state graduation minimums. As it relates to building an Equitable Core, the alternative means regulations can also allow high-quality course equivalents for the Equitable Core. Three critical alternative means allowances include dual credit/dual articulated college course work equivalents, integrated career-pathway-themed course equivalents, and language other than English course equivalents. These options must also be proactively monitored to ensure they are not tracked by race and/or ability. Examples include (a) allowing students to take a four-year transferable English class at the college instead of taking senior ELA at the high school, (b) allowing a course like Project Lead the Way Introduction to Engineering and Design to count as a high school physics credit, and (c) allowing students to take a university-approved LOTE (language other than English) exam to demonstrate proficiency at the second-year level in their home language as a two-year language graduation equivalent. More about this will be discussed in chapter 5.

FOUR COMMITMENTS FOR EQUITABLE SCHEDULING

After outlining specific examples in math and science, contrasting traditional practices with the importance of maintaining fidelity to the Equitable Core, there are four commitments that Architects of Equity can make during their scheduling process to ensure access for all students (see Figure 4.8).

> *Imagine a K–12 system that emphasized competencies that all students could master—not lowering the standards, but broadening the definition of success.*

Commitment 1: Stop Sorting by Ability

Consider Girl Scout merit badges. The assessments Girl Scout leaders use to determine who gets a badge aren't designed to measure who hiked the farthest or who wrote code the fastest but are instead designed to meet competencies. The hope is that everyone earns the badge. The assessments aren't designed to be competitions, pitting one scout against another. Now imagine a K–12 system that emphasized competencies that all students could master—not lowering the standards, but broadening the definition of success.

Commitment 2: Adopt Co-Requisites Over Prerequisites

As discussed, prerequisites add an additional layer that limits access. One solution to overcoming this barrier is allowing diploma-bound students access to equitable sequencing with appropriate supports like co-requisites. Students who are struggling with math, for example, should be enrolled in a co-requisite math course in addition to the core class. If possible, this co-requisite should be taught by the core content teacher.

Commitment 3: Allow Open Access to Advanced Course Work Options

Access also needs to be defined more broadly. Allow all students to earn advanced credit if they choose to complete work beyond defined

| Stop Sorting by Ability | Use Co-Requisites Rather Than Prerequisites | Allow Open Access to Advanced Course Work Options | Be Mindful of the Illusion of Choice |

FIGURE 4.8 FOUR COMMITMENTS FOR EQUITABLE SCHEDULING
There are four commitments Architects of Equity must make for scheduling equity.

competencies. Remember Griselda and the gatekeeping that prohibited her from enrolling in AP English Language and Composition. Don't separate advanced students from regular students. Indeed, equitable sequencing should break the relationship between ZIP Codes and predetermined student performance (Reardon et al., 2019). A student's address should no longer determine his or her destiny.

Commitment 4: Be Mindful of the Illusion of Choice

Some schools and districts place the responsibility of course sequence choices on the student, saying that they let the student "choose" their pathway. However, the student may have unknowingly agreed to take course work that would potentially prevent access to a four-year college. In other circumstances, similar student groups make "choices" about courses that derail any chance of graduating college ready. This illustrates why systems must reexamine the definition of personalized learning and choice. The problem is that personalized learning doesn't live in the sequencing of course work, especially when a path is determined for a student (Rickabaugh, 2016). This is the *illusion of choice*. These paths are paved with courses that are driven by sorting mechanisms, including grades, tests and test scores, prerequisites, special population designations, class size, and teacher loads.

> *Equitable sequencing should break the relationship between ZIP Codes and predetermined student performance.*

FOUR STRATEGIES FOR DESIGNING SYSTEMS THAT SUPPORT COURSE EQUITY

In addition to the four commitments Architects of Equity must make in creating equitable course sequences, districts must commit to building systems that protect access to the Equitable Core (see Figure 4.9).

Revision of the Course of Study

Revision of the Course Approval Process

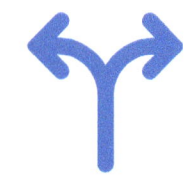

Develop a Rigorous Alternative Means Policy

Revise Course Selection and Credit Checking Tools

FIGURE 4.9 FOUR STRATEGIES THAT SUPPORT COURSE EQUITY
The Equitable Core is formed by using these strategies.

Strategy 1: Revision of the Course of Study

Once a course of study self-assessment has been completed (discussed in chapter 3), the district must use the findings to make decisions about how to revise the course of study to align options to the Equitable Core. The technical work of revising the course of study must be done in partnership with the adaptive strategies necessary to prevent significant and public push back. In collaboration with site leaders, district office staff should work to strategically develop a process to share information about the changes, consider how course assignments impact teacher identities, and understand the relationships that exist among individuals, departments, and schools in relation to these courses.

Strategy 2: Revision of the Course Approval Process

A critical step in ensuring course equity in a school district is to revise the course approval processes and establish a course approval committee at the district level. To ensure that courses are aligned to the Equitable Core, consider the questions in Figure 4.10.

Course approval committees are critical to maintaining course equity throughout the system. These committees must conduct ongoing monitoring of the creation of courses and the student outcomes associated with these courses. Establishing this committee with balanced voices from the district and the sites is always key.

Strategy 3: Develop a Rigorous Alternative Means Policy

An alternative means procedure is a companion policy to the Graduation Procedure that clearly outlines any acceptable course equivalents that require board approval outside of the course of study. This policy should be created, and board approved, to allow for rigorous and engaging course work opportunities that may extend beyond the district course of study, such as

- Transferable college course work
- Integrated pathway-themed course equivalents
- Language other than English equivalents

Strategy 4: Revise Course Selection and Credit Checking Tools

Course selection cards, and the subsequent course selection process, must be aligned to the Equitable Core. Using the Equitable Core templates (standard and pathways versions) that are provided in the appendices and online at https://companion.corwin.com/courses/equitableschoolscheduling, Architects of Equity can purposefully and transparently provide four-year course options to families at a glance and in alignment with meaningful district graduation expectations. This will enable scheduling teams to examine the

- ✅ What is the current internal process for approving courses before submitting them to the board for approval?

- ✅ Does the course approval process include an approval committee? Does representation include all content areas, special populations, operations specialists, and site leaders at all levels? Who leads this committee?

- ✅ If an Equitable Core has been established, what will be the criteria for this committee to consider any divergence from the Equitable Core course work?

- ✅ What constitutes a quorum for committee approvals?

- ✅ When a course is being considered, who must be there from the site? Who must be there from the central office? Does the site have to get approval from the principal's supervisor to submit the course?

- ✅ What approval criteria must be set for courses that are not college prep?

- ✅ How will the committee ensure that student need and access is a priority in decision making?

- ✅ Has a process been put in place to make sure that site staff submitting a course for approval has met with the core content department responsible for the suggested course and received their support and approval prior to submission to the committee?

- ✅ How will sites be notified about the results of their submission?

- ✅ Is at least one site leader from a high school, middle school, and elementary school on this committee?

- ✅ Is district staff participation on the committee equal to site representation?

- ✅ Is anyone who is not a voting member of the committee but would like to speak on an item allowed to attend?

- ✅ Does the chair of this committee have (1) a deep understanding of courses, course sequences and graduation requirements; (2) experience leading a school site; (3) the ability to facilitate adaptive and technical conversations grounded in data and evidence; and (4) the ability to cast the odd vote?

- ✅ Are representatives from Counseling, Career Technical Education, English Learner Support, and Information Technology regular members of the committee?

FIGURE 4.10 QUESTIONS TO CONSIDER WHEN DESIGNING A COURSE APPROVAL PROCESS

impacts of offering elective choices in relationship to the Equitable Core. Course choices, especially electives, should be carefully offered by grade level and teacher section availability to avoid fiscal impacts. (This will be covered further in chapter 7.)

In addition, credit check forms are used by counselors to tally the completion of courses required for graduation. These forms should be aligned to the Equitable Core. Credit check forms and transcripts should be discussed with students and families/guardians or at a minimum sent home to students and families/guardians after each grading period as they clearly articulate progress toward reaching course work and credit proficiencies. Too often, students and their families do not see credit checks and transcripts until the senior year, which may be too late for some students. In addition, sometimes it is assumed that families understand the requirements they have been provided. Sample high school and middle school credit checks are available in the online resources for this book at https://companion.corwin.com/courses/equitable schoolscheduling

PROACTIVE MONITORING TO ENSURE ACCESS TO THE EQUITABLE CORE

After gaining a deep understanding of the differences between traditional sequencing with the establishment of an Equitable Core, reviewing four commitments educators can make to ensure fidelity to the core, and following four strategies to build equitable course management systems, Architects of Equity must tightly monitor progress toward these goals and consistency of practice. Ultimately, the Equitable Core is nonnegotiable. Divergence from the core must only be considered after everything possible is done to support students to meet the competencies within core courses.

The Equitable Core must always default to college prep course work. It should be aligned to an alternative means policy that allows engaging, rigorous, and strategic course equivalents, **not** ability grouping tracks. Sequencing of the Equitable Core must develop a strong foundation for high-quality learning by leveraging structured-choice sequencing.

To ensure that a student's language or disability status is not a barrier to enrollment in the Equitable Core, staffing and budgeting must prioritize students with exceptional needs. No one right course sequence exists. No one-size-fits-all approach to scheduling students is recommended. However, systems and schools must establish an Equitable Core—a sequence of courses that all students are entitled access to as a guaranteed right, as a standard of excellence to meet college and career readiness.

Now that Architects of Equity understand the power and potential of equitable sequencing, it's time to discover how to monitor its impact on equity. Cultures of accountability are good for adults and students, but they must be designed and modeled by strategic scheduling teams who understand that at the core of any good instructional program are structures that guarantee ideal conditions for learning. Therefore, monitoring must be a regularly scheduled engagement including the site principal and the scheduling team. This is done by frequently collecting and analyzing data about the relationship among intentions, actions, and outcomes (see Figure 4.11). School and district leaders should examine the results of equitable sequencing regularly with an eye toward results: grades, summative test results, college admissions, course pass rates, and other data. And perhaps one of the most important questions to ask when reviewing this data is, What's the impact of this action on the neediest students?

When examining the relationship between intentions, actions, and outcomes, it's clear that leaders were successful in the technical act of identifying and enrolling students of color in AP classes. However, the adaptive challenges associated with teacher mindsets weren't addressed when students were enrolled without being tested (and therefore failed to earn weighted credits). Finding out this information at the end of the year is too late. Site leaders must work closely with staff to create a culture of accountability through frequent monitoring of enrollment and outcomes.

One reason why gaps exist in intention, action, and outcome in Figure 4.11, is that the right questions weren't asked on the front end of the decision making. This questioning process might include sitting down with the scheduling team at the start of the scheduling process to review the roster of first-time AP enrollees for the upcoming year and asking the questions in Figure 4.12.

While the questions in figure 4.12 apply to first-time AP students, any underestimated student group (or all student groups) could benefit from this type of personal and purposeful monitoring and accountability. It will disrupt dysfunctional trends in real time—when they can be changed, not when they are final.

FINAL THOUGHTS

To begin to peel back the layers of inequity in school systems, scheduling teams must get comfortable with assessing equity regularly, clarifying expectations based on those data, and monitoring the implementation of

Intention	Action	Outcome
Data revealed that many students of color in the school didn't have access to advanced studies courses and/or didn't earn weighted credits.	More sections of AP were opened, and growth mindset criteria were used to identify students of color who had AP potential. These students were enrolled in AP course work.	Enrollment of students of color in AP classes increased overall, but the number of students tested and the number of students passing AP tests declined significantly.

FIGURE 4.11 GAPS IN INTENTION, ACTION, AND OUTCOME
Architects of Equity must ensure that intentions, actions, and outcomes are aligned. What's missing from this model is a clear plan for monitoring and accountability.

- [x] Which AP courses are the friendliest for first-time students? What does the AP potential report say about the type of AP class in which the student might be successful?

- [x] Which teachers are the most successful in supporting students from diverse backgrounds and experiences to show mastery in the course competencies?

- [x] How can AP courses that first-time students are enrolled in be placed before lunch in the schedule?

- [x] How can first-time AP students and any other students who require additional support be placed in co-requisite course supports connected to the AP course?

- [x] How can we make sure that teachers and other staff members who reflect the gender and racial diversity of the first-time AP students have the opportunity to provide feedback on the courses, teachers, and experiences that are designed for success?

- [x] Do first-time AP students have one adult on the campus that they trust and believe cares about them? How do we know? Have these adults been activated as mentors to check in informally?

- [x] How will first-time teachers of AP receive ongoing, professional learning to support student success?

- [x] How are students doing in the AP class? Are they still enrolled?

- [x] Who will communicate student progress in AP with families and administration in a timely and proactive cycle?

- [x] Did students submit the proper paperwork and/or fees to take the AP exam, and how is any financial need being handled?

- [x] Do students need additional after-school or Saturday support for mastery of AP competencies?

- [x] Have the first-time students been collected and encouraged by the principal at least 30 minutes before school on the day of the exam?

- [x] On testing day: (1) Have the students eaten? Do they have something to drink? (2) Is a trusted and encouraging adult the proctor in the room? (3) Is the enrollment of the testing room small? (4) Is the room where the test is being given and the set-up of the seats legal but welcoming?

- [x] What is planned for the first-time students to celebrate this accomplishment after the test is over?

FIGURE 4.12 QUESTIONS TO CONSIDER WHEN PROVIDING MORE ACCESS TO ADVANCED PLACEMENT CLASSES

high-functioning staff teams. Architects of Equity create schools that are strategically organized to support the academic and social needs of students who have multiple risk factors for failure.

QUESTIONS ARCHITECTS OF EQUITY ASK BEFORE CONSIDERING COMPROMISING THE EQUITABLE CORE

- Has this decision produced significant results for students each year?
- Will this decision potentially end the ability for a student to be college and career ready?
- Will this decision ensure the best chance of grade-level mastery this year?
- What is the impact of this action on the neediest?
- Am I allowing special interest groups to dominate schedules?
- Are you meeting learning objectives by sorting or learning?
- Am I challenging course effectiveness?

TECHNICAL SELF-ASSESSMENT QUESTIONS (above the green line)	ADAPTIVE SELF-ASSESSMENT QUESTIONS (below the green line)
1. Has the district established an Equitable Core? If so, is it being equitably implemented across schools? 2. Does an alternative means to graduation administrative regulation exist? If not, how will our team help facilitate this process? 3. Does a course approval committee exist at the district level? If not, how will our team help facilitate this process? 4. Is the course of study revised yearly? 5. How are course enrollments monitored and acted upon in your district?	1. Will the establishment of an Equitable Core make any staff nervous? What will you do to provide meaningful input/feedback from staff throughout the process? 2. How will you build a shared purpose around the Equitable Core and approved alternative means course work? 3. How will you select or recommend staff for the course approval committee? How can you collaborate on designing the criteria for staff selection? 4. How will you involve staff in any course of study revisions? Are there union regulations defining engagement. If not, how will you create opportunities for input? 5. How will you present and discuss data that reveal course segregation by student group?

CHAPTER 5

SCHEDULING THE MARGINS

> *Changing Practice 3:* Scheduling Teams Must Prioritize the Historically Marginalized

Children in every community are born with the same potential, but not the same opportunity. This is often a result of systemic inequities beyond young people's control.
—San Diego Workforce Partnership

Marginalized: treated as **insignificant** or **peripheral** (Oxford Languages)

Kevin was excited to receive word that he had been accepted to the new magnet program at Mustang High. He had a passion for media arts, and he planned to specialize in video production so that he could one day work behind the scenes at a company like ESPN to shoot a variety of sporting events. He was sure that being bilingual, speaking Spanish at home and English at school, would be an asset as well.

When Kevin arrived at Mustang High for orientation, he and his parents were asked to attend a special meeting in the theater at 11 a.m. so that the ninth-grade counselor could talk to them about his schedule for the upcoming year. At this meeting, Kevin and the other students were told that because they did not score at a proficient level on the English Language Proficiency Assessment in eighth grade, they were required to take mandated courses in addition to their core course work. Kevin translated what was being shared for his Spanish-speaking parents as he was trying to digest the information in English for himself.

The counselor explained that students take six classes each day. In ninth grade, Kevin would be required to take English I, Algebra I, Physical Education I, Spanish I, Designated English Language Development (ELD), and a math intervention course. Kevin asked when he would take the media class. He was told that would happen in tenth grade if it fit into his schedule. He also asked why he had to take Spanish since he could speak it fluently. He was told that taking two years of Spanish was a requirement for graduation and since he didn't begin Spanish in middle school, he was behind. He also asked when he would take Biology because he knew other ninth-grade students had this course in their schedule. He was told that the designated ELD and math intervention courses were mandatory given his test scores so he would just take Biology later in high school. The counselor also asked him if he would like to take Algebra I or Quantitative Reasoning I for math. Kevin wasn't sure what to select. The counselor explained that Quantitative Reasoning was a class focused on data analysis and sometimes helped students prepare to do well in difficult courses like Algebra I. Kevin thought that sounded great and he "chose" Quantitative Reasoning without understanding that the course did not meet college admission requirements.

This experience left Kevin devastated. He left orientation feeling demoralized and began to think of ways he could convince his parents to place him in his neighborhood high school. He couldn't remember being told the importance of some of the tests he was given in eighth grade. He wasn't sure he even tried or took these tests seriously. Any enthusiasm Kevin had for school was gone.

Kevin's story is a typical example of how the schedule can become a vehicle of compliance rather than a pathway to potential. Because many student groups that are performing below grade-level expectations are required to participate in mandated course work, and because many traditional bell schedules have no room for "extras," students who need to be engaged, inspired, and filled with hope are denied access to courses that make learning relevant.

This chapter will focus on how Architects of Equity must operate with a growth mindset when scheduling traditionally marginalized students.

SCHEDULING THE MARGINS

As previously stated, Architects of Equity establish an Equitable Core set of course sequences that are the guaranteed pathway of excellence for each student. If the Equitable Core is the established road map of excellence for all students, it must be protected at all costs. When building equitable schedules, scheduling teams must be aware of how their perceptions, values, and experiences inform decision making. As the keeper of this compact with the community, Architects of Equity must be keenly aware that signs of deficit mindsets in scheduling are evidenced when the Equitable Core is compromised. Architects of Equity must act with urgency when there are signs that the Equitable Core is being compromised in the following ways:

- The **order of courses will be rearranged** for **some** students. Sometimes this results in math-heavy courses (both math and science courses) being diverted to upper grade levels.

- Some students will have **grade-appropriate courses removed** from their schedules during that grade level. This typically happens when mandates are added to a limiting bell schedule and/or when the scheduler thinks the student needs a lighter course load.

- Some students will be placed in **parallel courses.** These courses receive the same graduation credit but do not qualify for college entry. Many of these courses are taught by teachers without highly qualified core content, single-subject credentials.

- **Alternative means courses will be offered without proactive monitoring** of student group enrollments and meaningful graduation outcomes. Alternative means course option enrollments should be reflective of student interests not student group isolation and/or segregation.

- **Bell schedules that cannot support the demands of both mandated and meaningful courses** within the Equitable Core will continue to be used despite inequitable outcomes.

- **Multiple four-year diploma options will be offered in ninth grade**—separating advanced studies, special education, and college career and technical education pathways into separate tracks. These "options" become tracked course sequences.

This chapter will specifically discuss the equitable scheduling shifts that must be made to support traditionally marginalized students: special education students, English learners, students reading below grade level, and those ready for acceleration.

Schedules can be unforgiving and when faced with competing priorities, many times marginalized groups are scheduled on the periphery.

MINDSET AND THE MARGINS

If the Equitable Core is the road map for excellence at the school, it is important for the Architects of Equity to prioritize scheduling efforts to ensure that historically marginalized students are scheduled strategically. Nothing can be accidental or after the fact when scheduling the margins. Schedules can be unforgiving and when faced with competing priorities, many times marginalized groups are scheduled on the periphery.

Special Education

Architects of Equity must strategically use the site schedule as a road map to accessing the general education environment if equity is a priority:

> *The legal and scientific basis for special education services points to the positive outcomes for students with disabilities when they receive an inclusive versus segregated education. Yet nationally, students with disabilities, in particular students of color and students in urban settings, as well as students with specific disability labels (such as autism or intellectual disability), continue to be removed from general education, instructional, and social opportunities and to be segregated disproportionately when compared to White students who live in suburban and rural areas and those who have less intensive academic support needs.*
>
> *(National Council on Disability, 2018)*

For the purposes of this discussion, the special education students referred to are diploma-bound students with Resource Specialist Program and/or self-contained Special Day Class designations.

There is no group of students more impacted by mindset than students with disabilities. It begins with the special education referral process that focuses its attention on identifying potential causes of academic and/or behavioral performance concerns raised by a teacher or teachers, but rarely equally examines the classroom instruction the student is receiving and its potential impacts on learning. Additionally, once a student is identified as needing diploma-bound special education services, many decisions about these students are based on their perceived abilities, rather than evidence-based decisions about supports and services that must be used in the general education environment to support students to access tier 1 instruction (Shifrer et al., 2013). Evidence that this is a mindset issue is that many individualized educational plans (IEPs) include skills-based versus standards-based goals, and there are rarely IEP meetings focused on how to exit special education. Instead, many times being labeled special education leads to an underestimation of the student's true capabilities. And worst of all, the students (and sometimes their guardians) internalize these beliefs, which become their beliefs about themselves.

Mindsets about diploma-bound special education students are evident in scheduling practices.

Scheduling teams who believe in and act on the concept that the IEP is a road map for accessing the general education environment are going to design scheduling practices that encourage tier 1 access. Scheduling teams who believe the IEP is a sign that a student is not capable of achieving the standard course work for a meaningful graduation, many times use "poor you" scheduling practices like short scheduling, diverting course work, or encouraging course choices that are less math demanding.

Consider Figure 5.1. One student is scheduled with a growth mindset and reaches meaningful graduation outcomes. The second student is scheduled with a deficit mindset and meets basic graduation standards.

In Carol Dweck's (2006) research on mindset, she offers the idea that approaching learning with a "not yet" mindset sets the stage for belief that learning happens at different times for different people. If scheduling practices are anchored in a "not yet" frame of mind, the scheduler's strategy would be focused on how to best organize time and structure to support the student to perform at or beyond their grade-level peers. Figure 5.2 contrasts the difference in mindsets and the direct impact this has on student learning.

The reason why mindsets matter is that decisions that are made about students in ninth grade set students on a learning path that is rarely diverted. It is crucial in this moment that everything is done to make sure that scheduling mindsets are acting strategically to leverage fiscal and human resources to act urgently and meaningfully. Special education and general education pathway models are available for your review in the appendices and online. Additionally, Figure 5.3 outlines guiding questions that help teams focus on making decisions that support meaningful and equitable postsecondary futures for students who qualify for services and supports, and Figure 5.4 provides role clarity for collaborative co-teaching teacher teams at https://companion.corwin.com/courses/equitableschoolscheduling

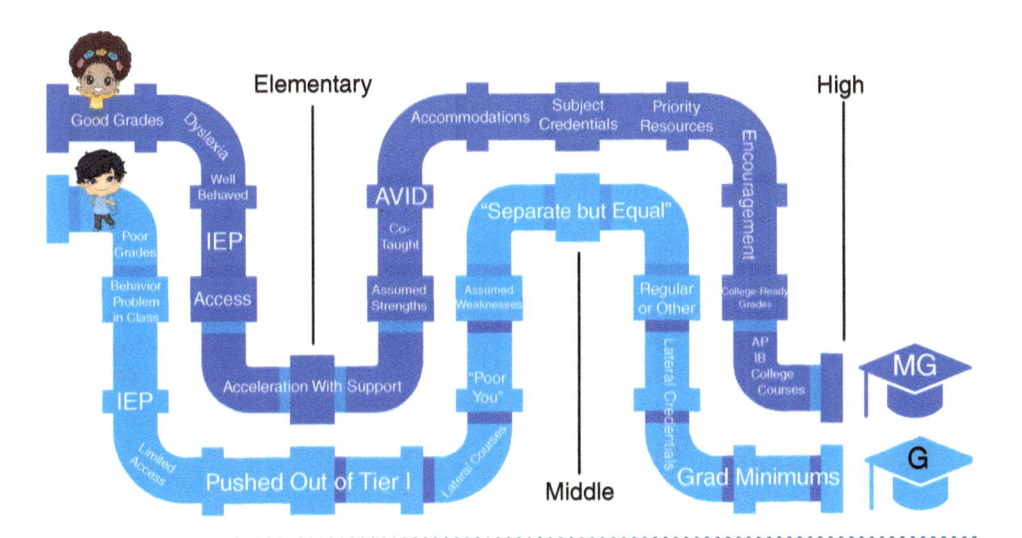

FIGURE 5.1 TWO STUDENTS WITH IEPS

Scheduling mindsets impact two pathways of students who are identified as having learning disabilities. One student achieves a meaningful graduation (MG) while the other, a typical graduation (G).

Note: AP is Advanced Placement; IB is International Baccalaureate.

Growth Mindset	Deficit Mindset
Diploma-bound special education students are placed in co-taught courses with highly skilled core content teachers delivering core instruction paired with highly skilled special education teachers implementing supports and services. Counts for graduation from high school and college access with appropriate grades, GPA, and so on.	Diploma-bound special education students are placed in "parallel" core content courses where a special education teacher who does not have a single-subject credential, delivers the course work and assigns grades. Counts for graduation from high school but will not be accepted for college.
Diploma-bound IEP-mandated courses *are* connected to the tier 1 environment. The special education teacher who is part of the co-teaching model uses the support class to master concepts from the co-taught classes. Alternatively, a general education support class like advancement via individual determination (AVID) or an engaging core class supporting reading could be the mandated course and this teacher could share common planning time with the co-teaching team.	Diploma-bound IEP-mandated courses *are not* connected to the tier 1 environment. Students attend IEP-mandated courses taught by special education teachers who are trained to deliver skills-based instruction, not core content instruction. Courses like study skills fall into this category.
Diploma-bound special education students are placed in the Equitable Core set of courses—the standard required course work for graduation that prepares students for college and career.	Diploma-bound special education students are placed in courses that are perceived to have less math demand, parallel core classes taught by a special education teacher, or are short scheduled to make the day "easier."
Diploma-bound special education students are given priority to math and English language arts (ELA) classes earlier in the day with the most skilled/experienced teachers. Special education students are organized strategically in co-taught sections by similar accommodation needs.	Diploma-bound special education students are scheduled in courses tagged as co-taught or special education. The numbers of special education students are balanced across sections. Less skilled/experienced teachers are assigned to these sections.
Financial and human resources are prioritized to use the summer months to provide necessary diploma-bound courses for these students to progress for an on-time graduation.	The only courses available over the summer are those that the special education division makes available and pays to offer. Many times, these courses are not college prep or graduation equivalent.

FIGURE 5.2 GROWTH AND DEFICIT MINDSETS AS THEY ARE TYPICALLY APPLIED TO STUDENTS WITH DISABILITIES

English Learners

There is no group of students underestimated more than English learners. Because they are not fluent speakers of English, it is difficult for educators to assess the rich prior knowledge that they bring to learning. Many times, these

- [✓] What do the individualized educational plan **assessments** tell the team about the student's strengths? Areas of need?

- [✓] What Information in the **assessment** reports describes how the students learn best in the classroom? What recommendations are provided for accommodations? Modifications? What would these look like in the classroom?

- [✓] Do the descriptions of the **present levels** provide a clear understanding of how the student is performing in each of these areas?

- [✓] Will focusing on the **areas of need** provide access for the student to grade-level curriculum or appropriate functional skills?

- [✓] Do these **goals** align with the identified areas of need? Note: Each identified area of need needs to have a goal.

- [✓] Are the **goals** aligned to grade-level standards?

- [✓] Are the **goals** measurable? How will these goals be implemented? Who will work with the student on them?

- [✓] Do the **goals** make sense? If you were a non–special education person, do you know what the student is working on?

- [✓] Are **service** minutes uniquely designed to meet the needs of the students (rather than offered based on the program the school provides or the site schedule)?

- [✓] Are **service** minutes designed to ensure goals can be met?

- [✓] How will **service** minutes be delivered (co-teaching, push in, pull out, etc.)? How will the student benefit from these services?

- [✓] Based on the student's goals and services, what **placement** does the student require to meet their needs?

- [✓] What **placement** is the most appropriate and least restrictive in which these services should be delivered?

- [✓] In which **placement** will the student have the most access to their typical peers and still be able to achieve their goals?

FIGURE 5.3 USING THE IEP PROCESS TO GUIDE EQUITABLE SCHEDULING FOR STUDENTS WITH DISABILITIES

Special Education and General Education Collaboration

Special Education Teacher	General Education Teacher
Write and distribute IEPs in student classes.	Review IEPs and communicate questions and comments with the case manager. Use case manager for resources, strategies, and methodologies.
Implement IEPs within classes in which the case manager or paraprofessional is teaching. Monitor student progress quarterly in other classes unless concern is noted by general education staff.	Implement IEPs within classes in which the case manager or paraprofessional is not teaching.
Plan, coordinate, and run IEP meetings.	Plan, coordinate, and run student/parent meetings.
Communicate concerns with parents. Address appropriate negative concerns with follow-up phone calls to parents when general education staff communicate concerns with the case manager.	Communicate student concerns with the case manager. Contact parents regarding concerns.
Advocate for student needs (scheduling, behavior, etc.) by communicating with counselor.	Collaborate with the counselor to address discipline when necessary. Communicate with the case manager regarding student concerns.
Review progress reports when distributed. Contact parents with negative issues. Meet with counselors on failing grades in core classes and poor attendance.	Contact parents with negative issues before a progress report is distributed. Contact case manager with the same concerns.
Identify need, refer to psychologist when necessary, and organize implementation of behavior support plans.	Implement behavior support plans. Contact case manager with difficulties and concerns. Involve case managers in all suspensions/expulsions.
Prepare for IEP meetings by requesting general education comments and concerns regarding student progress.	Respond to case manager requests.
Address behaviors as necessary when the case manager is "pulled out" of class.	
Initiate and coordinate transition services.	
Support IEP assessments and standardized testing.	
Attend professional learning with the co-teacher.	Attend professional learning with the co-teacher.

FIGURE 5.4 COLLABORATION BETWEEN SPECIAL EDUCATION AND GENERAL EDUCATION TEACHERS

learners' understanding of ideas, concepts, and/or standards is masked by their inability to communicate what they know in English. It is critical that scheduling structures support the belief that assessing a student's ability to read, write, and speak English is a separate assessment of whether a student understands, for example, an English language arts standard like point of view. If the concept was discussed in the students' home language, it may become apparent that the student has a grade-level appropriate understanding of the concept.

This raises the question of why schools don't deliver content courses like math, science, and social science in English and the home language simultaneously, while students are learning to read, speak, and write English. Imagine engaging the world history curriculum with a teacher who speaks the home language and English and taking English or the mandated English language support class with that same teacher so that the ideas in the tier 1 class transfer to the language-mandated work. Instead, many times students are siloed into content area courses and/or denied access to some content courses. They are placed into an English language learner support class with a teacher who has a specialized credential, but that teacher has no common planning time with the core teachers and subsequently the work that happens in the support class has no connection to what is happening in the tier 1 class. A structural must in equity-driven scheduling is that any push out mandate must be directly connected to the tier 1 environment through team teaching and/or be taught by the tier 1 teacher.

Scheduling mindset also plays a role in how schools view students' home language. A mindset focused on equity views the home language as a strength and uses structure to reinforce that belief. For example, many high schools offer Spanish as a language offering. Students who are not native Spanish speakers enter Spanish Year 1 and many times students who are native Spanish speakers are also placed in Spanish Year 1. The argument is made that while these students speak Spanish conversationally, they can't read and write in Spanish, so they need to go in the beginning level. Some people recognize the inequities in this and create Spanish for Spanish Speakers Year 1 classes that silo Spanish-speaking students into a Spanish Year 1 class that has a different name and no advanced weight on the school transcript. Unless the Spanish for Spanish Speakers classes are earning advanced weighted grades, these courses are segregating students by perceived ability.

> *A structural must in equity-driven scheduling is that any push out mandate must be directly connected to the tier 1 environment through team teaching and/or be taught by the tier 1 teacher.*

Growth mindset thinking would see the home language as a strength and allow the students to take a university-approved language other than English (LOTE) test in their home language to determine whether they had already met the second-year graduation requirement level of language. If the student passes, he or she should be offered a higher level of Spanish that earns weighted/advanced credit on the school transcript. Many schools use this strategy and place these students in advanced placement (AP) Spanish with a growth mindset educator who assesses what they already know and provides tailored instruction focused on exactly what they need to know. These teachers understand that literacy in a student's native language supports their transition to English and directly impacts their academic work across the content areas. In other schools that cannot afford to open additional AP sections, Spanish speakers who pass the LOTE exam are placed in an advisory period with a Spanish teacher to prepare for the AP exam. Regardless of the strategy, scheduling structures, including courses, should be evidence of the school's values and beliefs about learning. Using any legal means available to validate English learners' strengths is paramount.

As an example, there are six different ways students can qualify for language to enter the University of California system:

1. Completion of two years of district **world language courses**
2. Completion of two years of district-approved **Independent World Language School (IWLS) courses**
3. Passing an **SAT II** (Scholastic Aptitude Test) **or an AP or IB** (international baccalaureate) **exam**
4. Formal schooling in a **language other than English**
5. Passing a **LOTE Alternative Assessment** with principal certification
6. Assessment by a **college or university**

What cannot happen is death by compliance. For example, at one high school in the greater San Diego region, West African immigrants who spoke Kizagua entered high school and their counselors placed them in French Year 1. Why? Because the district graduation standard required two years of the same sequenced language and the school did not offer Kizagua. So now this group of students who must learn English have to simultaneously learn French. This is educational malpractice. The students could have been offered a LOTE in their home language or an opportunity to take a language course like ASL (American sign language) at school or through dual enrollment. It should be a fiscal priority for the school to implement strategic options for English learners. Fiscal priorities like this are offered to AP students consistently in schedules. It's all about mindset.

Another way to provide strategic structural support for English learners is to take advantage of college dual enrollment programs and college admission approved language other than English qualifying options. Most community colleges have high-quality English learner programs and accompanying labs. Savvy districts with established college partnerships can collaborate to provide access to these programs through dual enrollment. These programs can also provide additional language programs not offered by the school, and many times professors can teach these classes on the high school campus.

In addition, research around reclassified English learners reveals that once reclassified, many of these English learners outperform their native speaking peers (Saunders & Marcelletti, 2013; Villegas & Ibarra, 2022). Unfortunately, varying district interpretations and subsequent mandates about English learner reclassification criteria often make reclassification very difficult. In some districts, teacher recommendation is a barrier to reclassification. In other districts, passing the state/federal test is the barrier—and in many schedules English learners are passing AP and advanced classes but are still forced to take an additional English learner–mandated course because they didn't pass the test. It should be no surprise that most adolescent English learners are not foreign born, and most scaffolding isn't temporary (Walqui, 2006). Reclassification is simply an invitation to the standard general education course work and should be a priority in scheduling given the positive results for students.

Scheduling structures approached with a growth mindset can help shift support from mandates that are left to multiple interpretations to purposeful experiences that reinforce access and mastery within the tier 1 environment. Figure 5.5 contrasts the difference in mindsets and the direct impact this has on English learner students.

To ensure that English learners are scheduled with the mindset that they can and will graduate on time, it is important to be deliberative about their pathways. Examining the site bell schedule and creating a mindset-proof equitable scheduling road map is one way to shift scheduling toward equitable outcomes—including an on-time and meaningful graduation. There is an EL pathways template in the appendices and a sample ELD pathways document available for your review online at https://companion.corwin.com/courses/equitableschoolscheduling

Students Not Reading at Grade Level

There is no group of students more in need of strategy than students not reading at grade level. Unfortunately, students who enter high schools unable to read and write at grade level are not only special education and English learner students. Many native English-speaking students are also struggling with grade-level reading, writing, speaking, and numeracy. Like special education and English learner students, students who are not proficient in literacy and/or numeracy are forced into mandated support courses (sometimes for large blocks in the day) that have little or no connection to the tier 1 core course work. Regardless of progress in these courses—which are usually accompanied by words like "intervention," "support," "study hall," and so on —students remain in these classes year after year until they either pass their core classes or transfer to an alternative school to earn a modified diploma. In one Northern California district, students who don't read at grade level by the time they enter high school are placed on an IEP—as if not being able to read is a disability, and the responsibility for the deficit is on the student. But it's easier to do this than hold a system accountable to using effective strategies to differentiate instruction in the classroom for each student.

Growth Mindset	Deficit Mindset
Diploma-bound English learners (ELs) are placed in core courses with highly skilled core content teachers leading instruction. These ELA teachers also teach the mandated designated EL section to ensure that the additional language supports are connected to the core learning.	Diploma-bound English learners are placed in a "parallel" core content course taught by a teacher designated as the EL teacher. Sometimes these students remain isolated for years in this instructional model.
Courses count for graduation from high school and college access with appropriate grades, GPA, and so on.	Some courses count for graduation from high school, but many times students must take an additional year to meet requirements.
Reclassification is a priority given the fact that data reveal that many reclassified English learners outperform their English-only-speaking peers.	Reclassification is desired but not fiscally prioritized. Roadblocks to reclassification exist but are not addressed.
Diploma-bound English learners are placed in the Equitable Core set of courses—the standard required course work for graduation that prepares students for college and career.	Diploma-bound English learners are placed in courses that are perceived to have less math demand, courses that do not count for graduation, or courses that segregate them by their home language (e.g., Spanish for Spanish Speakers) but do not provide advanced/weighted credit for completion.
Financial and human resources are prioritized to connect the EL-mandated courses to the tier 1 courses through common planning time and/or using the tier 1 English teacher to teach the mandated course.	There is no connection between the EL-mandated course and the tier 1 core course work. Teachers who teach ELs are working in silos.
Financial and human resources are prioritized to use the summer months to provide necessary diploma-bound courses for these students to progress for an on-time graduation.	The only courses available over the summer are credit recovery.

FIGURE 5.5 GROWTH AND DEFICIT MINDSETS AS THEY ARE TYPICALLY APPLIED TO ENGLISH LEARNERS

The reality is that students know when they are being placed in remediated course work, thus telling them they are "lesser." Rather than continuing to offer disconnected interventions that are rarely monitored for effectiveness, why not set higher standards for students and adults? For example, in one Southern California high school the principal recognized that each year 70% of the ninth-grade students entered the school reading at the primer to fifth-grade level and most had either failed or never taken Algebra. Rather than approaching this situation with a deficit mindset, the principal used some outside-the-box thinking to design an experience that would benefit all ninth-grade students. She went to the best and most popular social science teacher on the campus and proposed that all ninth-grade students in the media pathway should be enrolled with him all year in a course called GLOPED (Global Political Economic Decision Making). Since the state social science graduation requirement was only three years this would benefit the students in multiple ways: (a) They would graduate with four years of social science; (b) They would be reading, annotating, writing, and arguing for an additional period during the day without it feeling like it was a punishment; and (c) This would benefit all students—it could even help accelerate students who were ready. This teacher worked closely with the English teachers to ensure uniform instructional practices, and the course yielded amazing results. Most students accelerated three reading levels per year. Figure 5.6 contrasts the difference in mindsets and the direct impact this has on student learning for those reading below grade level.

Growth Mindset	Deficit Mindset
Students reading below grade level are placed in core courses with highly skilled core content teachers leading instruction. A universal screener is used to understand reading levels so that differentiation strategies including balanced literacy and leveled texts can be implemented in all secondary classrooms.	Students reading below grade level are placed in course work without any understanding of their current reading levels. Grades are used to make determinations about placement.
Students may receive an additional class for reading, but it does not have a title that includes "intervention," "support," and so on. Instead, this might be a ninth-grade history class focused on current events where students are asked to argue, annotate, and write each day.	Students are placed in math and/or ELA intervention classes that are not continuously monitored for their effectiveness. Many times these courses are mandated. These courses are not taught by skilled and experienced teachers.
Secondary teachers across subject areas are well trained in balanced literacy strategies like shared reading/writing, guided reading/writing, independent reading/writing, annotation, and so on.	Secondary teachers believe it is the role of the English teacher to deal with students who are not reading at grade level.
Students reading below grade level are placed in the Equitable Core set of courses—the standard required course work for graduation that prepares students for college and career. Fiscal and human resources are prioritized to appropriately support mastery. Financial and human resources are prioritized to use the summer months to provide necessary diploma-bound courses for these students to progress for an on-time graduation.	The only courses available over the summer are credit recovery.

FIGURE 5.6 GROWTH AND DEFICIT MINDSETS AS THEY ARE TYPICALLY APPLIED TO STUDENTS READING BELOW GRADE LEVEL

Students Ready for Acceleration

There is no group of students more limited by a desire to keep the highest-achieving students in the high school than students ready for acceleration. The beauty with this group is that public schools do not have to solve for this group entirely on their own. There are many resources outside the traditional secondary setting that can be tapped to provide accelerated experiences for students. Dual enrollment with local and virtual postsecondary institutions is an excellent option for many districts.

There are many benefits to college dual enrollment programs for students ready for acceleration:

- Students don't pay for classes.
- Savvy agreements allow students to take four-year transferable courses like English Composition.
- Students can earn multiple credits before attending college, parents/guardians save money on college tuition, materials, housing, and so forth.
- Students can get ahead in college and graduate in less time.
- Students with disabilities receive IEP-mandated support.
- The number of teachers provided to the high school is never reduced because students attend college courses.

Logically, it makes sense that if families can save money on college while students earn four-year transferable courses in high school for free, this would be a good thing for the students. Unfortunately, it's not that simple. Access to students ready for acceleration in a high school is primarily done through access to AP course work and higher levels of mathematics. Typically, these are courses that staff do not want to lose to college programs. A by-product of tracking courses is that many times teaching assignments become ability tracked, and subsequently racially tracked, as well. While some teachers are assigned students who struggle in literacy/numeracy, co-taught special education sections, interventions, and so on, other teachers are assigned AP, IB, and other advanced course work. These course assignments can become a teacher's identity. As a result, conversations about whether the college courses are as rigorous as the AP courses and other challenges to college course quality surface. One work-around districts have used to satisfy concerned teachers is that if students choose to take a dual credit class at the college, they also must take the AP equivalent at the school. This can be a disadvantage for the student, however, if both classes meet the same graduation requirement.

In districts with unions, arguments have been made that decisions about dual credit options should be bargained. Others believe that the principal has the "right of assignment" and makes the final decision about teaching assignments after staff input. Because decisions about access to dual enrollment are often dependent on local context, considerable inequities exist in access from school-to-school, district-to-district, and state-to-state. As a work-around, parents/guardians have figured out that they can use concurrent enrollment to by-pass any denial of access. This creates considerable school and family tension when families want these classes to count for graduation.

Unfortunately, when the conversation is about whether high school students should take the AP English Literature class at the high school or take English 101 at the college, the opportunity to use dual enrollment for the benefit of all students is missed. For every section of college course work that students who need acceleration take, the vacant seats left due to their absence can be repurposed to lower the class sizes of regular classes where English learners, students with disabilities, and students who are not reading, writing, or numbering at grade level can be supported. It might not make people happy to lose one to two sections of AP English Literature to pick up one to two sections of regular or co-taught tenth-grade English, but is it the equitable thing to do? Figure 5.7 contrasts the difference in mindsets and the direct impact this has on student learning for those ready to accelerate.

Finally, one myth that surfaces about providing access to dual enrollment course work within the school day is that the number of teachers allocated to the school by the district would be reduced. To be clear, the number of teachers a school is entitled to under budget allocations should never be

Growth Mindset	Deficit Mindset
Students who are ready for college in high school have access to four-year transferable course work that can be used as dual credit for high school.	Students who are ready for college in high school are forced to take certain advanced options because teachers do not want to lose the "smart" kids.
These students can take a combination of college, AP, and/or IB courses if they choose. The course of study at the school reflects an understanding that students are judged against their own school's course of study.	In addition, because of a desire to teach AP courses, more AP courses are offered than a student can complete, which makes college admission more difficult because students are judged against their own school's course of study.
Students who are ready for college in high school have access to support classes like AVID, where a high school teacher is collaborating with the college to ensure success.	Students who are ready for college take college classes with no high school support.
Students who are ready for college in high school are taking classes in a bell schedule that allows for flex periods that do not compete with other core or elective course work.	Students who are ready for college are not able to take college courses or must take courses through concurrent enrollment outside of the school day.

FIGURE 5.7 GROWTH AND DEFICIT MINDSETS AS THEY ARE TYPICALLY APPLIED TO STUDENTS READY FOR ACCELERATED WORK

reduced due to dual enrollment. In some states this is illegal. Regardless, it should not be done.

DUAL ENROLLMENT STAFFING IN THE SCHEDULE

Because the rules around dual enrollment vary across states, colleges, and local school districts, schools must be strategic in how they think about solving potential dual enrollment limitations. Colleges determine the certification standards for how adjunct staff are hired, so school districts must be strategic in how they aid teachers to meet these standards. Typically, college faculty have priority to teach sections, but when colleges are not able to staff sections the opportunity for district teachers to become adjunct faculty presents itself. In some school districts, strategies including supporting teachers to earn certifications through school district funding are explored.

Before school districts and colleges agree to allow teachers to act as adjunct professors during the school day, discussions about the collection of apportionment, potential double dipping, and the potential need to prorate the adjunct teacher FTE (full-time equivalent) must be facilitated. Potential district finance and teacher retirement matters may be impacted in certain contexts.

BELL SCHEDULES AND MINDSET

Not all bell schedules are created equally, and because they impact the ability to schedule students equitably, they are a key factor when strategizing how to schedule the margins. While the course schedule organizes classes into teacher lines, the bell schedule defines how students and teachers access courses and how much time is spent within courses. Traditionally, high schools have used a six-period bell schedule. In this model, students move between six classes that are each approximately 58 minutes. Teachers usually teach five classes and have one preparation period. The six-period bell schedule is advantageous because teachers see their students every day all year. Unfortunately, however, the schedule is not built to provide equitable access for students who need support beyond the typical course sequences for graduation.

Figure 5.8 represents typical graduation requirements in a six-period schedule. Note that any language requirements would take one to two spots marked "open." In addition, the classes marked "pathway" are held to allow students to follow a passion like career technical education, visual and performing arts, and/or electives like student government, yearbook, and so on.

Figure 5.9 shows the inequities of the six-period system when trying to meet typical English learner mandates. If a mandated EL course is required each year, the schedule cannot accommodate this without removing a "pathway" course in tenth grade. In addition, if the student didn't finish language requirements in middle school, one to two pathway courses in grades nine,

Six-Period System

9th Grade	10th Grade	11th Grade	12th Grade
1. English	1. English	1. English	1. English
2. Math	2. Math	2. Math	2. Math
3. Science	3. Science	3. Science	3. Science
4. Pathway	4. Pathway	4. Pathway	4. Pathway
5. PE	5. PE	5. History	5. History
6. OPEN	6. History	6. OPEN	6. OPEN

FIGURE 5.8 A TYPICAL SIX-PERIOD DAY FOR A GENERAL EDUCATION STUDENT IN A PATHWAY PROGRAM

Six-Period System

9th Grade	10th Grade	11th Grade	12th Grade
1. English	1. English	1. English	1. English
2. Math	2. Math	2. Math	2. Math
3. Science	3. Science	3. Science	3. Science
4. Pathway	4. Pathway	4. Pathway	4. Pathway
5. PE	5. PE	5. History	5. History
6. EL 1-2	6. History	6. EL	6. EL

FIGURE 5.9 THE SIX-PERIOD DAY DOES NOT ACHIEVE EQUITY IN COURSE ACCESS

eleven, or twelve will have to be removed to accommodate this requirement. Is it equitable and/or strategic to remove the one class within a day that might keep students interested in attending school? And anyone who looks at twelfth grade and comments that English learners would typically not take math and science in twelfth grade should make sure that the Equitable Core indicates that this is best practice for *all* students.

Figure 5.10 reveals that like English learners, special education students who are required to take an additional IEP-mandated course, face the identical limitations and options in the six-period schedule. And anyone who looks at twelfth grade and comments that special education students would typically not take math and science in twelfth grade should make sure that the Equitable Core indicates that this is best practice for *all* students.

Six-Period System

9th Grade	10th Grade	11th Grade	12th Grade
1. English	1. English	1. English	1. English
2. Math	2. Math	2. Math	2. Math
3. Science	3. Science	3. Science	3. Science
4. Pathway	4. Pathway	4. Pathway	4. Pathway
5. PE	5. PE	5. History	5. History
6. Study Skills	6. History	6. Study Skills	6. Study Skills

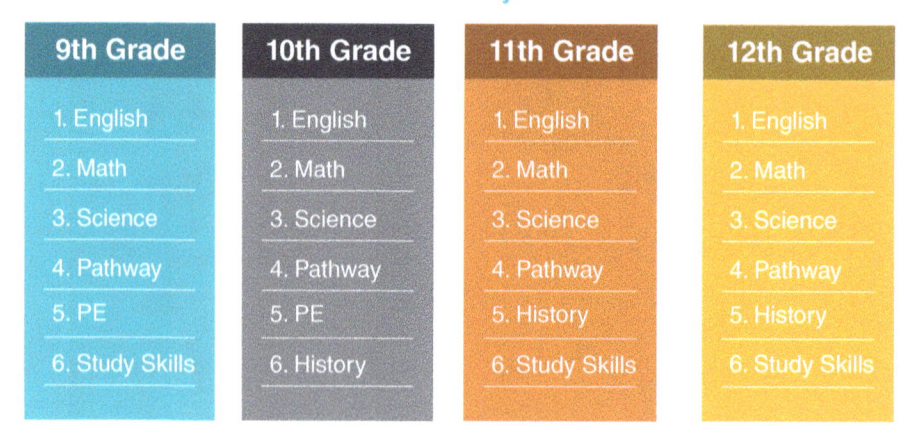

FIGURE 5.10 THE SIX-PERIOD DAY DOES NOT PROVIDE ACCESS TO THE EQUITABLE CORE FOR STUDENTS WITH DISABILITIES

Six-Period System

9th Grade	10th Grade	11th Grade	12th Grade
1. English	1. English	1. English	1. English
2. Math	2. Math	2. Math	2. Math
3. Science	3. Science	3. Science	3. Science
4. Pathway	4. Pathway	4. Pathway	4. Pathway
5. PE	5. PE	5. History	5. History
6. WL	6. History	6. Dual	6. Dual

FIGURE 5.11 THE SIX-PERIOD DAY IS CONSTRICTING FOR STUDENTS WHO REQUIRE ACCELERATION IN THEIR COURSE WORK

Figure 5.11 reveals that even students who are exceeding grade-level expectations have limited access to dual enrollment college options and additional electives in a six-period system. Students who are ready to accelerate would have to lose a "pathway" class in tenth grade to meet the second-year requirement for world language (WL) if needed. The only opportunities in this schedule exist if the "pathway" courses are removed.

While there is no one bell schedule that meets the needs of all schools, the following criteria should be considered when selecting an equitable bell schedule:

- All students get what they need without losing pathway and/or elective options.

- Teachers have more prep time each day to connect with grade-level teaching teams and nine to twelve department teams.
- Teachers teach fewer classes each day and for longer periods of time.
- Students make fewer transitions each day and/or each semester.
- The schedule promotes adult and student collaboration structures.
- Professional learning for teachers is embedded within the school day.
- Remediation and co-requisite support can occur within the school year rather than only during the summer or after school.

STRATEGIES FOR SCHEDULING THE MARGINS

To ensure that traditionally marginalized students become a priority in scheduling practices, Architects of Equity must commit to the actions presented in Figure 5.12.

Under the alternative means school district policy and the dual enrollment agreements with colleges, many college courses and integrated career technical courses meet graduation requirements. For example, in one district many courses count for graduation, gain weight on the transcript, and transfer to a four-year college. Some examples are shown in Figure 5.13.

BARRIERS TO SCHEDULING THE MARGINS

To ensure that traditionally marginalized students become a priority in scheduling practices, Architects of Equity must be aware of the barriers to scheduling the margins.

Barrier 1: Mindsets about student abilities

Barrier 2: Knowledge of best practices in schedule and bell schedule design

Barrier 3: Willingness to confront the status quo

Barrier 4: Continued delegation of the schedule process without oversight

Barrier 1: Mindsets About Student Abilities

Scheduling mindsets matter. Shifting scheduling practices from ability sorting to building pathways to potential is a crucial first step in the process. As stated in chapter 2, getting the scheduling team's MindSET requires a willingness to (a) start supporting rather than sorting, (b) engage collaboratively rather than in silos, and (c) transform strategically not just logistically. Because the stakes are so much higher for traditionally marginalized students, holding the scheduling team accountable to acting with a growth mindset is critical.

- ☑ Prioritize the scheduling of those in special education, English learner, students who are not reading at grade level, and students who need acceleration.

- ☑ Push supports and services into the core classroom so that all students can access tier 1 instruction.

- ☑ Design teaching lines where mandated English learner supports like designated ELD are taught by the same teacher who teaches the students the tier 1 ELA course so that supports are focused.

- ☑ Use co-teaching models where general education and special education teachers are paired in classrooms and share common planning time in the schedule.

- ☑ Ensure that diploma-bound special education IEP goals are standards based rather than skills based.

- ☑ Support diploma-bound special education IEP teams to make evidence-based decisions about student learning rather than relying on personal opinions.

- ☑ Support diploma-bound IEP teams to write IEP goals that focus on individual needs rather than grouping for schedules.

- ☑ Make scheduling expectations for English learners and special education students clear through bell schedule–aligned pathways.

- ☑ Raise awareness on how a school's course of study sets the standard for colleges to determine whether students have taken the most challenging curriculum.

- ☑ Support the use of differentiated syllabi so that students in every classroom can choose to earn honors credit for exceeding standard course expectations.

- ☑ Require that in order to teach an advanced, AP, IB or other weighted section of a course, the teacher must also teach the "regular" sections.

- ☑ Ensure that students have access to meaningful dual credit, dual articulated, and dual enrollment options through local colleges.

- ☑ Use summer months to offer first-time core course work taught by single-subject teachers for special education students, English learners, and students who are reading below grade level.

- ☑ Provide engaging alternative means courses to meet core course work. Rather than offering these courses as options, offer them as the Equitable Core.

FIGURE 5.12 STRATEGIES FOR SCHEDULING THE MARGINS
It is critical to schedule students on the margins prior to others to create access to the Equitable Core.

High School Graduation Requirement	Alternative Means to Graduation
Twelfth-grade English	English 101 at the community college
Ninth-grade English	ELD 5–6
U.S. History	Chicano and/or Black Studies at the community college
Physics	Introduction to Engineering Design (a Project Lead the Way career technical education [CTE] course approved by the University of California [UC]) Green UP and Go (a UC-approved CTE course)
Two years of a world language	Passing a UC-approved language other than English exam Spanish 4 for Patient Care (a UC-approved CTE-aligned course taught by world language teachers)
Twelfth-grade government	Political Science 101 at the community college
Algebra 2	Ag + Math = Calculated Sustainable Agriculture: Integrated Math 3 in Agriculture (a UC-approved CTE-aligned Algebra 2 class taught by a math teacher)
Third year of math or science	AP Computer Science

FIGURE 5.13 ALTERNATIVE MEANS TO GRADUATION
Using alternative means is a strategy to create access for greater numbers of students.

Barrier 2: Knowledge of Best Practices in Schedule Design

An important characteristic of a powerful and impactful scheduling team is ongoing familiarity with federal, state, and local policy that impacts scheduling. Many new scheduling teams are not aware of or do not have the historical knowledge of how state and local graduation requirements and alternative means to graduation impact scheduling. They are also not aware that local policy can be shaped and influenced to support desired scheduling shifts, thus scheduling teams have an enormous opportunity in front of them. It is a lot like being the coach of a sports team. How do you know how to organize the players meaningfully to achieve a goal if you don't know the rules and parameters of the game?

Strong scheduling teams understand that policy at the local level is influenced by state and federal policy decisions. It is imperative that someone at the district level, and someone high enough in the decision-making structure, convene regular growth mindset discussions about the impacts and parameters of the state education code, assembly bills, and so on to keep staff focused on what is possible rather than what restrictions are in the text. For example, most states include alternative means to graduation as part of their graduation standards and expectations. Rather than using this policy to "dumb down" the expectations for students to meet graduation standards, Architects of Equity with a growth mindset use this policy to provide rigorous and engaging options for students who just aren't as interested in the general curriculum options.

In addition, scheduling teams need to consider and understand the impacts that policy has on desired outcomes. For example, if a school district adopts the lowest possible expectations (education code minimums) as a graduation standard, it is likely that the result of that decision is inequality of outcomes. Why? Because privileged families who understand that there is a different set of expectations for students who plan to attend college, will set a parallel standard for their students and completely disregard the lower standard that is being presented to everyone else. The result is that some students will take the third years of math and science and others might not be encouraged to take those rigorous classes, with school personnel telling them they will meet graduation requirements. In addition, a school district that sets goals to increase the number of students meeting college readiness indicators but allows the graduation requirements to exist below that standard, will likely not meet their goals because the bar is not being held high for everyone. Scheduling teams with a growth mindset know that when the bar is held high for everyone, and students get the appropriate support they need, outcomes change.

SCHEDULING TEAM CONSIDERATIONS TO EQUITABLY SCHEDULE THE MARGINS

- Use the highest graduation expectations that the state allows and prioritize the fiscal and human resources necessary to support students on the freeway of excellence rather than create lesser off-ramps.

- Use one graduation diploma standard with several engaging options rather than multiple diploma options that track advanced, special education, and college and career readiness opportunities

- Ensure that definitions of student choice and personalization are not reinforcing inequities. Students should never be able to "choose" the lesser off-ramp.

- Personalization does not mean course choice. It means that students are known so well by staff that they have choices within courses.

Examine the district Alternative Means to Graduation Policy. If district outcomes by student group are inequitable, make sure that the well-intended options in this policy are not the root cause.

Barrier 3: Willingness to Confront the Status Quo

As stated in chapter 2, it is important for scheduling teams who want to equitably schedule the margins to confront their role in reinforcing the status quo. If there are concerns within the team about the personal impacts of prioritizing resources equitably and strategically, and/or leading courageous conversations about staffing toward equity, it will be important to revisit chapter 2 and complete the inner work necessary for equity work.

And consider this: It's not just scheduling teams that need to confront their role in reinforcing the status quo. Perhaps the college board's decision to stop releasing AP results through a student group (demographic) lens should be examined as well. Structural racism is in our control. The first step is acknowledgment of one's role in the process and a willingness to act to make a meaningful change. Excluding data is not that.

Barrier 4: Continued Delegation of the Schedule Process Without Oversight

The bottom line is that effective leaders NEVER delegate their vision—and the schedule is the greatest lever a school principal has to protect instructional practices that change marginalized students' lives. While it may not be the principal's role to build the sections in the School Information System and/or schedule the students in their classes, the design and subsequent student outcomes of the schedule are the responsibility of the school leader. This person leads the scheduling team and ensures that the vision is living in all decisions being made. An effective equity leader inspects what he or she expects—and builds a staff culture where this does not feel like micromanagement. Leaders must understand that equity doesn't happen because you read a book or gave a speech—equity is action and outcome accountability. The site leader may design a scheduling team, delegate tasks to that team, but the continuous messaging about the WHY behind scheduling decisions and the subsequent outcomes based on those decisions lies at the principal's feet. Period.

An effective equity leader inspects what he or she expects—and builds a staff culture where this does not feel like micromanagement.

FINAL THOUGHTS

TECHNICAL SELF-ASSESSMENT QUESTIONS (above the green line)	ADAPTIVE SELF-ASSESSMENT QUESTIONS (below the green line)
1. Has the district established recommended ELD pathways by bell schedule? If not, how will your team help facilitate this process? 2. Has the district established recommended special education IEP team questions that can be used to support discussions about scheduling? If not, how will your team help facilitate this process? 3. Does the district course of study include world language course work options that treat the student's home language as an advanced weighted strength? If not, how will your team help facilitate this process? 4. Does an engaging and high-quality alternative means to graduation administrative regulation exist? If not, how will your team help facilitate this process?	1. Will keeping English learners, special education students, and students who are not reading at grade level in the core tier 1 environment with support cause staff concern? How will you work with staff to support this shift? 2. Will implementing a co-teaching model cause staff concern? How will you work with staff to support this shift? 3. How will you build a shared purpose around scheduling traditionally marginalized students from a strengths-based mindset? How will you facilitate conversations about what might have to be removed from the schedule to accommodate this shift? 4. How will you facilitate discussions about access to college course work? Especially if courses act as high school equivalents? 5. How will you work with staff to examine the current bell schedule through an equity lens? How will you facilitate a discussion about potential solutions? 6. How will families and students be involved in conversations about scheduling shifts?

CHAPTER 6

STRATEGIC STRUCTURES

PATHWAYS, TEAMS, AND COHORTS, OH MY!

> <u>Changing Practice 4</u>: *Scheduling Teams Must Organize Strategically and Intentionally*

If you don't know where you want to go, then it doesn't matter which path you take.

—*Lewis Carroll*, Alice in Wonderland

Johnny was sure of one thing when he prepared to enter high school—he wasn't very good at school. Despite showing up for school each day, he consistently brought home D and F grades. He spent hours in dead-end intervention classes while his friends were having fun in courses like engineering, medical detectives, and computer science. The only thing he was looking forward to about high school was that it was over in four years, and he could get a job.

When Johnny registered for his feeder high school, they asked him to select a pathway theme—engineering, health, media, or business—so he chose engineering because they said it involved architecture and robotics. He had no idea what being a part of a pathway meant, but to his surprise on the first day of school all the ninth-grade engineering students were given a clipboard and told to report to the auditorium. When Johnny got to the auditorium, he met all his teachers and took a test that identified his personal strengths, interests, and values. He was assigned to a project-based learning team where all the students had different strengths and would collaborate for the semester as a team. There was a presentation by engineering industry professionals who discussed the semester-long project.

After the ninth-grade assembly, Johnny attended his first class. The teacher gave the students one syllabi for all his integrated courses (English, math, science, and engineering) and it revealed that these teachers all shared the same grading policies, classroom rules/consequences, argumentative essay outline, annotation key, and event calendar. They even shared some of the same reading documents. Johnny wasn't sure how to feel. This was different.

One day, Johnny's parents received a call requesting that they meet with the ninth-grade team. He was scared. What did he do? Was he failing again? When Johnny and his family attended the meeting, it occurred during a prep period that all the teachers shared. All of Johnny's teachers and his counselor were present. They began by sharing all the strengths Johnny was exhibiting. They went over Johnny's four-year course plan. They shared some samples of Johnny's work. They shared the results of the universal screener Johnny took to establish a baseline for reading comprehension and algebra readiness. Johnny was a little behind in reading, but the team provided some strategies for the family to use at home to help Johnny catch up. Johnny's family shared that they didn't have the internet or a computer at home. The counselor submitted his name for the free district internet partnership and issued a laptop to Johnny that could be brought to and from school so he could access the reading resources.

Johnny and his family left the meeting feeling very happy. Johnny was excited to hear that his teachers thought he had talents. He wanted to show them that he could catch up in reading so when he got home, he logged in and got started. Four years later when Johnny was completing his internship at Qualcomm, he reflected on how lucky he was to be at a school where teachers, students, and industry collaborated at such high levels.

Johnny was lucky. He accidentally landed at a school where the staff understood that innovative scheduling structures are vehicles for breaking down the traditional silos that dominate secondary systems. Rather than placing Johnny in a siloed career technical education (CTE) sequence of courses, what traditional schools call a pathway, this school understood that when teachers across content areas work together with a shared purpose, the concept of pathways and teaming can have new meaning and potentially produce new results. Unfortunately, schools like these tend to be one-offs. Despite all the research on the impacts of highly collaborative environments on student achievement, few high schools are truly making meaningful collaboration a priority.

Instead, professional learning communities (PLCs) have become a buzz word for department meetings that take place outside of the school day in early-release and/or late-start bell scheduling structures. The term itself, professional learning community, has become increasingly prevalent in educational discourse, yet its true essence is often misconstrued or misapplied. Originally, a PLC referred to a collaborative group of educators committed to continuous learning and improvement, focusing on student outcomes through shared goals and reflective practices. However, in many educational settings, the term has been diluted, sometimes reduced to merely indicating a group of teachers meeting periodically without truly engaging in meaningful, collaborative learning experiences. Such misuses not only undermine the transformative potential of PLCs, but also perpetuate superficial approaches to professional development. True PLCs demand a commitment to collective efficacy, mutual respect, and an unwavering focus on enhancing instructional practices for the betterment of all students (Fullan, 2015; Louis & Marks, 1998).

Sometimes PLC time is between 30 and 60 minutes once a week, which is not enough time to truly do the real work of a PLC, especially after it takes 5 to 10 minutes before and after these meetings to get settled and/or packed up. Many of these meetings also tend to lack structure. Administrators "trust" staff to run PLC meetings without the necessary oversight to produce results. Agendas are not reviewed by administrators prior to the meetings, and administrators are not typically consistent and regular members of the PLCs. The PLC itself is not the issue—PLCs implemented to fidelity are effective, impactful, and life changing for educators and students. The issue is implementation and the role that administrators take—or many times do not take—in the process.

This chapter will highlight the steps necessary to effectively use the school schedule to create intentional and impactful structures like pathways, teaching teams, and student cohorts. Because many school sites might believe that they are already implementing pathways under a traditional definition, it will be important to shift this construct into a definition of pathways as a system of highly effective interdisciplinary grade-level teams collaborating over many years within a shared purpose (Stern et al., 2010). This is an important shift to make as the typical siloed CTE course sequence being used as a pathway has not been a significant lever for equitable postsecondary readiness. That is why much of the funding for pathways has shifted to a more interconnected relationship between the CTE courses (technical core) and core course work (academic core) (Lafors & McGlawn, 2013; Rix, 2022). For the purposes of this chapter, the following definitions will be used:

Pathway: A two- to four-year grouping of interdisciplinary grade-level teams attached to student cohorts and linked by a shared purpose.

Teaching Team: An interdisciplinary group of teachers and support staff who share common planning time and dedicated student cohorts.

Student Cohorts: Groups of students who are attached to specific teaching teams.

Figure 6.1 illustrates the relationship between multiple pathways, teaching teams, and student cohorts within one high school.

THE EFFECTS OF BEING KNOWN WELL IN SCHOOL

When high schools are not organized intentionally and strategically, it is easy for students to get lost within a shifting bell schedule that moves people

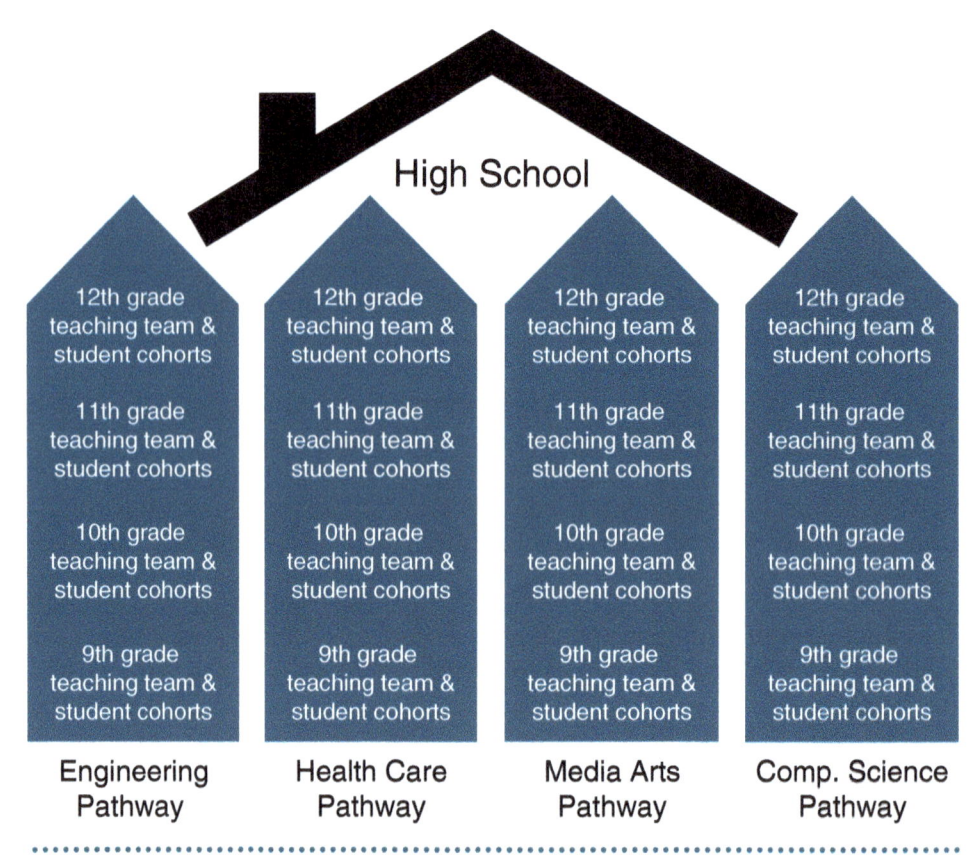

FIGURE 6.1 WALL-TO-WALL PATHWAYS IN A HIGH SCHOOL MODEL

between siloed subjects. A typical and very traditional bell schedule still used in many secondary schools is the six-period schedule. Students and teachers move between six periods for approximately 50 minutes per class each day. There is very little room in a six-period schedule for prevention, intervention, remediation, acceleration, or anything beyond the typical grade-level course offerings. The result of these traditional high school models is that there is no guarantee that students and staff will be connected meaningfully (Mehta & Fine, 2019).

> *When high schools are not organized intentionally and strategically, it is easy for students to get lost within a shifting bell schedule that moves people between siloed subjects.*

Rather than investing resources in connecting learning in powerful ways between subject areas, many high schools base school personalization on course choice—primarily elective course choice. In this model, the heart of personalization is grounded in the belief that because students and their families choose their courses, the high school experience will be meaningful and impactful. Postsecondary readiness data may not reflect a significant impact on achievement for student groups using this strategy, but it is still consistently implemented (Balfanz et al., 2016). In addition, being engaged at school is also typically connected to extracurricular clubs and sports that primarily occur after the school day. While participation is encouraged, it is not mandatory, and so connection might or might not happen for each student. Connection and collaboration should not be optional, which is why it is critical for scheduling teams to choose pathways, teams, and cohorts over a traditional model.

In addition, it is an unfortunate reality that many students arriving in high school are not reading and writing at grade level (Annie E. Casey Foundation, 2011; Nation's Report Card, 2024). Rather than using collaborative structures to collectively address reading, writing, and number sense across subjects, most high schools place the responsibility for reading, writing, and math intervention on English and math teachers. This seems like a futile strategy in a traditional high school context. It supports a belief that if a student who reads significantly below grade level attends a 59-minute intervention course that has no connection to the core English course or any other course in the student's schedule, significant reading progress will be the result.

Given the importance of reading as a precursor to accessing a typical ninth-grade textbook, and therefore course content, high schools need far more aggressive and collaborative methods for accelerating student reading while also supporting students to master grade-level standards and skills. If students in a high school cannot read at grade level, each teacher in the school must become a reading teacher. This does not mean that high school content needs to be watered down. Instead, it highlights the need for high school teachers to collectively use literacy strategies in their lesson planning (McCoss-Yergian & Krepps, 2010). In addition, rather than investing in common collaborative structures that allow teachers to connect subject areas meaningfully, schools will attempt to purchase their way out of reading and numeracy problems by buying programs that become the curriculum rather than enhance an integrated curricular experience crafted and owned by highly qualified teaching teams in the school. Teachers who feel supported and respected by their administrators are capable of amazing things—including collaborating to design lesson maps, create common syllabi, monitor student progress, and align strategies and skills across subject areas.

Making the connections between subject areas is critical for students to own information well enough to transfer it from one context to the next (Lafors & McGlawn, 2013; Rix, 2022). Teams that work collaboratively to identify, implement, and discuss common instructional strategies, pave the way for students to make these important connections. If a student recognizes a thesis in English, it is easier to recognize a hypothesis in science or a proof in mathematics. Collaborating is connecting. Scheduling teams that understand the power of the school schedule as the greatest lever for supporting students and teachers to engage more meaningfully around content will make collaborative structures a key strategy in knowing their students well.

Being known well at school is being more than a test score, a social security number, or a ZIP Code. It means more than choosing courses on a card. Being known well means that a student's strengths, interests, and values are used by his or her teachers to maximize achievement across the curriculum. Simply making an environment small is never enough. Creating the conditions for teachers and students to engage meaningfully with content requires clearly defining the explicit work of teaching teams (Lafors & McGlawn, 2013). Understanding this is part of developing an Architect of Equity MindSET.

Teaching Teams

The primary role of teaching teams is to make learning more accessible and transferable by using common strategies to make explicit connections across subject areas. Collaborative teams in secondary schools can take many forms. Some of these forms include

1. Department level: for example, mathematics team
2. Grade level: for example, tenth-grade team (English language arts, math, science, social science, CTE)
3. Course level: for example, Algebra I team
4. Co-teaching: for example, special education and English language arts teaching team
5. Dual language: for example, Spanish, math, and social science team (one teacher or two)

> *The primary role of teaching teams is to make learning more accessible and transferable by using common strategies to make explicit connections across subject areas.*

Figure 6.2 provides expanded descriptions of several collaboration models in secondary schools.

Regardless of the type of team that is provided collaborative planning time, the key to effective teaming is using the time provided intentionally and with accountability. In addition, in many or all of the examples above, counselors would be a part of each team and organize themselves by pathway rather than by alphabet. Counselors would still have a four-year looping experience with students, but it would be within a specific pathway.

> *The single most powerful lever for impacting instructional improvement is a highly effective teaching team.*

Department Collaboration	Teachers in the **same content area** share a common prep period. For example, all ninth- through twelfth-grade English teachers might share at least one prep period in the schedule.
Grade-Level Collaboration	Teaching teams connected in the **same grade level** share a common prep period. For example, the tenth-grade English, math, science, social science, and CTE teachers might share at least one prep period in the schedule.
Course-Level Collaboration	Teachers who teach the **same course** share a common prep period. For example, all Algebra I teachers might share at least one prep period in the schedule.
Co-Teaching Model Collaboration	The special education and general education teachers working in a co-teaching model within the **same course or courses** share a common prep period. For example, a math teacher and math co-teacher might share at least one prep period in the schedule to plan lessons together.
Dual Language Collaboration	Teachers in a dual language sequence **teaching two or more integrated courses** share a common prep period. For example, a Spanish teacher, math teacher, and social science teacher might share at least one prep period in the schedule to plan lessons together.

FIGURE 6.2 EXAMPLES OF COLLABORATIVE TEAMS IN SCHEDULES

Using Common Planning (Prep) Periods Effectively

The single most powerful lever for impacting instructional improvement is a highly effective teaching team (Stern et al., 2010). Teaching teams, especially those grounded in a grade level, are focused on daily, weekly, and monthly instructional improvement rather than simply focusing on change year-to-year. Figure 6.3 illustrates how teaching teams organize around common planning time to integrate learning for dedicated groups of students, The power of this thinking is that what a team does every day in the classroom can have a profound effect on learning. As a result, when teaching teams are anchored around specific student cohorts, teaching teams have profound effects on specific groups of students who are known well and supported to recognize and use their own personal strengths. But building a common prep period is only the beginning. Use of the prep period cannot be taken for granted. Figure 6.4 illustrates an example of collaborative tasks that teams may complete in common planning periods. In the beginning, this time must be highly structured. Teams will not be successful if they do not have a shared purpose. To help teams understand and internalize a shared purpose, administrators and teaching teams should collaborate to create the following mutually agreed upon items:

1. A *sacrosanct calendar* of meeting dates/times that administration, counselor(s), and teaching teams agree to meet during the school year. To build a cadence of accountability, this must be a weekly excuse-free and on-time attendance expectation that is modeled by the administration and

lead teachers. If administrators make excuses for not being there, staff will make the same excuses. Culture within the common prep will be developed over time as staff experience the benefits of their connection to their team.

2. A *standard agenda* format that prioritizes instructional conversations grounded in evidence. These agendas should be designed collaboratively in advance of the weekly meetings. Some schools design the following

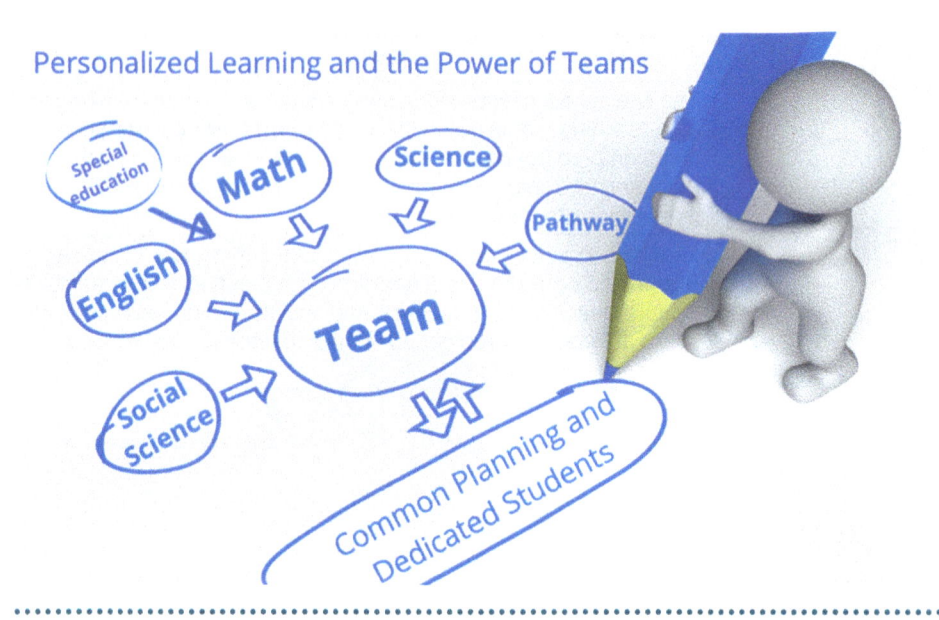

FIGURE 6.3 PERSONALIZED LEARNING AND THE POWER OF TEAMS TO CREATE ACCESS TO THE EQUITABLE CORE

How Highly Effective Teams Use Common Planning Time

- Designing and Implementing Common Classroom Routines & Expectations.
- Designing and Implementing Shared Grading & Discipline Practices.
- Engaging in weekly meetings focused on evidence-based discussions about student performance.
- Making weekly adjustments to curriculum and instruction to address evidence-based student needs.
- Designing and Implementing a Shared Team Syllabi.
- Collaborating with co-teachers, student teachers, interns, counselors, and other support staff in planning.

FIGURE 6.4 CREATING COMMON PLANNING TIME FOR TEACHERS WORKING IN PATHWAYS

week's agenda in the last five minutes of the current week's meeting. Operational items can be discussed at these meetings but should be limited to no more than 20% of the total meeting time. Teams should not use this time to discuss operational and/or logistical items that can be done over e-mail and that do not focus on student progress and any adjustments to lesson planning that need to be made to meet student needs. It is easy to talk operationally and logistically. It is hard to have powerful instructional conversations. Agendas should help teams structure time to focus on (a) reviewing student work and cross content progress to adjust instruction; (b) coordinating assignments, homework, and tests to ensure students are not overwhelmed with deadlines; (c) discussing student progress and potential supports on project timelines; and (d) identifying at-risk students and scheduling team meetings with guardians. To support staff to build a cadence of accountability around how they collaborate will require modeling.

3. A set of *shared documents* that reflect the team's purpose. Teams that collaborate on shared classroom routines and expectations, shared grading and discipline policies, a common syllabus, a common annotation key, common argumentative writing structures, and other powerful collaborative strategies develop a strong sense of who they are and what they are focused on doing. Teams that work within thematic college and career pathways might build project-based learning compendiums where, in addition to the items above, a project description, project calendar, and other collaborative structures would be available to students.

Before scheduling teams make common planning a priority in the schedule, it will be important to understand whether the administration has a plan to fully support and monitor this time. The credibility of the scheduling team is on the line as making the sacrifices necessary to build common planning time might compromise time given to other efforts. That is why it is essential to make sure that the Architects of Equity are clear about the order of competing priorities prior to beginning the planning process.

Competing Priorities

Teaming and pathway efforts are not new ideas—in fact, there has been considerable funding anchored toward these efforts in recent years—which begs the question of why implementation of these strategies has been so difficult in many school districts (Bottoms, 2022; Jones, 2024). What it really comes down to is whether staff views the school schedule as a lever for instructional improvement, whether high school teachers see their work as interdisciplinary, and whether the Architects of Equity are willing to prioritize resources equitably. Unfortunately, many people who lead schools, and therefore build schedules, attended and enjoyed traditional factory-model high schools. That experience consciously or unconsciously impacts what is believed to be a high-quality high school experience.

An examination of traditional school scheduling priorities reveals that a high-quality high school experience is grounded in having many elective course choices and providing an elite network of advanced courses for students who have been identified as exceptional as early as elementary school. Imagine how these priorities have impacted typical schedules: (1) Many advanced courses are isolated by student groups and have lower class sizes than regular course work, and (2) elective lines are offered beyond graduation-required course work specifications and as a result are typically under-enrolled and differentiated by course titles creating unmanageable singleton sections. In addition, all of this is impacted by school and pathway size. The bottom line is that the typical high school wants to be all things to all people—a strategy that has not produced equitable results, but that continues to be implemented across school systems. Figure 6.5 includes many of the competing priorities Architects of Equity face when building schedules.

FIGURE 6.5 COMPETING PRIORITIES MUST NOT UNDERMINE THE WORK OF CREATING PATHWAYS

COMPETING PRIORITIES IN SCHEDULES INCLUDE, BUT ARE NOT LIMITED TO

- Common planning periods (by course, grade, and/or pathway)
- Teaching teams and student cohorts
- Pathway course purity
- Integrated course work and/or project-based learning
- Elective access
- Tier 1 course access
- Athletics periods/coaching preps
- Advanced studies (honors, advanced placement, international baccalaureate, college courses)
- IEP, English learner, and/or other course work mandates
- Co-requisite supports
- Intervention courses
- Remediation course work
- Co-teaching models
- Limiting teacher preps
- Teacher certifications

While all the priorities listed in the box may sound important, scheduling teams must rank their priorities for the coming year so that if compromises need to be made, the Architects of Equity are clear about what will *not* be compromised. What is ranked highest must reflect the levers for instructional improvement over the next school year. If the schedule is the greatest tool for supporting staff to support student achievement in the coming year, the schedule must reflect the levers enabling the school's strategic vision. The death of any improvement effort is when scheduling compromises dilute the fidelity of the implementation efforts.

The ranking of priorities does not necessarily mean that items in the box must be removed. It means that scheduling teams must think strategically about implementation. In schools focused on pathways and/or teaming, the elements in Figure 6.6 must be considered to maintain equitable access and outcomes. A discussion of each of these elements follows.

Pathway Design Equity

- All pathways and teams must have advanced course work options
- Co-requisite supports, co-teaching, & course mandates should be offered within the pathway
- Pathways should not be built around programs
- Teachers should be assigned pure pathway courses and students

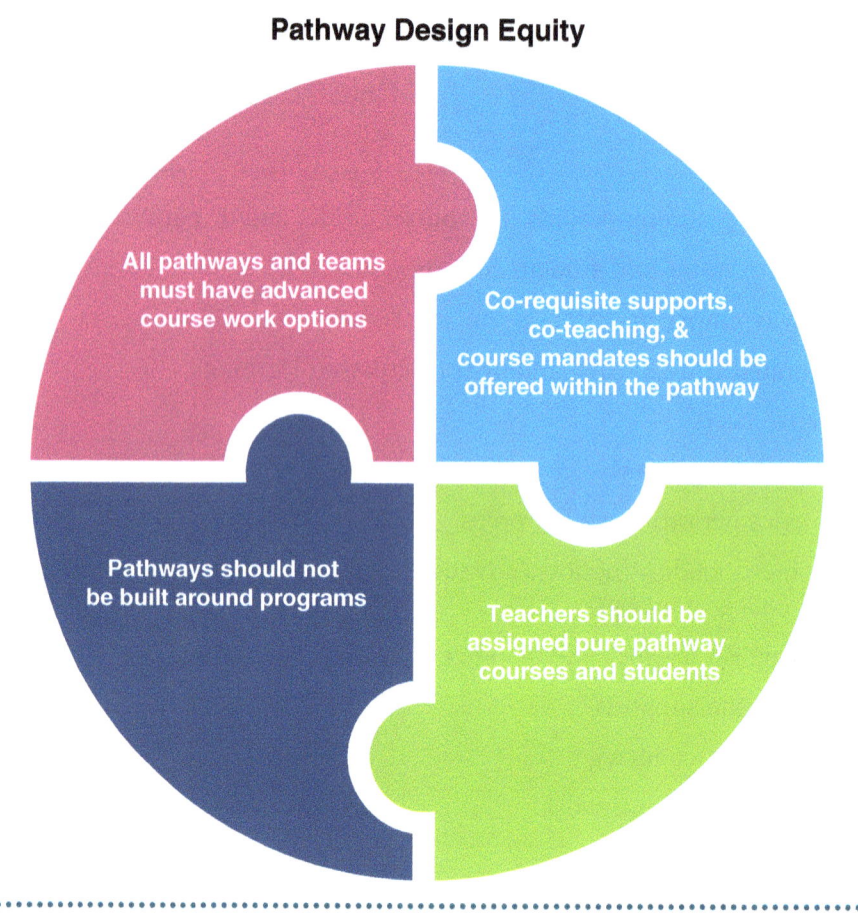

FIGURE 6.6 THE CRITICAL ELEMENTS OF PATHWAY DESIGN

- *All pathways and teams must have advanced course work options.* A teaching team is less effective when advanced students are funneled out to the only teacher qualified to teach advanced placement (AP) and/or international baccalaureate (IB) courses in any given subject. In a highly effective pathway and/or teaming structure, each set of teaching teams within pathways can teach any core class needed by the students arriving each year. This requires investing in teacher professional learning opportunities including AP, IB, and college course work teaching qualifications. In addition, highly effective teams will offer more advanced options to their students through strategies like layered syllabi, where students all have the option to do more to earn the weighted credit.[1] In a CTE pathway, dual college course work options will be used to support certification and capstone completion goals.

---

[1] An example of this would be co-seating Biology and Honors Biology, allowing students to submit additional assignments and/or take honors-level exams to earn the weighted credit at the completion of the course.

- *Pathways should not be built around programs.* The organizing principles of a pathway that operates within multiple pathways should not be based on programs like AP, honors, IB, advancement via individual determination (AVID), and so on. Why? Because this pathway will be the beginning of an ability track that will likely destroy all hope of building equitable pathways that produce similar results. Part of establishing an Equitable Core is ensuring that advanced options are part of the course sequencing. Why on earth would a school create an environment where all advanced students were funneled away from all other pathways? Why wouldn't all students choose a pathway of passion and/or theme that included a robust set of advanced options? If a school wants to adopt IB, can't it be IB for all? AP for all? College course work for all? A leader focused on equitable outcomes is not going to allow pathways to become ability tracks. Period.

- *Co-requisite supports, co-teaching, and course mandates should be offered within the pathway.* Highly effective teams know their students well and tailor their co-requisite supports to be an extension of the tier 1 core environments. Co-requisites, co-teachers, and mandates are cohorted within the teaming structure to ensure that supports are connected to general education–desired learning outcomes. This ensures access to the Equitable Core. (More about cohorting will be discussed later in this chapter.)

- *Teachers should be assigned pure pathway courses and students.* The more connected a teaching team is to the pathway, the more they develop and understand their shared purpose and assume ownership of the progress of their pathway cohorts. Occasionally, a pathway teacher may be assigned a "global" course like Student Government/Associated Student Body, but only if there is already room in that teacher's line for an additional course. Pure pathway teaching lines should not be compromised to place singleton global classes in schedules. Teachers who would prefer to keep singleton global electives should be placed in twelfth grade and teach courses that are not as tightly linked to a teaching team. For a teacher to be "all in" on the deep work of pathway integration, at least 80 percent of the teaching line should include pathway-aligned course work.

> *A leader focused on equitable outcomes is not going to allow pathways to become ability tracks. Period.*

Ranking competing priorities is a critical step in the work of the Architects of Equity. Teams that are not clear about their priorities and have systems of holding each other accountable to those priorities, are more susceptible to compromising fidelity and inadvertently desired student outcomes.

MAKING THE MATH WORK

Traditional scheduling math goes something like this: (a) course selection cards are provided to students/families; (b) courses are selected, verified, and tallied; (c) sections are built/scattered in the Student Information System (SIS) based on course tallies and desired class sizes; and (d) the students are loaded into the schedule sections. Adjustments are made to schedules depending on the percentage of students with full schedules after the load. To protect strategies in the schedule like pathways and teaming, this math will not be enough. There is a considerable amount of pre-thinking that schedule teams must do to make sure that what they intend is what will happen when all is said and done.

School schedules only work when the math works. Once priorities are identified for the upcoming school year, scheduling teams must consider the math before finalizing decisions. Consider this in the context of Sunport High School, a large comprehensive high school. Sunport staff identified three instructional priorities for the upcoming year:

- Implementing a ninth-grade wall-to-wall academy of teaching teams
- Implementing tenth- through twelfth-grade wall-to-wall CTE (career technical education) and/or arts pathways
- Shifting from a six-period bell schedule to a 4×4 a/b schedule (that is, a schedule that rotates four periods back-and-forth each day)

Before implementing any of these priorities, the scheduling team had to consider the impacts of these priorities within the site's unique contexts. The following had to be considered:

- Based on grade-level enrollment, how many teaching teams would best fit in a 4×4 a/b (students take 8 classes) schedule?
- How many CTE and/or arts pathways would best be offered in a 4×4 a/b anchored to grade-level teaching teams?
- How would the shift from a six-period to a 4×4 a/b schedule impact the types of teacher credentials needed to cover classes in the schedule?

Pre-Mapping Sunport High School

- Enrollments: ninth: 544; tenth: 571; eleventh: 510; twelfth: 491
- Desired class size ninth grade: 27
- Desired class size tenth- through twelfth-grade core: 34
- Desired school pathways: 4
- <u>Current CTE and arts programs</u>: Photography, Video Production, Health Care, Biotechnology, Welding, Automotive, Education, Computer Maintenance, Media Arts, Performing Arts

Checking the Math: Four Pathways

When making decisions about how many pathways should be implemented in alignment with grade-level enrollment constraints, schools should make it a practice to check the math in multiple scenarios. Figure 6.7 illustrates the connection between the student enrollment at each grade level and the corresponding number of sections aligned to contract class size staffing expectations within four proposed pathways.

What the Math Reveals About Sunport High School

- Teacher pathway sections of **four and/or five** in grades ten through twelve are going to require sharing of grade-level pathway courses or teacher assignments mixed with pathway and elective courses.
- Class sizes in grades ten through twelve will be much smaller than 34, given the need to round up on the sections to keep pathway sections pure.
- The ninth-grade teams will work if one team takes the two additional sections needed in addition to courses outside of the pathway.
- It might be better to operate with three overarching pathways with optional majors.

Checking the Math: Three Pathways

Given what has been revealed by checking the math if four pathways are implemented at Sunport, a next best step is to check to see if three pathways might result in class sizes closer to the contract maximums and more dedicated teaching team lines. Figure 6.8 illustrates the connection between the student enrollment at each grade level and the corresponding number of sections aligned to contract class size staffing expectations within three proposed pathways.

What the Math Reveals

- Teachers in grade ten will have full pathway teaching lines.
- Teachers in grades eleven through twelve will have to be assigned one additional course outside of their grade level. Not ideal but almost perfect. These teachers should be assigned a course in the pathway.
- One ten through twelve core teacher (ELA, math, science, and social science) can be assigned to one CTE teaching line in each grade level.
- Each ten through twelve grade level will have three teaching teams anchored to three CTE pathways.

Potential Overarching Pathway 1	Potential Overarching Pathway 2	Potential Overarching Pathway 3	Potential Overarching Pathway 4
12th: 123 students (491 divided by 4) 4 sections (min) (123 divided by 34)	12th: 123 students (491 divided by 4) 4 sections (min) (123 divided by 34)	12th: 123 students (491 divided by 4) 4 sections (min) (123 divided by 34)	12th: 123 students (491 divided by 4) 4 sections (min) (123 divided by 34)
11th: 128 students (510 divided by 4) 4 sections (min) (128 divided by 34)	11th: 128 students (510 divided by 4) 4 sections (min) (128 divided by 34)	11th: 128 students (510 divided by 4) 4 sections (min) (128 divided by 34)	11th: 128 students (510 divided by 4) 4 sections (min) (128 divided by 34)
10th: 143 students (571 divided by 4) 5 sections (min) (143 divided by 34)	10th: 143 students (571 divided by 4) 5 sections (min) (143 divided by 34)	10th: 143 students (571 divided by 4) 5 sections (min) (143 divided by 34)	10th: 143 students (571 divided by 4) 5 sections (min) (143 divided by 34)

Ninth-Grade Academy:
- 544 divided by desired class size of 27 = 20 sections
- 4x4 a/b teachers teach 6 classes
- 20 divided by 6 = 3.33 teachers

	P1	P3	P5	P7	P2	P4	P6	P8
Team 1								
English	Team Prep	ELA 9	ELA 9	ELA 9	Dept Prep	ELA 9	ELA 9	ELA 9
Math	Team Prep	Algebra I	Algebra I	Algebra I	Algebra I	Dept Prep	Algebra I	Algebra I
Science	Team Prep	Biology	Biology	Biology	Biology	Biology	Dept Prep	Biology
Career	Team Prep	Career	Career	Career	Career	Career	Career	Dept Prep
Team 2								
English	ELA 9	Team Prep	ELA 9	ELA 9	Dept Prep	ELA 9	ELA 9	ELA 9
Math	Algebra I	Team Prep	Algebra I	Algebra I	Algebra I	Dept Prep	Algebra I	Algebra I
Science	Biology	Team Prep	Biology	Biology	Biology	Biology	Dept Prep	Biology
Career	Career	Team Prep	Career	Career	Career	Career	Career	Dept Prep
Team 3								
English	ELA 9	ELA 9	Team Prep	ELA 9	Dept Prep	ELA 9	ELA 9	ELA 9
Math	Algebra I	Algebra I	Team Prep	Algebra I	Algebra I	Dept Prep	Algebra I	Algebra I
Science	Biology	Biology	Team Prep	Biology	Biology	Biology	Dept Prep	Biology
Career	Career	Career	Team Prep	Career	Career	Career	Career	Dept Prep
Team 4								
English	ELA 9	ELA 9		Team Prep	Dept Prep			
Math		Algebra I	Algebra I	Team Prep		Dept Prep		
Science			Biology	Team Prep	Biology		Dept Prep	
Career				Team Prep	Career	Career		Dept Prep

FIGURE 6.7 THE CONNECTION BETWEEN STUDENT ENROLLMENT AND STAFFING

The top of this figure represents the math that is needed to project the pathway sections needed in grades ten through twelve as these are distinctly different pathways with multiple industry themes. The second part of the figure represents the math needed to project the ninth-grade sections needed to create teams anchored with a pre-pathway career class.

Note: ELA = English language arts.

Potential Overarching Pathway 1	Potential Overarching Pathway 2	Potential Overarching Pathway 3
12th: 164 students (491 divided by 3) 5 sections (min) (164 divided by 34)	12th: 164 students (491 divided by 3) 5 sections (min) (164 divided by 34)	12th: 164 students (491 divided by 3) 5 sections (min) (164 divided by 34)
11th: 170 students (510 divided by 3) 5 sections (min) (170 divided by 34)	11th: 170 students (510 divided by 3) 5 sections (min) (170 divided by 34)	11th: 170 students (510 divided by 3) 5 sections (min) (170 divided by 34)
10th: 190 students (571 divided by 3) 6 sections (min) (190 divided by 34)	10th: 190 students (571 divided by 3) 6 sections (min) (190 divided by 34)	10th: 190 students (571 divided by 3) 6 sections (min) (190 divided by 34)

FIGURE 6.8 THE MATH ASSOCIATED WITH THREE PATHWAYS

Based on the math, the Architects of Equity must collaborate to identify and substantiate the best possible path(s) forward. In the case of Sunport, to get as close to the initial three site priorities, the model with three overarching pathways will help ensure the highest level of student cohort purity, grade-level teaming, and common planning periods.

Evaluating Sunport's Current CTE Offerings

One important task for the Architects of Equity is assessing whether the current CTE offerings will become the overarching pathways and/or majors. The course sequences below reflect the current CTE course offerings at Sunport High School. These programs *could* be used to frame the three overarching pathways needed above, but the scheduling team would need to assess the programs first. Some questions that scheduling teams might ask include the following:

- Have the current CTE programs increased in enrollment over the years?
- Does the ninth- or tenth-grade CTE pathway enrollment maintain through twelfth grade?
- Do some CTE programs have higher capstone completion rates?
- Are some programs so small that course work must be layered within the same periods?
- Are the current CTE and/or programs aligned to the high-wage, high-skill sectors in the local and/or state region?
- Are some CTE and/or arts programs better suited to overarching pathways and/or majors within pathways?

- Which CTE and/or arts teachers are suited to collaborate with an integrated grade-level team?
- Which CTE and/or arts courses are already aligned to Equitable Core equivalents?

Sunport High will need to inventory the current list of CTE and visual and performing arts (VAPA) electives offered to determine how current programs might be shifted to pathway options. Figure 6.9 illustrates the current elective courses offered at Sunport, organized as potential pathways.

Introduction to Digital Photo Digital Photo Digital Photo III	Introduction to Video Production Video Production Advanced Video Production
Health Care Assistant I Health Care Assistant II Prevention & Care of Sports Injuries Sports Medicine/Athletic Training	Biotechnology Concepts and Techniques Advanced Biotechnology
Auto Systems and Repair Auto System Diagnostics Advanced Automotives	Welding I Basic Welding II Intermediate Welding Materials and Processes
Early Childhood Progressions Teacher Training Program Education Professions Internship	Advanced Computer Maintenance
Beginning Ceramics Intermediate Ceramics Advanced Ceramics Beginning Painting Intermediate Painting Advanced Painting Beginning Drawing Intermediate Drawing Advanced Drawing	Concert Band Marching Band Jazz Band Choir I–II Concert Orchestra Symphony Orchestra Chamber Orchestra Theatrical Arts I–II Beginning Dance Intermediate Dance Advanced Dance

FIGURE 6.9 CURRENT SUPPORT CTE AND ARTS PROGRAMS
It is important to examine current elective course offerings to determine potential pathway possibilities.

Potential Pathway Themes and Sequences for Sunport

The digital photo and video production courses could become part of a **media arts** pathway.

- The health care and biotechnology courses could become part of a **health care** pathway.
- The auto, welding, and computer maintenance courses could become part of a **business entrepreneurship and/or clean engineering** pathway.

- The education courses could live as a **major and/or freestanding elective** experience. So could the auto, welding, and computer maintenance courses.

- As a note, this high school currently has a robust arts course of study that could also become a **performing arts** pathway—although the number of students currently enrolled in the performing arts sections is too small for the three ability tracks being used in several disciplines. This is requiring courses to be layered and adding too many singletons to balance in a schedule focused on prioritizing teaching teams and student cohorts anchored by common preps within thematic pathways.

NINE ENABLING CONDITIONS FOR PATHWAY DESIGN

Enabling conditions are factors that help increase the likelihood of an intended change. When designing equity-focused pathways, there are nine conditions that must be understood by the Architects of Equity. Figure 6.10 lists these conditions.

> *There is nothing more destructive to pathways than ever-changing teaching teams that are the result of unstructured student choice.*

FIGURE 6.10 THE NINE ENABLING CONDITIONS
Enabling conditions are a critical part of the Architect of Equity's role in getting their Mindset during the pathway and teaching team design phase.

Enabling Condition #1: Setting Consistent Pathway Enrollment

There is nothing more destructive to pathways than ever-changing teaching teams that are the result of unstructured student choice. Pathways must be grounded in structured choice. Using a ranking system for pathway access is one way to make sure balance is achieved and maintained in pathway structures. When one pathway meets desired enrollment targets, the enrollment in that pathway should close to allow for enrollment in other pathways to fill to capacity. All boats must float. Part of balancing pathways includes making sure that student group access is also balanced. Unstructured student choice can lead to pathways that are overrepresented by students with IEPs, English learners, boys, students of color, and/or advanced students. It is imperative that the choice process is structured in a way to ensure that pathways are equitably enrolled across student groups. Schools that are unwilling to make this commitment usually end up with ability-grouped and/or gender-isolated pathways.

Enabling Condition #2: Choosing Broad Pathway Themes

Overarching pathways should be broader than a major. For example, placing students in a welding pathway and expecting core teaching teams to integrate with that theme/discipline for three to four years is not a good idea. Any pathway focus that could be taken at the community college in one to two semesters to earn a certificate should not be broken into four courses and stretched over an entire high school experience. This doesn't mean welding shouldn't be part of a high-skill engineering pathway—it should. The point is that engineering as a pathway allows for many paths: civil engineering and architecture, machine tool technology, digital electronics, welding, and so forth. Welding is a discrete optional major within an engineering pathway. The arts must also be considered when planning for pathways. If there is a student and teacher interest in a performing arts pathway it should be considered as an overarching theme.

Enabling Condition #3: Limiting Pathway Course Sequences

Pathway sequences do not need to be differentiated by many courses. Differentiation of ability and interests can be managed within broad pathway courses. Keep the pathway course lines clean and simple if there is a desire to integrate them with core classes. Only add additional courses and/or majors if grade-level/pathway/school enrollment numbers work. Use resources that already exist to help with integrated core courses. A resource like the University of California Curriculum Institute (https://ucci.ucop.edu) provides integrated course work by content area and industry pathway focus, and the syllabi and lessons associated with each course. This will allow the title of the core course to change without introducing another separate course into the scheduling mix. In addition, in the Sunport example above, the multiple ability tracks within the arts are going to create scheduling constraints across the entire schedule. It is not necessary to create these tracks in the schedule.

Enabling Condition #4: Integrating Interests Within Courses/Pathways

If a student is interested in fashion design, does he or she have to have access to a fashion design course or pathway? Why can't a student be in a business pathway focused on marketing and selling fashion? Why can't a student be in an engineering pathway and learn the science behind design? Why can't a student be in an environmental and/or health pathway and study the impacts of (and potential solutions for) the dispersal of fashion design dye in the environment? Isn't knowing students well enough to support them to focus on their passions more important than offering one or two courses for every interest that they verbalize? High schools are not large colleges where students take specialized courses to select a discrete major.

Enabling Condition #5: Designing Teacher Lines

It is important to focus teachers on becoming specialists in a course/grade level/pathway—not create competing priorities within teaching lines. What teachers are allowed to offer in blank spaces should be purposeful. Be mindful about coaching preps and/or additional preps. Athletics and coaching periods must be discussed by scheduling teams prior to the scheduling process as these decisions can have significant impacts on teaming. Sometimes teaching lines that include coaching periods must be assembled at the twelfth-grade level to protect the ninth- through eleventh-grade–level teaming. As stated previously, 80% of the teaching line should be focused on pathway work.

Enabling Condition #6: Matching Teacher and Student Interests

Pathway selection should be aligned to the high-wage, high-skill local sector, but it should also marry student and teacher interests/passions. Creating a survey of high-wage, high-skill industry themes that can be supported in the school's local context is a good way to make decisions about pathway themes. A template for a pathway selection application is available in the appendix and online at https://companion.corwin.com/courses/equitable schoolscheduling

Enabling Condition #7: Organizing Teacher Teams

It is important to think about the composition of teaching teams based on teaching strengths and specialty courses. It is not a good idea to build teams consisting of the strongest teachers and/or all of the advanced classes. It is also not a good idea to build teams with the least-experienced teachers or lowest-level courses. In addition, if two groups of students need Geometry versus Algebra, how those sections are distributed across teams have important impacts on equity.

Enabling Condition #8: Providing Clarity on Integration

Course integration doesn't mean standard-by-standard alignment. It means the identification of cross-content skills and strategies that can be implemented across subject areas in the service of mastery. Modeling this for teachers early in the process will be critical for teams to develop mental maps of what shifts they are being asked to make.

Enabling Condition #9: Holding the Student Information System Accountable

In the Sunport model above, it is not possible to load course requests into the scheduling frame in a traditional process. The student information system (SIS) must be able to team, lock in groups, set priorities in the load, mass schedule, and so on. It should also produce reports that reveal student cohort purity levels.

USING COHORTING AS A SCHEDULE-BUILDING TOOL

One critical step for the Architects of Equity is to design a pathway and/or teaming map that incorporates and protects the scheduling priorities for the upcoming year. Establishing and protecting common preparatory periods is not a simple task—especially if the nonnegotiable is that all teaching teams share common planning time. The common prep periods must be framed in the schedule first. In addition, the Architects of Equity must have a strong understanding of how the student information system will allow for the necessary tagging of teachers, sections, and/or students who will be aligned around particular prep periods. This kind of design cannot be done by simply "pushing the loader" in the SIS. In addition, singleton sections can complicate the scheduling process if team coding and loading priorities are not preset in the SIS. The student information system should be a support for innovative and equitable scheduling design. If it isn't, rather than succumbing to allowing an inanimate object to make equity decisions for the school, make sure that the contacts at your chosen student information system provider are aware of what is needed to be done. If the provider can't make it happen, find a company that can execute the vision. Making sure that staff and students have what they need to succeed is priority number one.

To map the common preparatory periods and pathway course sections into the scheduling frame, it is always a good idea to use a cohorting tool. The definition of cohorting can differ depending on who is asked. For some, cohorting is the locked in traveling pattern of a group or groups of students through the same courses during the day. For others, it reflects groups of students assigned to specific teaching teams via specific course sections. Both definitions and others may be true. It depends on the user and his or her desired scheduling outcomes. A blank cohorting tool is available in the appendix and online at https://companion.corwin.com/courses/equitable schoolscheduling

Often when the word or concept of cohorting is introduced, there is an immediate question about the ethics of tracking of students within a cohorting model. This reaction is ironic given that many traditional secondary schedules reflect multilayered ability tracking through their current courses—especially elite programs like accelerated math, honors, IB, AP, and so on. Like current scheduling practices, if sites choose to ability-track students within courses in a standard schedule build, placing those same ability-tracked courses in a cohorting tool will also track students in the schedule. It's not the cohorting tool that tracks the students. It's the courses they are separated within that creates the tracks. When building equitable schedules, it is necessary to limit or eliminate course tracks before beginning the cohorting process.

For the purposes of scheduling pathways, teaching teams, and student cohorts, the concept of cohorting will be defined as a tool for mapping the school schedule grounded in the concept that the traveling patterns of students within teams defines the placement of courses in teaching assignments. The next few pages will illustrate how a cohorting tool can be used to protect priorities like common preps, teaching teams, and student cohorts. The process will result in a partial schedule built with specific criteria that do not include course requests. The schedule will be adjusted after the course-request process, and the course-request process will be defined by the draft schedule built with the cohorting tool. This is how Architects of Equity build schedules that are within their fiscal resources and grounded in instructional improvement strategies. Figure 6.11 highlights the items that are necessary to begin the process of cohorting a schedule.

WHAT IS NEEDED TO COHORT A SCHEDULE

- Graduation requirements (by grade level)
- District-mandated course work
- Projected enrollment by grade level and pathway
- Bell schedule (number of courses and preps per teacher)
- Class sizes by subject area and overall teacher load limits
- Desired teams (course, department, grade level, pathway)
- Desired prep periods for teams
- Desired pathway sequences (aligned to enrollment constraints)
- Support teachers who should share the common prep (special education, English language learners, etc.)
- Teacher certifications and credentials
- Union contract details (overall teacher load, number of preps, etc.)
- Constraints (that is, teachers with medical notes defining prep periods, coaches, and/or specialty assignments with additional prep periods, etc.)

Items Needed to Cohort a Schedule

- Mandated Course Work
- Projected Enrollment
- Bell Schedule
- Class Sizes and Teacher Loads
- Desired Prep Periods
- Teacher Credentials and Certifications
- Desired Teams
- Co-Teachers
- Site-Specific Constraints
- Graduation Requirements

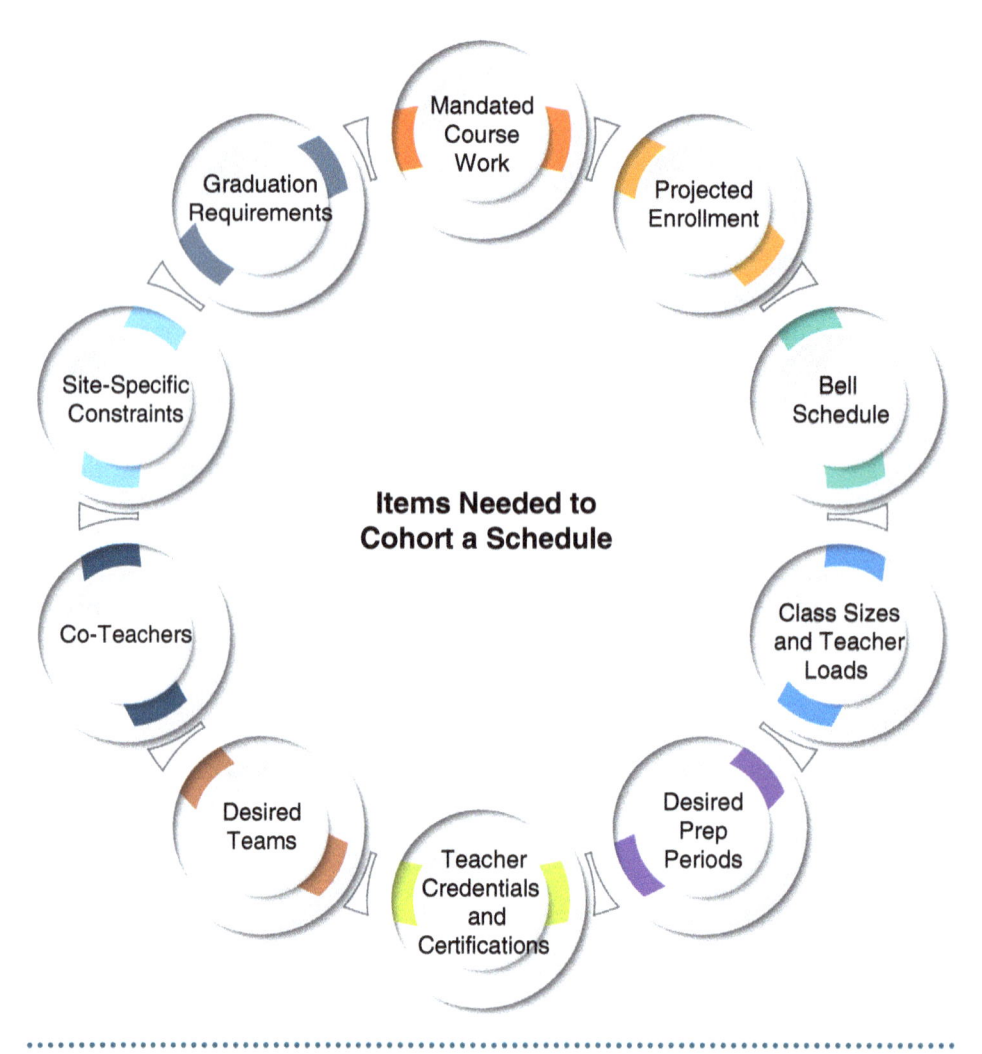

FIGURE 6.11 "MUST-HAVES" FOR CREATING A COHORTED SCHEDULE

Seven-Period Schedule Cohorting Model

The cohorting model below outlines the thinking and actions taken to fill out a cohorting tool focused on specific site priorities. The process will help determine where the classes associated with an engineering pathway should be placed within a multi-pathway comprehensive school. The partial frame that is developed through this cohorting process will reflect the priorities of the specific school and pathway: common planning, grade-level teaming, and pure student cohorts. Prior to cohorting a schedule there are some questions that must be considered to ensure that your framing of the process matches the site constraints:

- How many periods do students take daily? *Seven*
- How many periods do teachers teach daily? *Six*

- Are there any constraints in teacher credentials, additional assignments (i.e., coaching, Student Government), limited/shortened assignments, and/or medical notes? *Student Government is only offered during period 4 and athletics is only offered during period 7. These are priority-access courses for eleventh- and twelfth-grade students.*

- How many students are in the pathway and/or school overall? *500*

- How many students are in each grade level in each pathway? *Ninth, 130; tenth, 125; eleventh, 125; twelfth, 120*

- What are the class sizes for various courses (core, PE, CTE, etc.)? *Core: 32; PE: 50; CTE: 32.*

- What are the desired prep periods for grade-level teams and/or departments? *Staggered by grade level. Younger grades later in the day.*

- Are there any support teachers (special education, English language learners [ELL], and/or general education teachers) that should be teamed and share a common prep? *Designated ELL and co-requisite supports should be cohorted.*

- What are the expected courses that ALL students take each year? *See sample graduation requirements below.*

- Which courses should be linked in each grade level? *They are highlighted in Figure 6.12.*

- What are the mandates that must be scheduled prior to any extras?

9th Grade	10th Grade	11th Grade	12th Grade
English	English	English	English
Math	Math	Math	Math
Science	Science	Science	Pathway
PE	PE	Pathway	Government/Economics
Pathway	Pathway	U.S. History	
Language	World History		
	Language		

FIGURE 6.12 PRIORITIZING GRADUATION REQUIREMENTS TO ENSURE STUDENT SUCCESS

Note: Priority order of courses for cohorting: ELA, math, pathway, social science, science, designated ELL or co-requisite, PE.

Graduation Requirements (Seven Periods)

The first step in cohorting a schedule is getting clear about the courses that will be linked by a common planning period. Figure 6.12 illustrates which courses will be linked and which will remain outside of the cohort. Courses highlighted in yellow will be cohorted around a common planning period as a scheduling priority.

Seven-Period Schedule Cohorting Tool

The second step in cohorting a schedule is building the grade-level cohorts. Figure 6.13 illustrates how grade-level enrollments and contracted class size maximums are used to determine the number of sections needed to link student cohorts in a pathway. In the figure, four cohorts are mapped for each grade level. These maps will support the placement of courses strategically in a site scheduling frame.

Schedule Frame Built With Cohorting Tool

The third step in cohorting a schedule is using the grade-level cohorts to build a frame. Figure 6.14 represents where course work would be placed to ensure that the engineering pathway teaching teams, student cohorts, and common preparatory periods are balanced around priorities.

Notice and Note

- The Figure 6.14 frame is built with generic courses so that decisions can be made before specific course tallies are considered.

- The cohorts in Figure 6.13 are determined by dividing the total number of students in a grade level by the desired class size of the Core courses. (CTE class sizes are not smaller or larger than the Core classes. When the class size of the CTE class is reduced, every linked class is reduced in size.)

- To ensure that common preps are the priority, courses have been assigned to teachers by grade level.

- Elective opportunities were filled into vacancies in each teaching line to ensure that cohorts stay with their teachers before classes outside of the pathway are assigned to the teachers. These elective courses could be co-requisite tier 1 supports, additional senior science and math options, AVID, designated EL courses, and so on.

- There are dedicated PE, language, and VAPA lines—although one language would be offered unless a teacher had multiple credentials; and one VAPA sequence would be offered.

- This schedule reflects that access to the Equitable Core is the priority for all students—not multiple strands of elective options. Courses like music would have to be shared across pathways and could be reflected in an elective line at the bottom. Student government, journalism, and so on would have to be shared but could be added in an elective space.

9th Grade
130 students
32 Core and 50 PE
Core: 4 sections; PE: 3 sections

Period	Cohort 1	Period	Cohort 2	Period	Cohort 3	Period	Cohort 4
P1	ELA 9	P1	PE	P1	Elective	P1	Physics
P2	Algebra	P2	ELA 9	P2	PE	P2	PE or Algebra or Elective
P3	Engineering Design	P3	Algebra	P3	ELA 9	P3	Algebra or Elective
P4	Physics	P4	Engineering Design	P4	Algebra	P4	ELA 9
P5	Designated ELL 1–2 or Elective	P5	Physics	P5	Engineering Design	P5	Geometry
P6	PE	P6	Elective	P6	Elective	P6	PE or Elective
P7	Elective	P7	Designated ELL 3–4 or Elective	P7	Physics	P7	Engineering Design

Note: Cohorts reflect course priorities of ELA, math, pathway, and science in grades nine and ten. Mandated ELLs are also part of the cohort if students are required to take it.

10th Grade
125 students
32 Core and 50 PE
Core: 4 sections; PE: 3 sections

Period	Cohort 1	Period	Cohort 2	Period	Cohort 3	Period	Cohort 4
P1	ELA 10	P1	PE or Elective	P1	World History	P1	Biology
P2	Geometry	P2	ELA 10	P2	PE or Elective	P2	World History
P3	Principles of Engineering	P3	Geometry	P3	ELA 10	P3	PE or Elective
P4	Biology	P4	Principles of Engineering	P4	Geometry	P4	ELA 10
P5	Designated ELL 1–2 or PE	P5	Designated ELL 1–2 or PE	P5	Designated ELL 1–2 or PE	P5	Designated ELL 1–2 or PE
P6	World History	P6	Biology	P6	Principles of Engineering	P6	Algebra II
P7	Designated ELL 3–4 or PE or Elective	P7	World History	P7	Biology	P7	Principles of Engineering

Note: Social science is added to the cohort in grade ten and the designated ELL sections were strategically added to the ninth-grade English teaching line so the cohorting moved around it.

(Continued)

(Continued)

11th Grade
125 students
32 Core and 50 PE
Core: 4 sections; PE: 3 sections

Period	Cohort 1	Period	Cohort 2	Period	Cohort 3	Period	Cohort 4
P1	U.S. History	P1	Chemistry	P1	Digital Electronics	P1	Precalculus
P2	Elective	P2	U.S. History	P2	Chemistry	P2	Digital Electronics
P3	ELA 11	P3	Elective	P3	U.S. History	P3	Chemistry
P4	PE 11–12 or Elective	P4	PE 11–12 or Elective	P4	PE 11–12 or Elective	P4	PE 11–12 or Elective
P5	Algebra II	P5	ELA 11	P5	Elective	P5	U.S. History
P6	Civil Engineering	P6	Algebra II	P6	ELA 11	P6	Elective
P7	Chemistry	P7	Civil Engineering	P7	Algebra II	P7	ELA 11

Note: The cohorting pattern of eleventh grade changed to ensure that twelfth-grade classes would be bunched up in the same periods. ELA, math, pathway, science, and history are still priorities.

12th Grade
120 students
32 Core and 50 PE
Core: 4 sections; PE: 3 sections

Period	Cohort 1	Period	Cohort 2	Period	Cohort 3	Period	Cohort 4
P1	ELA 12	P1	Engineering Design and Development	P1	Elective	P1	Elective
P2	Elective	P2	ELA 12	P2	Engineering Design and Development	P2	Elective
P3	Government/Economics	P3	Elective	P3	Elective	P3	Engineering Design and Development
P4	PE 11–12 or Elective	P4	Government/Economics	P4	PE 11–12 or Elective	P4	PE 11–12 or Elective
P5	Engineering Design and Development	P5	Elective	P5	Elective	P5	Elective
P6	Elective	P6	Elective	P6	ELA 12	P6	Government/Economics
P7	Elective	P7	Elective	P7	Government/Economics	P7	ELA 12

FIGURE 6.13 COHORTING TOOL TO CREATE PATHWAYS IN GRADES NINE THROUGH TWELVE IN ONE SCHOOL

Note: In twelfth-grade cohorting priorities are limited to ELA, social science, and the pathway—the order has also changed to ensure that periods available in the schedule frame are filled. No common prep in twelfth grade.

- Because of the limits on enrollments at each grade level, some teachers had to absorb twelfth-grade classes. The initial cohorting pattern was broken, but instead used to best determine where twelfth-grade courses would be placed to maintain fiscal responsibility.
- Some electives in the last few lines may be absorbed into the lines of the other pathways being cohorted in the same school.

Cohorting as a strategy begins as a tool for building a scheduling board that protects priorities for the upcoming year, but transitions to a useful tool for making difficult student scheduling decisions. For example, if a counselor wanted to schedule a tenth-grade student in seventh-period athletics, he or she would use the tenth-grade cohorts shown in Figure 6.13 to determine that this student had to take course work within a variation of cohort one. If the same student was an English learner who needed Designated ELL 3–4, the student would not be able to access the athletics period within the day. If this same student was in the ninth grade, he or she could access athletics in period seven through a variation of cohort one.

	P1	P2	P3	P4	P5	P6	P7
ELA	ELA 9	ELA 9	ELA 9	ELA 9	Des. ELL 1–2	PREP	Des. ELL 3–4
ELA	ELA 10	ELA 10	ELA 10	ELA 10	PREP	ELA 12	ELA 12
ELA	ELA 12	ELA 12	ELA 11	PREP	ELA 11	ELA 11	ELA 11
Math	Elective	Algebra	Algebra	Algebra	Geometry	PREP	Elective
Math	Elective	Geometry	Geometry	Geometry	PREP	Algebra II	Elective
Math	Precalculus	Elective	Elective	PREP	Algebra II	Algebra II	Algebra II
Physical	Physics	Elective	Elective	Physics	Physics	PREP	Physics
Biological	Biology	Elective	Elective	Biology	PREP	Biology	Biology
Physical	Chemistry	Chemistry	Chemistry	PREP	Elective	Elective	Chemistry
Social Science	World History	World History	G/E	G/E	PREP	World History	World History
Social Science	U.S. History	U.S. History	U.S. History	PREP	U.S. History	G/E	G/E
Engineering	Elective	Elective	IED	IED	IED	PREP	IED
Engineering	EDD	EDD	POE	POE	PREP	POE	POE
Engineering	DE	DE	EDD	PREP	EDD	CEA	CEA
PE	PE 9	PE 9	PREP	PE 11–12	PE 10	PE 9	PE 10–12
PE	PE 10	PE 10	PE 10	PE 11–12	PE 10	Elective	PREP
Language	Elective	PREP	Elective	Elective	Elective	Elective	Elective
VAPA	Elective	Elective	PREP	Elective	Elective	Elective	Elective
Elective	Elective	Elective	Elective	Elective	Elective	Elective	PREP
Elective	PREP	Elective	Elective	Elective	Elective	Elective	Elective

FIGURE 6.14 SCHEDULING FRAME TO ENSURE ALIGNMENT OF STAFF WITH PATHWAYS EMBEDDED IN THE SCHEDULE

Note: IED is introduction to engineering design; EDD is engineering design and development; DE is digital electronics; CEA is civil engineering and architecture; G/E is government/economics; POE is principles of engineering.

Cohorting is a tool for thinking through the building of schedules and the scheduling of students in strategic ways.

ADDITIONAL PATHWAY-BUILDING CONSIDERATIONS

Because building schedules that support pathways, teaching teams, and student cohorts requires careful attention to the fidelity of the implementation model, there are four additional items that must be considered when scheduling teams design their maps:

- **Pathway Size:** Pathways are best when at least three groups of students are connected at each grade level (approximately 100 students.)
- **Pathway Balance:** An important part of checking to see if a pathway is sound is a vertical count of sections. It is important to make sure that the total number of students in the school have a seat each period of the day. This vertical check will also need to be done by grade-level section access as there will need to be an appropriate number of seats for each grade level. Having the right overall count doesn't necessarily mean having the right grade-level count.
- **Pathway Failure:** If students in integrated pathways are still experiencing failure, the reasons are usually in a compromise of fidelity of implementation. Make sure that the monitoring systems are in place and provide opportunities for staff to examine how they are responding when students are not demonstrating high levels of learning.
- **CTE Course Failure:** If students are failing their CTE courses, this is a major problem. The CTE course work should be highly engaging, hands-on, and give life to the core course work. If large numbers of students are failing the CTE course, this is not a sign of rigor and high expectation. In addition, if students who fail CTE course work are forced to retake CTE course work with the class behind them, the anchor for the grade-level-project focus has now been removed. CTE course work failure should be dealt with like failing an ELA class. They move to the next class while they make up the previous class. This is the difference between implementing a CTE sequence and implementing a pathway.

These items must be attended to early in the schedule design process as failure to consider size, balance, and failure within the design of a pathway can compromise fidelity of implementation and subsequently the effort itself.

FINAL THOUGHTS

If the purpose of scheduling is to support instructional strategies that accelerate the learning of all students in a school, shifting the way students, staff, and content interact is a critical step in achieving equitable outcomes. Shifting to a model of thinking where it is the responsibility of an entire team of grade-level experts to ensure that entire grade-level cohorts have what they need to master content in service of preparedness for the next grade level is essential. Designing highly effective collaborative teams that operate under a cadence of accountability is the beginning of building a culture where it is assumed that all students will succeed when the right conditions are created around them.

TECHNICAL SELF-ASSESSMENT QUESTIONS	ADAPTIVE SELF-ASSESSMENT QUESTIONS
1. How does the school site/district currently define pathways? How will the administration support a shift in thinking? 2. Are the number of courses in pathway sequences congruent with grade-level enrollment projections? Has a course of study self-assessment been conducted? 3. Are visual and performing arts classes offered as electives or sequenced pathways like CTE course work? How might this change in a pathway model? 4. Are counselors and other support staff currently assigned to pathways or last name alphabets? How might their organizational structure change in a pathway model? 5. How will administrators be organized to participate and monitor pathway efforts? How will a cadence of accountability be developed at all levels? 6. Does the student information system currently have the tools and reports needed to build a cohorted pathway schedule?	1. Do staff members value collaborative opportunities that are built into the schedule? How will discussions about the benefits of highly collaborative teams begin? 2. How will teams be formed? How will staff, student, and family voices be part of the design? How will the strengths of interdisciplinary teams be balanced? 3. How will discussions about desired student learning outcomes and ongoing progress monitoring be framed and supported in the pathway model? How will the structure of common planning be constructed with staff? 4. Does staff believe their role is to teach courses or cohorts? How will discussions about this shift begin? 5. How will discussions about differentiation support a shift from pushing services and supports out of the tier 1 core environment to pushing them in? 6. How will implementation efforts support quick wins for staff so that they value the collaboration and integration processes?

CHAPTER 7

RESOURCE EQUITY

THE COSTS OF INEQUITABLE SCHEDULING PRACTICES

> *Changing Practice 5: Scheduling Teams Must Understand How to Use Resources Strategically*

In the end, a strategy is nothing but good intentions unless it's effectively implemented.

—Clayton M. Christensen

The newly hired Sand Ridge High School district superintendent had a problem. Declining enrollment and shifting demographics within the district required a changing set of resource needs within a continuously shrinking budget. One practice that the district had employed was the allocation of site staffing at the same levels each year despite ongoing enrollment changes. In addition, there was very little district oversight over bell schedule selection, which resulted in several school sites employing bell schedules that required additional staffing to implement. The biggest problem for the superintendent was not identifying what needed to change, but rather dealing with the perceptions of stakeholders who were comfortable with the precedents that had been set. The superintendent understood that to achieve resource equity, his decision making had to be evidence based.

The superintendent started with an assessment. He conducted a vacant seat analysis to determine the cost of the under-enrolled sections within each high school schedule. He was not only able to identify the cost of course under-enrollment, but the root causes of under-enrollment, which he identified as advanced course work offerings and several singleton electives. Additionally, he examined the impacts of high school enrollments and their unique bell schedules. He noticed that in some cases sites had to add filler electives and/or support classes into teacher lines to make them whole. When he did the math on how many sections might be needed to meet English language arts (ELA) graduation expectations over four years, the sections in some schedules far exceeded what would have been expected. Finally, he examined the impacts of intervention courses on student achievement and found that these courses were not having the impacts that should have been the result of their financial investments in the schedule.

The superintendent knew what he needed to do. First, he worked with the chief financial officer to establish an enrollment-based allocation model that would provide an equitable distribution of resources to schools. Before he released these new staffing numbers, he examined the overall staffing impacts. He worked closely with the school board and labor unions to make sure that they were aware of this process, its outcomes, and all impacts. Second, he collaborated with stakeholders at all levels to create a list of expectations around site autonomy as it related to bell schedule selection. He met with each principal around these philosophical and financial nonnegotiables to support messaging and potential shifts in schedules within each community's unique context. These nonnegotiables included limiting teacher preps, prioritizing the Equitable Core, filling, supporting opportunity youth in advanced course work, and monitoring interventions for effectiveness and subsequent use. The superintendent worked alongside site leaders throughout the entire process to ensure that his principals, the staff, and their families felt safe and supported throughout this difficult but necessary process. Within a few years the district realized resource equity through the collaborative development of clear and supportive processes, procedures, and expectations around staffing.

The superintendent's journey to resource equity began with the identification of the technical and adaptive shifts that were necessary to support intentional and purposeful changes in the way staffing was allocated and implemented across the system. He used an evidence-based and collaborative approach to engaging the system around needed changes. He did not leave the site principals alone in the transition. He stood next to them as an ally and model throughout the change management process. This support allowed site staff to approach needed changes without working in a culture of fear, which was critical to reach desired outcomes.

RESOURCE EQUITY

There is a growing focus in education on what has been deemed "resource equity," or the "allocation *and* use of resources—people, time, and money—to create student experiences that enable all children to reach empowering, rigorous learning outcomes, no matter their race or income" (Travers, 2018, p. 1). According to Travers, there are eleven dimensions to resource equity, one of which touches on scheduling at the secondary level: instructional time and attention. The author focuses on both extending the school year for students who need additional instructional time as well as ensuring students are taking the courses they need to graduate on time during their four years in high school. To bring this approach to the school schedule, it is important to consider the costs of staffing resources and what the schedule says about the Architect of Equity's values and decision making.

There are significant human and fiscal costs associated with implementing schedules that do not consider equitable resource allocation at their core. While it may be true nationally that schools are underfunded, this chapter focuses on what is within the control of educators who seek to achieve resource equity with the funding they are provided. It will highlight the three critical enabling conditions that must be aligned to achieve resource equity:

Enabling Condition #1: Understanding the Relationship Between Graduation Requirements, Student Enrollment, and Site Funding

Enabling Condition #2: Understanding the Alignment Between Selecting Courses, Building Sections, and Staffing the Schedule

Enabling Condition #3: Understanding the Impacts of Bell Schedules, Schedule Balance, and Scheduling Experience on Resource Equity

ENABLING CONDITION #1: UNDERSTANDING THE RELATIONSHIP BETWEEN GRADUATION REQUIREMENTS, STUDENT ENROLLMENT, AND SITE FUNDING

To achieve resource equity in scheduling, Architects of Equity must recognize and understand the significant relationship between graduation requirements, student enrollment, and site funding for staff (see Figure 7.1).

This relationship begins when the board of education approves the course work required to graduate from district high schools. An established set of course requirements defines a need for specific teacher credentials. The number of students in each school, the desired class sizes by content area, and the selected bell schedule impact the number of credentialed personnel who

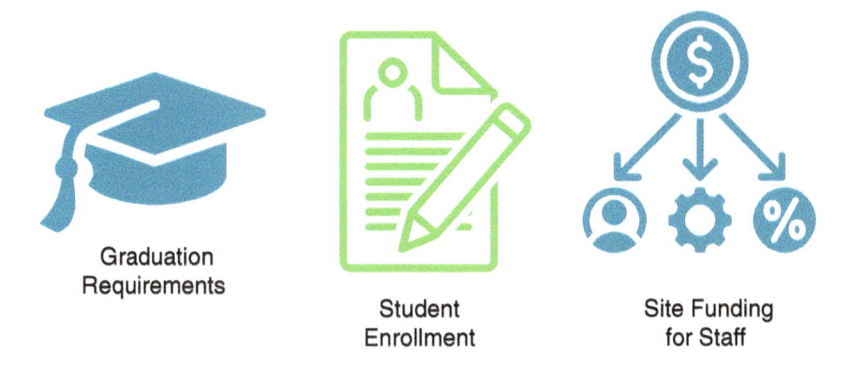

FIGURE 7.1 THE INTERSECTION OF GRADUATION REQUIREMENTS, STUDENT ENROLLMENT, AND SITE STAFFING

Note: In most districts, there is a significant relationship between graduation requirements, student enrollment, and site funding for staff.

are needed to cover the required course work to graduate. To simplify this idea, imagine that there are 500 students in a six-period school and the desired class size in English is 25. If each student must take English all four years, a minimum of 20 sections of English are needed—which means a minimum of four full-time English teachers would be needed to cover the graduation-mandated course work. (This number may increase if grade-level enrollments are not evenly divided by grade level.) Ideally, these four teachers would be a priority in staffing and would be able to focus on becoming core course experts to ensure that the Equitable Core mastery of ELA was a priority for each student in the school. This commitment to tier 1 excellence in each graduation-required content area within the Equitable Core is what the district is funding (see Figure 7.2).

To complicate this idea further, many districts allocate funds overall, rather than allocating funds by projected grade level, which allows for variances in the way FTE (full-time equivalent) is used. This has consequences on many levels. First, many times when principals/site leaders are provided FTE for the upcoming year, the natural inclination is to "save" or maintain what already exists in the schedule. Principals may receive allocations and do a quick check to see how many FTE are gained or lost within the current schedule. This is problematic for many reasons—especially since strategic thinking about student needs and the levers that will be funded to support any achievement gaps is not facilitated simply by a rollover of the current schedule.

One might argue that allocating FTE overall is a sign of allowing decisions to be made at the local level to empower communities to design school systems that reflect local priorities. The truth is that given how underfunded schools are, there are very few decisions in the general fund that

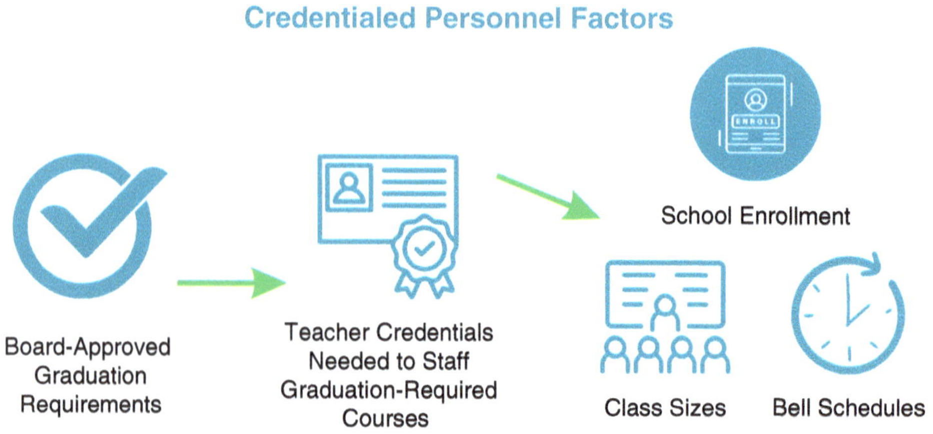

Credentialed Personnel Factors

Board-Approved Graduation Requirements → Teacher Credentials Needed to Staff Graduation-Required Courses → School Enrollment, Class Sizes, Bell Schedules

FIGURE 7.2 STAFFING ALLOCATION TO MEET THE GRADUATION REQUIREMENTS AND ENSURE ACCESS TO THE EQUITABLE CORE

can be made collaboratively with communities. Most funding discussions with communities are most congruent with categorical and/or supplemental funding opportunities governed by school site councils, and so on. This is why the use of equitable staffing allocation formulas and an allocation tool grounded in the prioritization of the Equitable Core is essential for resource equity.

Understanding the Allocation of Teacher FTE

One critical step in site scheduling is receiving FTE staffing allocations from the district. In many cases, FTE is initially based on a demographer predicting incoming enrollment each year. To illustrate how enrollment projections may be established, consider two models currently being used in large urban school districts.

MODEL 1: STANDARD MODEL

Staffing Allocations Based on Total Enrollment Projections

Step 1: Overall projected student enrollment is divided by the desired class size to determine "A" (might have to be an average if multiple core class sizes have been bargained).

Step 2: Multiply "A" times the number of periods in the bell schedule to determine "B."

Step 3: Divide "B" by the number of periods taught, which equals the teacher allocation.

Example:

- 500 overall students divided by desired class size of 34 students equals 14.7.
- 14.7 times 6 periods equals 88.2.
- 88.2 divided by 5 periods taught equals 17.6 general education teachers.

Note: This is the base general education allocation and does not include special education teachers, counselors, other supplemental resources, and so on.

MODEL 2: SUPPLEMENTAL SERVICES REMOVED MODEL

Staffing Allocations Based on Total Enrollment After the Removal of Supplemental Support

Step 1: Supplemental enrollment numbers are subtracted and/or prorated from the overall projected student enrollment to determine "A"—the total projected student enrollment. Figure 7.3 provides examples of the types of student groups that may be prorated due to the use of other funding sources directly allocated for these groups.

In the example above, ROTC teachers, English learner teachers, and special education teachers are not paid out of the general fund. They are covered with supplemental funding. If students are taking required graduation course work with these teachers, they are not using general fund–covered seats. This might occur all day and/or for one or more periods so prorating might be required. To illustrate prorating, consider students who take English language arts and math with a special education–funded teacher rather than a general education–funded teacher. On a six-period system, two periods of these students' days are now allocated within the special education funding, so this student is now a .6 student in the general fund rather than a 1.0 student. If 50 students follow this pattern, 50 projected students are 30 students in the general fund (.6 times 50.)

Total Enrollment	Students Who Take the Equitable Core Outside of the General Education Environment	Total General Education Enrollment
The overall number of students projected to attend school in the upcoming year	Examples: • Students in special education self-contained classroom settings for any portion of the day • Newcomer and/or English learner program sections (if funded outside of general fund) • ROTC students • Students with free periods	The total number of students projected to be accessing general education courses

FIGURE 7.3 DETERMINING ENROLLMENT FOR FTE ALLOCATION IN GENERAL EDUCATION

Note: SDC is self-contained special day class; RSP is resource specialist program; IEP is individualized educational plan; ROTC is reserve officers' training corps.

Step 2: Multiply the total projected student enrollment ("A") times the number of periods in the bell schedule to determine "B."

Step 3: Divide "B" by the number of periods taught by teachers, which equals the teacher allocation.

Example:

- 500 overall students **minus 18 students** is 482 students.

  - 20 special education students taking math and ELA outside of general education (20 times .6 equals 12, so **8** students are removed from overall projected student enrollment)

  - 50 students taking ROTC for one period (each student becomes .8 student in general funding which is 40, so **10** students are removed from overall projected student enrollment)

- 482 students are divided by desired class size of 34 students equals 14.2.
- 14.2 times 6 periods equals 85.2.
- 85.2 divided by 5 periods taught equals 17 general education teachers.

While it may not seem like much of a difference in general education funding between option 1 and 2 (.6 or three sections), please remember the examples involve 500 students. When dealing with middle and high schools with enrollments in the thousands, and within districts that have multiple school sites, this savings could be significant depending on the numbers of supplemental-funded sections. In addition, some districts will allocate an additional one or two teachers or create a staffing ratio that is slightly above contractual staffing maximums to allow for additional staffing flexibility in the schedule.

USING AN ALLOCATIONAL TOOL

This section of the book is best shared between the business, human resources, and education services leadership of a school district as resource equity is the result of a carefully structured staffing and budgeting cycle each school year.

An important step in crafting equitable schedules is using an allocation tool to project staffing needs each year. While some traditional schedulers may see the following exercise as unnecessary, one could argue that it is essential in shifting mindsets from reinforcing the status quo (just rolling last year's schedule over) to thinking strategically each year about resource equity. In addition, the exercise of understanding what, how, and why resources are provided to the site is pivotal in helping site leaders understand how and when to engage stakeholders in shared decision making. Allocation tools also provide a context for site leaders and their supervisors to have conversations about how resources are being used each year to meet student performance goals.

In addition, it is important to recognize that not all districts allocate staff to school sites based on enrollment projections. In some cases, this has become problematic in the current context of declining enrollment and shifting demographics. Some school districts simply reallocate the same number of teachers to sites year after year, which has set a precedent that is difficult to reverse. For these districts, an allocation tool can help examine the funding discrepancies between what each site *needs* to staff the graduation-required course work, and what the sites are receiving and using. The result is typically a realization that additional resources that could be used to close achievement gaps between student groups are being employed for many other purposes. Regardless of the staffing model within a district, allocation tools allow for equitable conversations about resource equity.

Using an allocation tool requires that the Architects of Equity understand the following:

- The allocation tool is **not the school schedule.** It is a tool to examine the number of minimum sections needed to staff the Equitable Core. Teaching preps are not part of the tool, but the number of sections in each line reflects the number of courses teachers are assigned.

- The **class sizes** expected and/or bargained by **subject area** and/or **course.**

- The **actual funding formula**, including how supplemental funding is allocated. If the funding formula adjusts total enrollment by subtracting supplemental funds this must be done prior to using the tool.

- **Non-diploma–bound students** who do not take Equitable Core course work should be removed from the total enrollment numbers.

- The expense of **bell schedule decisions** and their impact financially.

- The impacts of **section rounding.** Rounding up or down on the minimum number of sections depends on the impact to the desired class size. If the impact is 1 additional student (31 instead of 30), round down. If the impact exceeds +1, round up—which will naturally lower the class size of all grade-level sections.

Figure 7.4 represents the information that must be collected and understood prior to using a cohorting tool. Equity High School is a generic high school created for the purposes of demonstrating how cohorting works.

Equity High School Allocation Tool

In the example below, the following is true:

	9th Grade	10th Grade	11th Grade	12th Grade	Overall
Enrollments	383	370	409	316	1,478
Graduation Requirements (minimum)	ELA Math Science PE Language[a]	ELA Math Science Soc. Science PE Language[a]	ELA Math Science Soc. Science	ELA Soc. Science VAPA[a,b]	4 yrs. ELA 3 yrs. Math 3 yrs. Science 3 yrs. Soc. Sci. 2 yrs. PE 2 yrs. Language 1 yr. VAPA

Note: There may be additional courses needed to earn the credits required for graduation. These course options will be discussed in the additional strategies section of the tool.

Class Sizes	30 students maximum in the core; 50 students maximum in PE
Bell Schedule	Six-period bell schedule. Teachers have one prep period.

[a]These courses could be scheduled in any grade level or year.
[b]VAPA is visual and performing arts.

Graduation Requirement 1: 4 years of English language arts
9th Grade: 383 students/30 class size average = Minimum of 13 sections
10th Grade: 370 students/30 class size average = Minimum of 12 sections
11th Grade: 409 students/30 class size average = Minimum of 14 sections
12th Grade: 316 students/30 class size average = Minimum of 11 sections

ELA 1	English 9	English 9	English 9	English 9	English 9
ELA 2	English 9	English 9	English 9	English 9	English 9
ELA 3	English 9	English 9	English 9	English 10	English 10
ELA 4	English 10	English 10	English 10	English 10	English 10
ELA 5	English 10	English 10	English 10	English 10	English 10
ELA 6	English 11	English 11	English 11	English 11	English 11
ELA 7	English 11	English 11	English 11	English 11	English 11
ELA 8	English 11	English 11	English 11	English 11	English 12
ELA 9	English 12	English 12	English 12	English 12	English 12
ELA 10	English 12	English 12	English 12	English 12	English 12

(Continued)

(Continued)

Graduation Requirement 2: 3 years of social science
10th Grade: 370 students/30 class size average = Minimum of 12 sections
11th Grade: 409 students/30 class size average = Minimum of 14 sections
12th Grade: 316 students/30 class size average = Minimum of 11 sections

SS 1	World History	World History	World History	World History	World History
SS 2	World History	World History	World History	World History	World History
SS 3	World History	World History	U.S. History	U.S. History	U.S. History
SS 4	U.S. History	U.S. History	U.S. History	U.S. History	U.S. History
SS 5	U.S. History	U.S. History	U.S. History	U.S. History	U.S. History
SS 6	U.S. History	Govt./Econ.	Govt./Econ.	Govt./Econ.	Govt./Econ.
SS 7	Govt./Econ.	Govt./Econ.	Govt./Econ.	Govt./Econ.	Govt./Econ.
SS 8	Govt./Econ.	Govt./Econ.			

Graduation Requirement 3: 3 years of mathematics
9th Grade: 383 students/30 class size average = Minimum of 13 sections
10th Grade: 370 students/30 class size average = Minimum of 12 sections
11th Grade: 409 students/30 class size average = Minimum of 14 sections

Math 1	Math 9	Math 9	Math 9	Math 9	Math 9
Math 2	Math 9	Math 9	Math 9	Math 9	Math 9
Math 3	Math 9	Math 9	Math 9	Math 10	Math 10
Math 4	Math 10	Math 10	Math 10	Math 10	Math 10
Math 5	Math 10	Math 10	Math 10	Math 10	Math 10
Math 6	Math 11	Math 11	Math 11	Math 11	Math 11
Math 7	Math 11	Math 11	Math 11	Math 11	Math 11
Math 8		Math 11	Math 11	Math 11	Math 11

Graduation Requirement 4: 3 years of science
9th Grade: 383 students/30 class size average = Minimum of 13 sections
10th Grade: 370 students/30 class size average = Minimum of 12 sections
11th Grade: 409 students/30 class size average = Minimum of 14 sections

Sci 1	Biology	Biology	Biology	Biology	Biology
Sci 2	Biology	Biology	Biology	Biology	Biology
Sci 3	Biology	Biology	Biology	Chemistry	Chemistry
Sci 4	Chemistry	Chemistry	Chemistry	Chemistry	Chemistry
Sci 5	Chemistry	Chemistry	Chemistry	Chemistry	Chemistry
Sci 6	Physics	Physics	Physics	Physics	Physics
Sci 7	Physics	Physics	Physics	Physics	Physics
Sci 8	Physics	Physics	Physics	Physics	

Graduation Requirement 5: 1 year of visual and performing arts (VAPA)					
9th Grade: 383 students/30 class size average = Minimum of 13 sections					
VAPA 1	Arts	Arts	Arts	Arts	Arts
VAPA 2	Arts	Arts	Arts	Arts	Arts
VAPA 3	Arts	Arts	Arts		

Graduation Requirement 6: 2 years of the same world language (WL)					
9th Grade: 383 students/30 class size average = Minimum of 13 sections					
10th Grade: 370 students/30 class size average = Minimum of 12 sections					
WL 1	WL 9	WL 9	WL 9	WL 9	WL 9
WL 2	WL 9	WL 9	WL 9	WL 9	WL 9
WL 3	WL 9	WL 9	WL 9	WL 10	WL10
WL 4	WL 10	WL 10	WL10	WL 10	WL10
WL 5	WL 10	WL 10	WL10	WL 10	WL10

Graduation Requirement 7: 2 years of physical education					
9th Grade: 383 students/45 class size average = Minimum of 9 sections					
10th Grade: 370 students/45 class size average = Minimum of 9 sections					
PE 1	PE 9	PE 9	PE 9	PE 9	PE 9
PE 2	PE 9	PE 9	PE 9	PE 9	PE 10
PE 3	PE 10	PE 10	PE 10	PE 10	PE10
PE 4	PE 10	PE 10	PE10		

FIGURE 7.4 RESOURCE ALLOCATION TOOLS IN PRACTICE

Summary: Graduation Requirement Teacher Minimums

Figure 7.5 reflects the summary of the minimum FTE that would be needed to staff Equity High's Equitable Core as it is aligned to graduation requirements.

	9th Grade	10th Grade	11th Grade	12th Grade
ELA	2.6 teachers	2.4 teachers	2.8 teachers	2.2 teachers
Social Science		2.4 teachers	2.8 teachers	2.2 teachers
Math	2.6 teachers	2.4 teachers	2.8 teachers	
Science	2.6 teachers	2.4 teachers	2.8 teachers	
VAPA	3.0 teachers			
Language	2.6 teachers	2.4 teachers		
PE	1.8 teachers	1.8 teachers		
Totals	15.2 teachers	13.8 teachers	11.2 teachers	4.4 teachers

FIGURE 7.5 GRADUATION REQUIREMENTS WITH TEACHER MINIMUMS FOR FTE

To summarize:

- The overall teacher FTE needed to staff minimum graduation requirements is 44.6 (Equitable Core number). This number is not generic. For example, the site doesn't need 10 teachers to staff the Equitable Core in ELA. The site needs 2.6 ninth-grade, 2.4 tenth-grade, 2.8 eleventh-grade, and 2.2 twelfth-grade teachers to staff the Equitable Core. There is a difference.

- The overall FTE allocations is 59.2 (as determined using the standard allocation model).

- The balance of general fund FTE that can be used for site-specific strategy is 14.6.

- In some cases, the decision to round up to the nearest whole number during the creation of sections in the grid created a need for additional sections. If this had not been done, the additional students would have been placed in subsequent grade-level sections, which would have raised class sizes in grade-specific courses.

Equitable Core Course Work Versus Additional Strategies

The allocation tool grids reflect the minimum sections needed to place students in the Equitable Core. These grids do not include items that will be purchased as **additional strategies** beyond the core. Among these items are the following: double-blocking classes; co-requisite supports; English learner, special education, and other mandates; ability tracking (advanced placement [AP], honors, regular, co-taught, and other course work); math tracking (specifically singletons created by small groups of elite accelerated students); responses to course failure (retaking failed courses simultaneously with the next course), tracking students in science by math readiness; additional visual and performing arts offerings beyond the one year dictated by graduation expectations; additional years of language beyond the two years dictated by graduation expectations (the district is funding the completion of two years of the same language—not multiple language choices); additional electives (including those that are needed to meet overall graduation credits); courses that meet any college requirements beyond graduation requirements; and retaking failed course work.

Decisions about additional strategies should accelerate the learning of all students. These are decisions that should be monitored closely with the site leadership to ensure that all students are getting what they need, when they need it, and in the way they need it. These decisions must prioritize what students need over what students might want. In addition, if sites use ability course tracking in each grade level, the site will likely exceed the district allocated FTE in many content areas. That is why keeping the allocation around generic course placeholders is crucial.

Prioritizing Additional Strategies

The most important allocation discussions between site leaders and their supervisors take place during the decision-making process about additional strategies. After having established and staffed the Equitable Core, how will the remainder of site general fund allocations and any categorical/supplemental funding support the site vision for improving student achievement over the next 10 months? Figure 7.6 reflects four strategies that have been organized in the order of site priority.

Priority 1: Supporting Student Access to Tier 1

- How many co-requisite supports are needed? In which subjects, grade levels?
- If sites are already using strategies like double blocking, is it producing the desired student outcomes compared to the financial commitments? In 10 months? Does research support this, and/or any strategy being used for remediation and/or intervention?

Priority 2: Supporting Mandate "Must Do's"

- How many English learners are mandated to take English Language Development support as a separate class period? (If this is paid through additional categorical funding it would not be allocated here.)
- Is there a mandatory career technical education (CTE) and/or VAPA pathway program in the school? (If not, pathways would be discussed under "additional decisions" in priority 4 below.)

Four Additional Strategies Priorities

- Access to Tier 1
- Mandate "Must Do's"
- Acceleration
- Additional Decisions

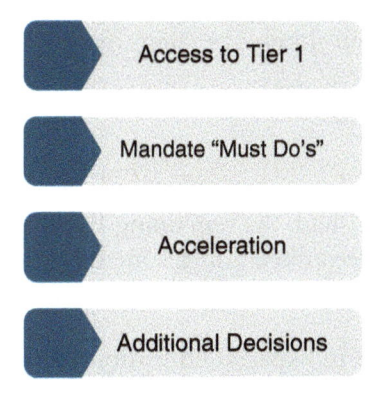

FIGURE 7.6 PRIORITIES TO CONSIDER WHEN STAFFING THE EQUITABLE CORE

- How many students need to remediate course work within the school day to graduate on time? Which subjects/courses? Will they do this while continuing in the core sequence or instead of moving to the next course?

Priority 3: Acceleration

- How many students will take math in twelfth grade?
- How many students will take science in twelfth grade?
- How many students will take world language in eleventh and/or twelfth grade?

Priority 4: Additional Decisions

- How many additional course sections are needed to support ability tracking and random course sequencing in each content area?
- What staffing will be needed for athletics?
- Which additional electives will be offered? (student government, yearbook, advancement via individual determination, etc.)?
- What additional courses would the site like to offer? Will these desires cause a need for partial core teachers and/or credentials that are hard to staff?
- How many singletons are in the schedule? How can singletons be reduced?
- Do any staff typically receive additional prep periods? Will this continue?

As a reminder, co-requisites can be purchased from the categorical/supplemental funds as they are not supplanting the district's responsibility to fund the core. Also, any additional credits needed to meet graduation requirements will likely be met by anything in the additional strategies section.

Additional Strategies in the Allocation Tool

Once priorities are established, the remaining FTE from the original Equitable Core allocation should be ranked and resourced. In the Equity High example above (see Figure 7.4), the following additional strategies were identified:

- Implementing a "push in" special education co-teaching model in all regular ELA and math courses (no impact to the general fund)
- Offering math course work to half of the seniors to support four-year college preparation (6 sections/1.2 teachers)

- Offering science course work to half of the seniors to support four-year college preparation (6 sections/1.2 teachers)
- Offering a wall-to-wall CTE pathway teaming strategy (additional 7.2 teachers)

Figure 7.7 reflects the minimum FTE needed after additional strategies are factored into the process. These strategies include offering math and science to 50% of the senior class and implementing a mandatory three-year CTE pathway model.

Additional Math: **1.2 teachers**					
12th Grade: 316 students/30 class size average = Minimum of 11 sections (Ratio: half is 6)					
Math 1	Math 12	Math 12	Math 12	Math 12	Math 12
Math 2	Math 12				

Additional Science: **1.2 teachers**					
12th Grade: 316 students/30 class size average = Minimum of 11 sections (Ratio: half is 6)					
Science 1	Science 12	Science 12	Science 12	Science 12	Science 12
Science 2	Science 12				

CTE Pathway Strategy: **7.2 teachers**					
10th-Grade Core: 370 students/30 class size average = Minimum of 12 sections					
11th-Grade Core: 409 students/30 class size average = Minimum of 14 sections					
12th-Grade Core: 316 students/30 class size average = Minimum of 11 sections					
Pathway 1	Pathway 10	Pathway 10	Pathway 10	Pathway 10	Pathway 10
Pathway 2	Pathway 10	Pathway 10	Pathway 10	Pathway 10	Pathway 10
Pathway 3	Pathway 10	Pathway 10	Pathway 11	Pathway 11	Pathway 11
Pathway 4	Pathway 11	Pathway 11	Pathway 11	Pathway 11	Pathway 11
Pathway 5	Pathway 11	Pathway 11	Pathway 11	Pathway 11	Pathway 11
Pathway 6	Pathway 11	Pathway 12	Pathway 12	Pathway 12	Pathway 12
Pathway 7	Pathway 12	Pathway 12	Pathway 12	Pathway 12	Pathway 12
Pathway 8	Pathway 12	Pathway 12			

FIGURE 7.7 STAFFING PRIORITY FTE OUTSIDE THE EQUITABLE CORE

ADJUSTED TEACHER MINIMUMS WITH MATH, SCIENCE, AND PATHWAY STRATEGIES

Figure 7.8 reflects the summary of the minimum FTE that would be needed overall to staff Equity High after additional strategies are factored into the process.

To summarize:

- The overall adjusted teacher FTE needed to staff minimum graduation requirements and additional strategies (math, science, CTE) is 54.4.

- The overall FTE allocations are 59.2.
- The balance of general fund FTE that can be used for site specific strategy is 4.8 FTE.

In some cases, students will fail classes and need to take the failed class and their grade-level-appropriate class simultaneously. The strategy for staffing failed courses must be established prior to using this allocation tool. Placing students back in their failed ELA class will change the grade-level allocation by course, not the overall staffing number. However, placing students in the course they failed and the course they should be taking simultaneously is more complex. One allocation is dealt with in the staffing of the Equitable Core (the standard access to ELA course) and the second (the credit recovery strategy) is dealt with in the additional strategy section of the process above.

	9th Grade	10th Grade	11th Grade	12th Grade
ELA	2.6 teachers	2.4 teachers	2.8 teachers	2.2 teachers
Social Science		2.4 teachers	2.8 teachers	2.2 teachers
Math	2.6 teachers	2.4 teachers	2.8 teachers	**1.2 teachers**
Science	2.6 teachers	2.4 teachers	2.8 teachers	**1.2 teachers**
VAPA	3.0 teachers			
Language	2.6 teachers	2.4 teachers		
PE	1.8 teachers	1.8 teachers		
CTE		**2.4 teachers**	**2.8 teachers**	**2.2 teachers**
Totals	15.2 teachers	16.2 teachers	14 teachers	9 teachers

FIGURE 7.8 FTE NEEDED TO STAFF SCHOOL

THE IMPORTANCE OF ALIGNING ALLOCATIONS CONNECTED TO MANDATES

Because allocations are aligned to expectations, it is imperative that the general education, special education, and English learner divisions of a school district collaborate on how to allocate resources if these resources are coming from multiple departments. While mandates must be met, they must not dilute the fidelity of the district's overall instructional strategy. There is nothing more devastating to building equitable schedules than to have misaligned mandates.

As an example, one large urban school district in Northern California decided to implement a pathway strategy to address inequities through connecting adults and students meaningfully in teams. In the model, students in each grade level travel through the same English, math, science, social science, and CTE teachers' classes each day, experiencing project-based learning. Although this is the primary instructional improvement strategy in the district, not all students have access to the "treatment" because of well-intended mandates. First, the special education division took a stance that resulted in many diploma-bound students being required to take ELA and/or math outside of the tier 1 general education environment in the pathway, so many students missed the ELA and/or math instruction that is directly connected to the grade-level project. In addition, English learners who scored below expected standards on state and local assessments are required to take additional course work as a mandate. When these course sections are allocated in a silo, they are not cohorted as part of the pathway teaming, which creates another constraint for scheduling. These misaligned staffing mandates made it almost impossible to implement the interdisciplinary strategy to fidelity—and the students most in need of the engagement associated with the strategy were the ones excluded from the full experience. The result was inequitable access and opportunity for historically marginalized students, which is not equity.

There is nothing more devastating to building equitable schedules than to have misaligned mandates.

ENABLING CONDITION #2: UNDERSTANDING THE ALIGNMENT BETWEEN SELECTING COURSES, BUILDING SECTIONS, AND STAFFING THE SCHEDULE

To achieve resource equity in scheduling, Architects of Equity must recognize and understand the alignment between selecting, tallying, and verifying courses; building sections; and staffing the schedule as each becomes a component of the articulation process (see Figure 7.9).

The articulation process has several steps:

- *Course Selection Process:* The process where students and their families select courses for the upcoming school year.

FIGURE 7.9 THE ARTICULATION PROCESS

Course Selection Process | Course Tally and Verification Process | Section Building, Loading, and Balancing | Staffing Assignments

The articulation process, or course selection process, is a critical part of the scheduling process. Enabling condition #2 requires action beyond simply offering and choosing courses as the choice process directly impacts resource equity.

- *Course Tally and Verification Process:* The process where the courses selected by students and families are tallied and verified for counselors.

- *Section Building, Loading, and Balancing:* The process where course tallies are used to determine the number of sections that need to be built, loaded, and balanced in the student information system.

- *Staffing Assignments:* The process where teachers are assigned to specific courses and students.

It is easy for fiscal responsibility to be compromised due to pressure to offer discrete course work despite low enrollments.

AVOIDING MISALIGNED COURSE SELECTION PROCESSES

During the articulation process, students fill out course selection cards (usually Google forms or some online version within the student information system). Typically, students are guided by their school counselors to select the required core classes they need including AP, honors, college prep, and so forth, and any additional course work the student might be interested in taking. The course selection process is the most anticipated process for students and their families because course access has a powerful connection to how students are perceived by staff, how students are perceived within their families, and how students are perceived as members of their peer group. Similarly to how teachers are leveled by the titles of the courses they teach, students wear course access like a badge of honor. As a result, it is easy for fiscal responsibility to be compromised due to pressure to offer discrete course work despite low enrollments.

Each year, comprehensive high schools release their programs of study, enticing students with their elective offerings while also including the courses they need to meet state requirements for graduation. Some high school programs are stacked with a variety of courses on a par with small liberal arts colleges. There are many exciting choices for students, ranging from Sports Marketing to Beekeeping to Business in a Global Economy—courses that might be beyond the course work needed to graduate. A consequence of offering a large elective course of study beyond the graduation requirements and/or not in alignment with the overall student enrollment, is that resources tend to benefit the options over the expectations. What this means is that the core classes students must take for graduation are usually scheduled with higher class sizes (typically 30 or more in urban areas), while the variety of electives are offered at smaller sizes, such as 20–24 since there are more elective seats offered than students can take. Since many students on the margins (English learners and students with disabilities) do not have the room in their schedules for electives, offering elective course work at class sizes lower than core course work is a glaring issue in many schools and a significant resource issue.

The bottom line is that a course selection card and/or process should not offer more than the site can afford or offer an experience that is not aligned to the site leadership vision for increased student performance, including mastery of the Equitable Core. In an equitable system, the course selection process facilitates the implementation of a sequence of courses designed to accelerate student performance strategically each year and over four years. Unfortunately, in many districts a siloed course selection process acts as the most impactful lever in the schedule. Instead of offering an experience, it facilitates singular courses as the be-all and end-all to an educational experience. A course selection card that is provided as a list of courses available, without any strategic offering of courses at specific grade levels and/or attached to specific pathways and/or experiences is a threat to equity. And if this list of courses includes a series of unmanageable and/or schedule-dominating singletons, the course selection process becomes a threat to equitable student outcomes.

The course selection process should facilitate access to the Equitable Core for each student. It should be an extension of the staffing allocation process completed with the allocation tool. Once a draft schedule designed with fiscal responsibility is created, the course selection process should be a tool to staff that vision.

In large comprehensive settings, it appears as if efficiency and logistics are the primary concerns when scheduling. Members of traditional scheduling teams might ask, Do we have enough sections? Are teachers working within the contract? Does every student have a schedule? Architects of Equity would ask those questions in addition to considering the following:

- Is it equitable or efficient to run smaller electives and larger core classes?
- Is it equitable or efficient to run many electives that dilute the student enrollment in each class, often leading to many sections with about 20–22 students, rather than filling electives to run closer to 28–30 students?
- Is it equitable or efficient to have the most experienced teachers assigned to higher-level courses with small enrollments while less experienced teachers are assigned to larger groups of students in classes where most students are struggling?

Before starting the course selection process, the Architects of Equity should also know exactly what is available for each grade level, and how student groups will be able to access those options. Consider the following:

- At each grade level, how many course opportunities are possible in students' schedules? For example, on a six-period system, if students must take ELA, math, science, and PE in grade nine, how many choices do they really need to fill two course periods?

- At each grade level, how many students are required to take mandated English learner, special education, and/or co-requisite courses? For example, on a six-period system, if students must take ELA, math, science, PE, and a mandated course in grade nine, how many choices do they really need to fill one course period?

- Should access to singletons take priority over access to teams, cohorts, pathways, and/or other collaborative strategic structures?

- Do the offerings of courses match district graduation requirements? For example, if the district requires the completion of one year of visual and performing arts, but the site offers enough seats for multiple years of VAPA, can the site afford the additional expenditures—and at the expense of which other possible offerings?

- Is it necessary for every elective course to be offered in grades nine through twelve or could electives be grade specific to allow for teaming, cohorts, and common planning time for core teams?

- Which competing priorities need to be addressed and/or ranked before starting the course selection process?

These questions (and possibly more) should be considered before starting to design and/or implement an equitable course selection process.

AVOIDING SINGLETON MADNESS

In scheduling lingo, a singleton is a class that is offered for only one section. This means that if one class of Band is offered during fourth period, and it is not offered anywhere else in the schedule, it is called a "singleton." The effect is that if a student wants to take Band, they must have fourth period free in their schedule or there is no other opportunity to take the class. Singletons are more common in smaller high schools, typically under 1,000 students, and can often wreak havoc on the schedule.

Higher-level (e.g., AP) courses are often singletons as well as many electives being offered through layered ability tracks. By offering these classes once, and sometimes keeping them open despite low enrollment numbers, singletons create a class hierarchy often serving the most elite and advantaged students with extremely small class sizes while their peers' classes must be overloaded to meet FTE limitations. Many scheduling teams believe that certain students are entitled to AP, international baccalaureate (IB), and advanced access regardless of class size, without considering opportunity youth to maximize sections, which may inadvertently create a culture of inequity through the establishment of ability tracks.

All singletons are not created equally. Some are necessary, because they may be the only option to offer a course at all in a schedule. Others may be the relic of inequitable practices. For example, each year Central City Academy, population 2,300, offers AP Chemistry and AP Biology. Both classes are double blocked due to the need for conducting labs and periods being only 48 minutes each. For several years, the classes have consistently enrolled less than 15 students, far from the contractual cap. Rather than offer the classes each year, Central City could offer AP Chemistry in odd years and AP Biology in even years. As established practice, this could both increase class size as well as allow students to take both courses more easily throughout their four years, since they are both singletons taking up two classes in the students' schedule. By making this shift, students can have a more comprehensive and individualized four-year plan for their studies. Figure 7.10 provides examples of typical singleton situations and potential scheduling solutions.

Singleton Situations	Singleton Solutions
A teacher speaks German and wants to offer the course even though it would be hard to staff if he left the school.	Encourage the teacher to incorporate his love for the German language into his current courses. Do not offer a singleton language course that will be hard to staff in the teacher's absence. Students might not be able to complete the number of years needed for college admissions.
Several single-period electives in the schedule have enrollments under 8.	Conduct a vacant seat analysis to determine costs associated with under-enrollment. Look for opportunity youth to increase enrollments if these are advanced studies sections. Eliminate singleton sections after attempting to find course equivalents and/or opportunities to layer course work.
A course has three levels: introductory, concentrator, and capstone. All sections have low enrollments, leaving three small singletons.	After layering all three levels in one period as a last option, meet with the department lead and teacher to discuss additional potential strategies for the upcoming year. Can course titles be consolidated to increase enrollment? Can the course work be offered after school or virtually across many schools and/or at the community college?
The school has historically offered one period of student government before lunch.	There could be another section of student government opened for students in grades 9–10 who are not elected officers. In this scenario, the underclassmen might work on posters, marketing, and so on. The standard student government class might cover Friday music, the prom, dances, and graduation.
Single AP classes are very small due to low enrollments.	Identify opportunity youth to increase enrollment and/or rotate AP opportunities each year. For example, AP Biology one year and AP Chemistry the next.

FIGURE 7.10 SOLVING THE SINGLETON CONUNDRUM

online resources: The entire 9–12 course selection card is in this book's appendix and available for download at https://companion.corwin.com/courses/equitableschoolscheduling

Too many singletons in a schedule is the first sign of an identity crisis in a high school. High schools are not colleges, and they are bound by the state graduation requirements to offer the most student-centered schedules that support grade promotion and completion for all students. By diluting the course selection and creating conflicts for students, high schools with too many singletons create more problems than they solve, all too often while offering inequitable programming.

Pathways and the Course Selection Process

When beginning a course selection process for CTE-driven pathway schools, the following items should be aligned: the Equitable Core, the course selection card, and the bell schedule. Figure 7.11 presents an engineering pathway in a seven-period system. Examples for six-period and eight-period schedules are available online. Figure 7.11 also depicts a sample course selection card for an engineering student at https://companion.corwin.com/courses/equitable schoolscheduling.

THE IMPORTANCE OF THE COURSE TALLY PROCESS

The course tally is a grid that shows the course, the total number of students who requested the course broken down by grade level, and the number of sections allotted. When denoted MU (make-up), this indicates students retaking the course due to a previous failure. The example in Figure 7.12 is a view of one content area in a course tally sheet. A blank version of the course tally sheet is available in the appendix and online at https://companion.corwin.com/courses/equitableschoolscheduling.

Notice and Note

Prior to building sections from this sheet, decisions need to be made that impact funding and priorities.

- If this is the tally sheet of a pathway-focused school, the tenth-grade students who need to make up ELA 9 must be placed in ELA 10 first to ensure access to the integrated grade-level team, and the ninth-grade ELA make-up must become the elective.

My 7-Period High School Plan Worksheet

	Grade 9	Grade 10	Grade 11	Grade 12
CTE Course Sequence (Indicate A–G)				
Linked Learning: Minimum 3-year sequence	Introduction to Engineering Design	Principles of Engineering	Civil Engineering and Architecture	Engineering Design and Development
Academic Core Classes (Indicate A–G)				
English Language Arts	ELA 9 Advanced ELA 9	ELA 10 Advanced ELA 10	ELA 11 AP Language	ELA 12 AP Literature
Math	IM I Advanced IM I IM II Advanced IM II	IM II Advanced IM II IM III Advanced IM III	IM III Advanced IM III Pre-Calculus Honors Pre-Calculus	
Science	Physics Advanced Physics	Biology Advanced Biology	Chemistry Honors Chemistry	
Social Science		World History AP World History	American History AP U.S. History	Government/Econ. AP Govt./Econ.
Language other than English	Language 1	Language 2		
Physical Education	PE 9	PE 10	Waiver after passing fitness test	Waiver after passing fitness test
Electives	Health/Ethnic Studies		Fine Art	4 electives

Board-Approved Graduation Requirements:
English: 4 years required
Mathematics: 3 years required
Science: 3 years required
Social Studies: 3 years required
Physical Education: 2 years required
Fine Art: 1 year required
World Language: 2 years or equivalent required
CTE: Four-course pathway completion required

Note: All students must maintain an overall 2.0 grade point average.
Student: _____
Parent: _____
Counselor: _____
Date: _____

Note: AP is advanced placement; CTE is career technical education; IM is Integrated Math.

Course Selection Card
9th Grade: 7-Period System

Pathway Course	
✅	Intro to Engineering Design

English Language Arts	
☐	ELA 9
☐	ELA 9 Adv.

Social Studies	
Not Applicable	

Mathematics	
☐	Integrated Math I
☐	Adv. Integrated Math I
☐	Integrated Math II
☐	Adv. Integrated Math II

Physical Education	
✅	PE 9

Science	
☐	Physics
☐	Adv. Physics

Student Supports	
☐	Designated EL 1
☐	Designated EL 2
☐	Math Support
☐	IEP Mandated Support
☐	ELA Mandated Support
✅	Health 0.5
✅	Ethnic Studies 0.5

World Language*	
☐	Spanish I
☐	Spanish II

Additional Electives**	
☐	Orchestra
☐	Art
☐	Band
☐	Choir
☐	Dance
☐	Student Government
☐	Yearbook
☐	Theater
☐	Journalism

*If a student needs **additional mandated support** these courses are not an option within the school day.

If a student needs **world language or additional mandated support these courses are not an option within the school day.

▨ Must Do

▨ Must Do if Failed PE Fitness Exam

FIGURE 7.11 SAMPLE FOUR-YEAR ENGINEERING PATHWAY PLAN AND FRESHMAN COURSE SELECTION CARD FOR AN ENGINEERING STUDENT

- If there are 50 tenth-grade students who need to make up ELA 9 and the class size of ELA 9 is 32, will two sections of ELA 9 MU be opened at 25 students each to accommodate this? What about the 35 ELA 10 make-up students? Will one or two sections be built to accommodate a 32-student class size? Each class opened is potentially a $28,000 decision that can have considerable impacts if not considered before the build.

- Because of the bargained class size of 32, many of the courses on the list are going to require the site to round up in the number of sections needed, which will also lower class size.

Course Tally Sheet

Type	Number	Title	Total Req.	No. of Sects.	Class Size	9th	10th	11th	12th
Req.	1000	ELA 9	400	12.5	32	350	50 MU		
Req.	1001	ELA 9 Honors	150	5	32	150			
Req.	1010	ELA 10	360	12	32		325	35 MU	
Req.	1011	ELA 10 Honors	125	4	32		125		
Req.	1020	ELA 11	330	11	32			300	30 MU
Req.	1120	AP English Language	100	3	32			100	
Req.	1220	ELA 12	200	6	32				200
Req.	1230	AP English Literature	50	2	32				50
Req.	CC	English 101	100	3	32				100
Elect	1050	Yearbook	40	1	32	5	5	20	10
Elect	1060	Theater	20	1	32	10	6	3	1
Elect	1070	Journalism	30	1	32	5	5	10	10
Elect	1080	Sci-Fi Literature	50	1	32		10	25	15
Req.	1001.1	Designated ESL 1	60	3	25	20	20	10	10
Req.	1010.1	Designated ESL 2	75	3	25	25	20	30	
Req.	1020.1	Designated ESL 3	50	2	25		30	20	

FIGURE 7.12 SAMPLE COURSE TALLY RECORD
Note: Req. is required; Elect. is elective; MU is make-up.

- If 100 students request AP Language at a class size of 32, three full sections is 96. Does the site place the 4 remaining students in the three sections and raise the class size to accommodate? Does the site look for 28 opportunity youth in the eleventh grade and open a fourth section of AP Language? What the site should not do is open four sections of AP Language for 100 students at a class size of 25. The cost of the vacant seats (7 seats times 4 sections) is almost an entire section. This is the same situation with AP Literature. A total of 50 students selected the course with a class size of 32. Is one full section opened? Are opportunity youth in twelfth grade identified to open the second section? What the site should not do is open two AP Literature sections at 25 students each. If this is done, course after course, the financial impacts are tremendous. In addition, if the regular courses have full classes and the AP classes do not, this is not resource equity.

- Can a theater class run at 20 (12 vacant seats) or might this program have to be supported after school? And this question is not just about theater. Can multiple programs run at class sizes well below the maximum across the schedule? The answer is no if resource equity is a priority.

Figure 7.13 demonstrates how the original projected section allotments stack up against the course-request tally.

	Number of Students	Minimum English Sections Needed Over 4 Years	English Course Request Tally Sections
9th Grade	500	17 sections	18 sections
10th Grade	450	15 sections	16 sections
11th Grade	400	14 sections	14 sections
12th Grade	350	12 sections	11 sections
Total	1,700	58 sections projected	59 sections requested

FIGURE 7.13 ORGANIZING THE COURSE TALLY RECORD TO PROJECT SECTIONS

The course tally in Figure 7.13 reflects a difference of one course in ELA, but it also reflects a need for fewer twelfth-grade, and more ninth-/tenth-grade course sections. The course tally process is essential because it typically dictates the number of sections that are built into the site schedule. The course tally process is the result of students making course selections during the articulation process. When the course tally process is not a highly structured process, it can result in financial inequities within the schedule. The point of this exercise is to illustrate that a course tally sheet is the beginning of the discussion not the end of it. Course tally sheets must be discussed and verified prior to being used to determine the number of sections in a section build.

Figure 7.14 illustrates the three important components of an equitable course tally process.

- *Counselor Verification:* It is imperative that before courses are officially and formally tallied that there is verification that each student has a full and accurate set of courses.

    The right number of courses: For example, in a seven-period schedule each student should have seven courses. If schools are going to allow

Equitable Course Tally Process

Counselor Verification · Mandate Verification · Accurate Enrollment Counts

FIGURE 7.14 STEPS TO A SUCCESSFUL COURSE TALLY PROCESS

"free periods," there should be a course placeholder like *assigned time home*, *off-site college*, and/or *internship* to account for student enrollments. Not paying attention to this step will result in the appearance that more sections and/or fewer sections of courses are needed than is true, resulting in schedule problems during the loading process.

- *The right courses:* Students may have selected the wrong level of courses, courses they have already passed, the wrong sequence of courses, and/or courses they don't have room for in their schedules due to mandates and/or course failures. Counselors and/or other designated staff must clean the course tallies prior to creating course sections as these items may impact course numbers and enrollments.

- *Mandate Verification:* For students to experience an equitable course selection process, it is important to know how mandates will affect articulation. If historically marginalized students are to be given priority in the scheduling process, it is imperative for any data (including IEP mandates) that might impact courses in the schedule be collected prior to the schedule build. This means that assessments and subsequent parent meetings must be conducted/completed on a timeline consistent with the course selection process. In addition, for English learners and special education students to be provided priority scheduling, accurate information about placement must be provided on the site scheduling timeline—not the timeline of the IEPs and/or other technical processes.

- *Accurate Enrollment Counts:* Sometimes students submit course selection cards in the spring before the following school year, and then don't return in the fall. When students' requests remain in the system, even though they have been unenrolled, this becomes a scheduling problem because phantom students hold seats in courses, which can completely throw off the counts. This is why it must be a priority for schools to clear their rosters of students who have not returned, so sections can either be opened or closed as necessary. This must be an ongoing process throughout the year to ensure accurate course tallies.

BUILDING SECTIONS

Once the course request tally sheet is in order and has been verified, the build begins in the student information system. The scheduler inputs the courses based on the course request tally sheet. Parameters such as class sizes, rooms, student lists, and so forth are input as well. Once the system populates the sections, the scheduler can create a spreadsheet with teachers assigned to the courses. For pathway schools trying to protect common planning, grade-level teaming, and/or student cohorts, it is imperative to understand how to tag students, teachers, and pathways prior to building and loading. Building a cohort purity report in the student information system is essential in monitoring the building and cohorting of sections and students. In the cohort purity report in Figure 7.15, it is apparent that courses that were intended to be pure by pathway, have not all been scheduled that way.

ASSIGNING TEACHERS

Traditionally, in large high schools, the assignment of teachers to sections falls to the department heads. These leaders know their colleagues and what they have been teaching. This is another point in the process to pause

Cohort Purity Report

Health Academy Biology	**Biology I** Health: 26 Engineer: 2	**Biology I** Health: 32 Media: 3	**Biology I** Health: 30 Engineer: 1 Media: 2	**Biology I** Health: 25	**Biology I** Health: 23	**PREP**
Health Academy ELA	**ELA I** Health: 27 Media: 1	**ELA I** Health: 27 Engineer: 2	**ELA I** Health: 27	**ELA I** Health: 25	**ELA I** Health: 30 Engineer: 1	**PREP**
Health Academy Medical	**PBS** Health: 32	**PBS** Health: 30	**PBS** Health: 24	**PBS** Health: 24 Media: 2	**PBS** Health: 26	**PREP**

FIGURE 7.15 A SNAPSHOT OF A PORTION OF A COHORT PURITY REPORT FOR THE SCHOOL'S HEALTH ACADEMY

Note: If a pathway is trying to integrate curriculum, the teaching sections must be filled with pathway-specific students. In schools with multiple pathways, there must be monitoring to ensure that students are not scheduled in the wrong pathway-dedicated sections. In the health academy example here, engineering and media pathway students have been scheduled in health pathway courses, which must be corrected. PBS is the mandatory ninth-grade pathway course, Principles of Biomedical Science.

and include the Architects of Equity, so that students are placed at the center of the process. Are the most experienced teachers being given the most "desirable" sections, for example, advanced placement and honors? Do the regular classes, such as ninth-grade English and English as a second language classes, have revolving doors of teachers? When assigning teachers to sections, it is imperative to center student needs and assign teachers where they can make the biggest impact on student learning. More about how to engage teachers meaningfully in the scheduling process will be covered in chapter 8.

ENABLING CONDITION #3: UNDERSTANDING THE IMPACTS OF BELL SCHEDULES, SCHEDULE BALANCE, AND SCHEDULING EXPERIENCE ON RESOURCE EQUITY

To achieve resource equity in scheduling, Architects of Equity must recognize and understand the impacts that bell schedules, schedule balance, and scheduling experience have on scheduling (see Figure 7.16).

BELL SCHEDULE SELECTION

The bell schedule a school chooses to use can affect seat capacity and a need for more FTE than the district has allocated. In this case, the bell schedule refers to how many classes students take each year (six, seven, etc.), how long the classes meet (straight periods each, block scheduling alternating days, rotating "drop one or two" days, etc.), or how much flexibility students have in terms of taking courses outside of the school schedule (adult education, remote learning, community college, etc.). A school's overall enrollment must be aligned to the bell schedule selected. For example, if there are fewer than 300 students in a school's tenth-grade class and a class size maximum is 30, a minimum of 10 ELA sections might be needed. In a nine-period bell schedule this might mean that two teachers pick up five English sections each, requiring the remaining four sections in the teachers' schedules to become two preparatory periods and two filler

Bell Schedule Selection Schedule Balance Scheduling Experience

FIGURE 7.16 EQUITABLE SCHEDULING CONSIDERATIONS
Meeting enabling condition #3 requires the Architects of Equity understand how bell schedules, schedule balance, and scheduling experience impact scheduling.

courses. Additionally, some union contracts have limitations on how many sections teachers may teach and how many students may be enrolled in a teacher's course load overall. Given any of these conditions, additional teachers might be required to cover sections.

Bell schedule decisions have serious consequences financially. Traditional bell schedules have typically been very limiting six-period models. In recent years, districts have been shifting to bell schedules that allow for more access. Some districts have moved to a seven-period bell, but in the process added an additional teacher prep period, which is an incredible expense because while students get access to an additional course, teachers still teach five classes. Districts that don't do the math to consider the increases in certain teaching credentials in this model may find out after the fact that they simply cannot afford the cost—and once precedent is set it is hard to reverse. Some districts have considered moving to a 4×4 block schedule, which would typically cost approximately 9% more than a traditional six-period schedule. However, because many courses in typical schedules are under-enrolled, a focus on making sure classes are tightly cohorted and filled to the desired class size would likely make the move to the 4×4 block far less expensive. Finally, some districts have chosen to implement other schedules that require students to attend eight-plus courses in one day. This just doesn't make sense for accelerating learning. How do students manage eight or more transitions, homework assignments, tests, and so on? These are just not student-friendly schedules, and they end up containing more filler classes than are necessary.

Consider the decision to shift to an eight-period bell schedule because of a desire to implement the international baccalaureate (IB) curriculum. The decision between shifting to eight periods of course work in a row versus a 4×4 rotating block can have serious consequences for students. IB students who are reading at grade level might be able to handle eight classes a day—including the homework associated with these classes. On the other hand, students who are learning English, not reading at grade level, or who need more co-requisite support, may not be able to handle this structure. Too often, decisions like this are made to accommodate a segment of the student population (25%) rather than making a decision that works for everyone. A solution to this problem is not implementing the option that best meets the needs of the 25% by short scheduling and/or adding filler classes to the schedules of the other 75%. A compromise might be a hybrid 4×4 where some students experience a rotating a/b while other students take limited course work for semesters.

The Cost of Bell Schedules

Example: Equity High is currently running a six-period bell schedule. Teachers have one prep period and teach five classes. There are 1,900 students in the school. The staffing to contract class size in core classes is 32 students.

Basic Formula (does not include prorating of supplemental allocations):

Student enrollment divided by desired class size equals "A."

"A" times the number of periods in the bell schedule equals "B."

"B" divided by the number of periods taught by teachers equals allocation.

COST OF A 6-PERIOD BELL SCHEDULE	COST OF A 7-PERIOD BELL SCHEDULE	COST OF AN 8-PERIOD BELL SCHEDULE
1,900 students divided by 32 students is 59.4. 59.4 times 6 periods is 356.4. 356.4 divided by 5 periods taught by teachers is **71.28** teachers.	1,900 students divided by 32 students is 59.4. 59.4 times 7 periods is 415.8. 415.8 divided by 6 periods taught by teachers is **69.3** teachers. If the site is providing two teacher preps rather than one in this model, divide by 5 not 6. 415.8 divided by 5 periods taught by teachers is **83.16** teachers.	1,900 students divided by 32 students is 59.4. 59.4 times 8 periods is 475.2. 475.2 divided by 6 periods taught by teachers is **79.2** teachers.

Conclusions (based on a teacher plus benefits costing $140,000):
- The cost of shifting from a 6-period schedule to a 7-period schedule with one teacher prep costs approximately 2 FTE less (or $280,000 less) than running the traditional 6-period schedule.
- The cost of shifting from a 6-period schedule to a 7-period schedule with two teacher preps costs approximately 12 FTE more (or $1,680,000 more) than running the traditional 6-period schedule.
- The cost of shifting from a 6-period schedule to an 8-period schedule with two teacher preps costs approximately 8 FTE more ($1,120,000 more) than running the traditional 6-period schedule.
- Shifting to a 4×4 with two preps is less expensive than shifting to a 7-period with two preps.
- How the bell schedule is organized over days does not mitigate the cost as students still need to be assigned to the same number of periods in the bell schedule.
- Prorating the (a) students receiving supplemental supports and (b) students with free periods will lower the general education enrollment and reduce the number of FTE needed.

Regardless of the bell schedule that is selected, Architects of Equity must stay focused on what a bell schedule is supposed to do: allow for students and teachers to behave purposefully and intentionally around content. Research illuminates that highly collaborative teaching teams are powerful levers in the mission to serve diverse groups of students (Stern et al., 2010). Unfortunately, many traditional bell schedules have prioritized collaboration at the department level instead of the grade level, which is really a decision about working with an eye on yearly goals versus daily and weekly goals. It's all about urgency.

Regardless of the bell schedule that is selected, Architects of Equity must stay focused on what a bell schedule is supposed to do: allow for students and teachers to behave purposefully and intentionally around content.

Not all bell schedules are created equally, so Architects of Equity must support awareness and selection of a structure that allows for access that leads to equitable academic outcomes. Decisions about bell schedules should be evidence based. Too often bell schedule decisions are based on unsubstantiated claims about learning, such as (a) I must see the students every day or they won't master competencies; (b) Some students just don't come to high school prepared so they can't be expected to achieve at the highest level; (c) Access to a wide variety of elective courses as a priority keeps students engaged in school; and (d) Students won't get into college unless the site offers more advanced course work than other schools. When these ideas are presented as a justification for selecting bell schedules that prioritize multiple transitions for students and inequitable access to high expectations for historically marginalized students, Architects of Equity must require that decisions are evidence based.

BELL SCHEDULE SELECTION CONSIDERATIONS

- Enrollment
- Transitions
- Approach to acceleration
- Meaningful collaboration
- Ability to earn credits—remediate credits, take support classes, and so forth
- Graduation requirements

BALANCING THE SCHEDULE

To balance a schedule properly, scheduling teams must know how to look at the schedule in a grid organized by period and grade level, so they can balance class offerings both vertically and horizontally. To put it simply, are there enough classes offered each period for each overall student to be in a seat, and for each grade-level student to be in a seat? What are the steps to determining this once you have a draft of your schedule input in the system?

HOW TO BALANCE A SCHEDULE
Section and Enrollment Balance

1. Start with a copy of the site schedule that includes teacher course assignments, teacher preps, and the periods within the bell schedule.

2. Use the total enrollment of the school to count sections vertically (in each period) to determine whether all students would have a seat with the current projected courses.
   For example:
   - Count the courses being offered to students in grades nine through twelve in period one.
   - Determine the total enrollment in those classes. If class sizes are typically scheduled at 30, and there are 55 classes available, there are 1,650 seats available.
   - If there are 2,000 students enrolled, and only 1,650 seats in period one, the scheduling team knows that more sections must be added to period one.
   - Continue this exercise for every period.

3. Use the total enrollment of the grade level to count vertically (in each period) to see whether each grade-level student would have a seat with the current projected courses.
   For example:
   - Count how many courses are being offered that ninth graders can take in period one.
   - Determine the total enrollment in those classes. If there are 30 ninth-grade classes and each can hold 30 students, there are 900 seats available.
   - If there are 500 ninth-grade students, there are too many ninth-grade seats in period one. The scheduling team knows that fewer sections are needed for the ninth grade in period one.
   - Continue this exercise for every period and every grade level.

Preparatory Period Balance

1. Start with a copy of the site schedule that includes teacher course assignments, teacher preps, and the periods within the bell schedule.

2. Count the number of teacher preps in each period vertically.

3. The number of preps do not have to be equal by period but they should be close.

Course Assignment Balance

This step is taken when there are contractual agreements on course/teaching assignments that must be monitored for implementation. For example, the Architects of Equity might encounter union agreements that state

- Teachers can only be assigned three consecutive core classes before they must have a prep period assigned.
- Teachers can only be assigned up to three different courses that require preparation.
- Teachers can only have a maximum load of 180 students on their caseloads—and this must also be balanced against the bell schedule (e.g., 180 students on a six period is different from 180 students on an eight-period 4×4 a/b).

AVOIDING A BAD BUILD

There is no doubt that scheduling is a complex and detailed process. Scheduling will become more complex as Architects of Equity pay increased attention to the inequities and unintended consequences that result from sloppy scheduling. As it is said, the devil is in the details when scheduling, which is why scheduling is best done in teams and as a collaborative and inclusive process. Teams are helpful in the balancing stage of scheduling. Not understanding this process or not having teams to double-check the work can contribute to schedules that are either out of balance or possibly even impossible to execute.

Too often, scheduling is done in an isolated environment by either someone new and without institutional knowledge, or by someone who has been doing it so long, they may not know what they don't know, and there is very little incentive to examine practices. In these cases, the resulting schedules can be "bad builds," or ineffectual schedules that create more problems than necessary.

An example of a bad build could be when classes are run at inefficient sizes, and there is no system in place to check the allotment of sections to the actual number scheduled. If a district does not have tight oversight and use a formula to allot FTE, a bad build may result in class sizes that are too large or too small with much variation across.

ADDITIONAL TOOLS TO MONITOR RESOURCE EQUITY

Previously in this chapter, the importance of using an allocation tool for staffing and a cohort purity report for scheduling and monitoring pathways was discussed. Another useful tool for measuring resource equity is the vacant seat analysis. In a vacant seat analysis, the district measures the cost of under-enrolled classes by completing the following steps:

- Extract all the courses in the current schedule by course alphabetically in Excel (or another spreadsheet tool).

- List the current enrollment, maximum capacity, and the difference between the two next to each course in the Excel file. This will reveal the total number of seats not filled in each course.

- Take the total number of seats not filled across all offered courses and divide this number by the district's determined average course size to determine the number of sections that would not have been used if courses were filled. For example, in Figure 7.17 the district chose an average class size of 30. In a maximum class size of 30, 28 was used as the average class capacity, to allow for room in the scheduling.

- Because all classes are typically not filled to maximum capacity in a schedule, a district might choose to examine capacity at 80% rather than 100%. In a maximum class size of 24 at 80%, 24 was maintained as the average class capacity, as that allows for room above the 80% average.

Figure 7.17 is an example of how one district in Connecticut conducted a vacant seat analysis to assess the cost of allowing many under-enrolled sections in the schedule. This chart was reprinted without modifications.

The vacant seat analysis reveals that this comprehensive high school of over 2,000 students has several areas where savings can be found. It is important to note that the analysis does not include special education and English learner classes, since these are mandated courses with maximum enrollment limitations and staffing requirements. In this high school, there are 788 sections of general education classes across ten disciplines. In examining the open seats per class as relative to the maximum capacity determined by the district, the chart reveals 4,442 open seats if the classes were scheduled at 100% capacity and 1,810 open seats if the classes were scheduled at merely 80% capacity. To compute the savings at 100% capacity, the 4,442 seats are divided by 28 students per class, giving us 158 sections that could have been removed from the schedule if the classes had been properly balanced. If each teacher teaches five sections, divide 158 by 5, meaning 31.6 FTE could have been saved by consolidating under-enrolled classes. In this example, each section is valued at $17,000 by the district. This equates to almost $2.7 million in savings at just one high school. Computed at 80%, the savings are just over $1.2 million. Whereas these are large amounts of savings, it is reasonable to assert there may be classes that need to run under the ideal enrollment, such as singletons and classes for targeted populations. That said, even if the savings aren't as extreme as the chart may suggest, certainly there is room to trim this schedule as it stands.

@ 100% Capacity 4442 Empty Seats in 788 sections 74 sections @ Under 50% Capacity Average Class Size 21 Students	28 average class capacity @ 100% 4442/28 = 158 unfilled sections			158 unfilled sections = 31.6 FTE (teach 5 periods) 158 sections x $17K = $2,686,000			
@ 80% Capacity 1810 Empty Seats in 788 sections 74 sections @ Under 50% Capacity Average Class Size 21 Students	24 average class capacity @ 80% 1810/24 = 75 unfilled sections			75 unfilled sections = 15 FTE (teach 5 periods) 75 sections x $17K = $1,275,000			

*SPED, Independent Study, and Other Small Intervention Classes have been removed from the data. Smaller sized EL classes are included, affecting the average class size.

Class	Period	Term	Enrollment	Full Capacity	Underenrolled By #	Enrollment	80% Full Capacity	Underenrolled By #
Accounting 1	7(A-G)	21-22	15	24	9	15	19	4
Accounting 1	5(A-G)	21-22	23	24	1	23	23	0
Accounting 1	2(A-G)	21-22	24	24	0	24	24	0
Adobe Photoshop	6(A-G)	S1	17	21	4	17	17	0
Adobe Photoshop	5(A-G)	S1	20	21	1	20	20	0
Adobe Photoshop	6(A-G)	S2	20	21	1	20	20	0
Advanced Algebra and Geometry	7(A-G)	21-22	15	30	15	15	24	9
Advanced Algebra and Geometry	5(A-G)	21-22	29	30	1	29	29	0
African American/Latino PR Studies	5(A-G)	21-22	25	30	5	25	25	0
African American/Latino PR Studies	3(A-G)	21-22	27	30	3	27	27	0
African American/Latino PR Studies	2(A-G)	21-22	23	30	7	23	24	1
Algebra 1	2(A-G)	21-22	22	30	8	22	24	2

172 EQUITABLE SCHOOL SCHEDULING

Algebra 1	3(A-G)	21-22	28	30	2	28	0
Algebra 1	6(A-G)	21-22	20	30	10	24	4
Algebra 1	1(A-G)	21-22	19	30	11	24	5
Algebra 1	5(A-G)	21-22	23	30	7	24	1
Algebra 1	3(A-G)	21-22	24	30	6	24	0
Algebra 1	7(A-G)	21-22	25	30	5	25	0
Algebra 1	6(A-G)	21-22	14	30	16	24	10
Algebra 1	2(A-G)	21-22	18	30	12	24	6
Algebra 1	4(A-G)	21-22	14	30	16	24	10
Algebra 1 Honors	6(A-G)	21-22	20	30	10	24	4
Algebra 1 Honors	1(A-G)	21-22	15	30	15	24	9
Algebra 2	7(A-G)	21-22	16	30	14	24	8
Algebra 2	3(A-G)	21-22	23	30	7	24	1
Algebra 2	5(A-G)	21-22	26	30	4	26	0
TOTAL 788 Sections					4442		1810

FIGURE 7.17 SAMPLE USE OF A VACANT SEAT ANALYSIS TOOL

FINAL THOUGHTS

Resource equity begins by considering the costs of staffing resources and what the schedule says about the school's values and decision making. When making the shift to becoming the Architects of Equity, the scheduling team must step back from what has always been done and assess the current practices and processes from a new lens. Gaining an understanding of the fiscal impacts of discrete decisions made during the scheduling process is a critical step in the process. Resource equity is achieved when awareness is heightened across the staff about the financial impacts of scheduling decisions. Architects of Equity are always working to support staff to consider the intersection between good ideas and alignment of actions to the site's vision for instructional improvement.

TECHNICAL SELF-ASSESSMENT QUESTIONS	ADAPTIVE SELF-ASSESSMENT QUESTIONS
1. How is staff currently allocated to schools? 2. Do the number of sections created match the forecasted enrollment and the FTE allotted? 3. How do mandates currently affect scheduling each year? What could be done to improve these processes? 4. How many singletons are currently in the schedule? Are they all necessary? 5. Do course selection processes align to Equitable Core expectations?	1. Does the current bell schedule allow for equitable access and opportunities for all student groups? If not, what shifts would improve the schedule? 2. How are discussions about student outcomes connected to schedule design each year? 3. How are discussions about the course tally sheet facilitated prior to a schedule build? 4. Does the schedule reflect a belief that personalization is a function of course selection or knowing students well? How are conversations about course selection and personalization facilitated?

CHAPTER 8

EQUITY BY DESIGN

ESTABLISHING GUIDING STRUCTURES FOR SCHEDULING TEAMS

> <u>Changing Practice 6:</u> *Scheduling Teams Must Structure Time and Input Intentionally*

With organization comes empowerment.
—Lynda Peterson

The scheduling process at Mission High School was always a mystery. Early in the fall, once the staffing and student enrollment settled, the principal and vice principal would disappear behind closed doors and begin to play with whiteboard magnets in the room from where next year's schedule would eventually emerge months later. Sometimes counselors and/or other support staff would be invited into this secret space and eventually rumors would begin to swirl about potential funding and program cuts that might need to be made. These rumors always came right before winter break, and by the time January rolled around the budgeting process was beginning and the fight to protect perceived losses would begin. This made for a terrible culture at the school, especially in the spring months. The lack of frequent, timely, and authentic information was resulting in staff filling the empty spaces with their own possible versions of the truth. Despite the vice principal's suggestions about how they might organize the scheduling process more meaningfully, the principal held on to the way things had always been done as this was his comfort zone.

When the current principal eventually announced his retirement, the vice principal applied for the job and was promoted. She knew this was an opportunity for the scheduling process—an impactful undertaking that extended from September to August—to be reformed in the service of true collaboration and instructional improvement. The new principal decided to create a transparent scheduling timeline that would provide ongoing information about the process, opportunities for collaboration, and engagement with current best practice teaching strategies. The first thing the principal did was identify a cross-discipline scheduling team that consisted of the head counselor, pathway lead teachers, vice principals, and classified support staff. She also developed a calendar of engagement, where the scheduling team would present the current work of the schedule and vet ideas with staff. These engagement opportunities included union leadership meetings, department meetings, pathway meetings, grade-level team meetings, student leadership meetings, and family/community meetings. In addition, the principal took all the deadlines she was provided from finance and human resources and organized them alongside the site scheduling actions so that staff could understand what was being done, why it was being done, and the deadlines things had to be done by. Not only did this transparency help staff understand the process, but it also helped the scheduling team work more efficiently.

While it was overwhelming to be that transparent in the beginning, the principal started to notice a shift in the culture of the school. People were not as angry about the schedule. While there were certainly moments of posturing about perceived losses, the conversations were more collaborative about what could be done to make the fiscal changes that were needed while attempting to preserve what the staff, students, and families valued most. Over the years, the principal took the overarching scheduling timelines and developed job-specific timelines within the organizational chart so that there was no mystery about who should be doing what, when, and where. She learned that clarity was appreciated and that she did not have to fear regular input from staff—even if that input did not always match her own thinking. Because she had clear, collaborative, and transparent procedures, she was able to make the scheduling experience more about process and less about people, which allowed the scheduling team to engage differently around matters of equity.

What the new principal did successfully is create a concrete timeline that made the scheduling process transparent and inclusive allowing everyone to participate meaningfully. Participants knew their roles and understood that their input would be an integral part of the ongoing planning process. This is not a typical scenario. Many teams operate within a comfort zone, treating their time together like the movie *Groundhog Day*, a repetitive cycle of yearly scheduling tasks, rather than the start of something transformative. This chapter will provide concrete examples of how Architects of Equity can schedule their time purposefully and intentionally through powerful structures. At the conclusion of this chapter, districts and site leaders should be prepared to identify and empower scheduling teams who work collectively as the *visible* hand of equitable scheduling.

THE INTENTIONAL STRUCTURING OF TIME

In chapter 1, it was established that through the site schedule students gain access to course work, teachers, and opportunities that define the difference between graduation and a meaningful graduation. Because schedules are defined as the invisible hand of equity, the need to identify, establish, and support a scheduling team operating within a growth mindset is offered as the primary solution for moving from the current scheduling reality to the ideal state.

Architects of Equity operate within powerful and intentional structures. First, personal and group accountability is key. Once a scheduling team addresses their role in the status QUO and develops their mindSET, these teams must establish operating norms. These norms should be collectively identified, discussed, and codified in service of equity. These norms might include a commitment to (a) designing with a growth mindset, (b) using asset-based (deficit-free) language when discussing students, (c) managing personal fears, (d) admitting when something is not understood or known, (e) being open to new possibilities, and (f) holding team members accountable to equitable scheduling practices. Many highly effective teams also use strategies like design thinking to support them to push past traditional thinking about schedules.

> *Architects of Equity operate within powerful and intentional structures.*

In addition, because Architects of Equity act strategically and intentionally, scheduling timelines are a critical piece of their planning processes. These timelines should be developed at the district and site levels to align scheduling systems equitably across the district, while attending to the unique contexts of each school community. The district should collaborate with site leaders to create the schoolwide timelines below. Once those timelines are established, school sites should develop site-level, community-specific timelines that include more details.

Some important scheduling timelines include, but are not limited to

- Overall District and Site Scheduling Timelines
- Dual Enrollment Timelines
- Counseling Activity Timelines
- Registrar Timelines
- Site/Tech Builder Timelines

OVERALL DISTRICT AND SITE SCHEDULING TIMELINES

These timelines focus on the scheduling cycle that aligns business services, educational services, and human resources through the budgeting, staffing, and scheduling process.

Suggested details:

- Choice/Enrollment Options Application Opening and Closing Dates
- Student Information System (SIS) New Year Rollover Dates
- Course Selection Process Opening and Closing Dates
- Information Technology and/or SIS Scheduling Training Dates
- Schedule Building—Loading, Balancing, and Finalizing Dates
- Teacher and Student Schedule Preview Dates
- Pre-Scheduling Data and Transcript Review Dates
- Bell Schedule Change Submission Dates
- Budgeting Timelines (including projections, allocations, and budget submission dates)
- Staffing Timelines (including hiring and excessing dates)
- Staff/Union Engagement Cycle Dates (including instructional leadership team, school site council, governance team, and/or any other formal engagement teams)

It is important to identify and assign tasks meaningfully to help the Architects of Equity understand how they will each play a critical and timely role in the scheduling process. Figure 8.1 provides a list of items that might be considered in a schedule planning process. The columns to the right allow for the team to consider who might be responsible and what month the task must be addressed. A downloadable version of Figure 8.1 is available on the companion website.

To establish a district scheduling timeline, the **Scheduling Timeline Roles and Responsibilities** drop-down tool online at https://companion.corwin.com/courses/equitableschoolscheduling can be used to identify the department, role, and/or months that scheduling items might be addressed. In addition, there are district and site timeline examples in the appendices.

Dual Enrollment Timelines

These timelines focus on the cycle that aligns the college and school district timelines for dual enrollment college programs.

Suggested details:

- College Enrollment, Admission, and Registration Events/Dates
- Student and Guardian Orientation and Information Dates
- College Course Start and End Dates (including withdrawal dates)

Scheduling Timeline Roles and Responsibilities

Item	Responsible	Month
Seat cost analysis of under-enrolled sections in prior/current year		
Enrollment projections are provided		
Projected allocations are provided		
Budget is provided to the principal		
Budget is finalized and submitted by the principal		
Single Plan for Student Achievement goals are written and submitted		
Inter/intra district transfer opens		
Inter/intra district transfer closes		
Open enrollment begins		
Open enrollment ends		
Create and distribute teacher preference sheets		
Collect teacher preference sheets		
Engage the union representative		
Engage the instructional leadership team		
Engage the School Site Council and site English Learner Advisory Committee teams		
Engage department chairs and/or pathway leads		
Engage the special education and English learner support staff		
Review the current credentials of staff		
Review any changes to labor contracts regarding staffing		
Teachers provide input on future student courses		
Teachers provide input on schedule frame without lines assigned		
Schedule frame is vetted with all stakeholders prior to budget build		
Additional staffing requests are submitted		
Sites submit any teacher/staff reductions		
Staffing descriptions are due		
Hiring of staff ends		
Preview draft schedules/courses with students before summer		
Preview teaching lines with teachers before summer		
Make final staffing adjustments based on enrollment		
Rising/future students are rolled over in student information system (SIS)		

(Continued)

(Continued)

Task		
Data report of advanced studies outcomes and enrollment shared with staff		
Summative data trends from last year and over multiple years are reviewed with staff		
Course requests are loaded and evaluated against the schedule expectations analytics		
Counselors verify schedules in SIS		
Schedule is built in SIS		
Course requests are submitted in the SIS		
The schedule is loaded		
Summer school grades are used to make course adjustments		
The schedule is revised after the load		
The schedule "goes live"		
Before courses are loaded, counselors verify that students have the appropriate number of course requests in relationship to the bell schedule		
Create/update special education and English language learner–mandated course sheets		
Use data to identify gaps and strategies to address		
Data analysis is used to justify fiscal and human expenses		
Distribute final schedules to students		
Distribute a final copy of the schedule to staff		
Course selections are reviewed and edited by the counselor		
Classes are balanced		
The cohorting tool is initially loaded		
Schedule frame is built (estimated)		
The course tally sheet is used to define cohorts and course names		
Student course selection begins		
Student course selection ends		
Counselor articulation and site visits begin		
Eighth-grade course selection begins		
Development of course selection cards and catalog		
Approval of course selection cards and catalog		
Determine core course minimums by grade level		
Identify scheduling team and roles/responsibilities		
Review scheduling expectations		
Review scheduling timeline		

FIGURE 8.1 MAINTAINING A SYSTEM TO TRACK SCHEDULING TIMELINE ROLES AND RESPONSIBILITIES

online resources: Available for download at https://companion.corwin.com/courses/equitableschoolscheduling

- College Course Interest and Verification Dates
- At-Risk Student Timelines
- College Grade Submission Dates
- Board Approval of Memorandum of Understanding (MOU) and/or Dual Enrollment Contract Dates
- Dates That College Course Codes Are Placed in the School District Student Information System

An example of a district college course work timeline is in the appendices. This type of timeline must be developed in collaboration with the college staff as the timeline must be consistent across all high schools aligned to a particular college feeder. A template is available for download at https://companion.corwin.com/courses/equitableschoolscheduling.

Counseling Activity Timelines

These timelines are activity sequences that make up the cycle that aligns the work of counselors across secondary schools.

Suggested details:

- Transcript Evaluation and Academic Review Dates
- Student Enrollment and Scheduling Dates
- Schedule Development Dates
- Articulation (course selection) and Preparation of Materials Dates
- Financial Aid Dates
- Progress Report and Report Card Dates
- Testing Dates
- Attendance Monitoring Dates
- Early Warning System Review Dates

An example of a district counseling timeline is in the appendices and available for download at https://companion.corwin.com/courses/equitableschoolscheduling.

Registrar Timelines

These timelines outline the cycle that aligns the work of the registrars across secondary schools. **Note:** It is critical to have a position like registrar in a school to act as a check and balance between the principal and counselors as it relates to management of student graduation verification/diplomas.

Counselors and principals should not be directly making changes to student transcripts.

Suggested details:

- Graduation Document (Grad Doc) Dates (Mid-Year, End-of-Year, and Summer)
- Principal Certification of Graduates Dates (Mid-Year, End-of-Year, and Summer)
- Graduation Waiver Dates (Mid-Year, End-of-Year, and Summer)
- Summer School Dates
- Review of Transcript (errors, inconsistencies, and/or need for grade replacement) Dates
- Credit Review/Check Dates
- CAL Grant Grade Point Average Update Dates
- Establishing Files for Incoming/New Student Dates
- Verifying District "Leaver" Dates
- Verifying "Class of" and Grade-Level Changes Dates

An example of a district registrar timeline is in the appendices and available for download at https://companion.corwin.com/courses/equitable schoolscheduling.

Site Tech/Builder Timelines

These timelines outline the cycle that aligns the work of the schedule builder across secondary schools.

Suggested details:

- Schedule Building and Committing Dates
- Ongoing Schedule Clean-Up Dates
- Updating Staff Access to the Student Information System (SIS) Dates
- Complete Student Schedule Monitoring Dates
- Adding Bell Schedule (and other cycle data) to the SIS Dates
- Grade Reporting, Storing, and Changing Dates
- Exiting Student Management Dates
- Upload CAL Grant Dates
- Testing Information Dates

An example of a district site tech/builder timeline is in the appendices and available for download at https://companion.corwin.com/courses/equitable schoolscheduling.

THE RISKS OF OPERATING WITHOUT TIMELINES

When scheduling teams do not organize around timelines, they risk acting at the last minute throughout a process that requires attention to detail to achieve equitable outcomes. Anyone who has worked in a high school knows that there are many unpredictable daily and weekly events that can monopolize time around putting out fires. Architects of Equity cannot live in a state of reaction. Proactive planning must be at the center of the scheduling process. This is especially important at the district level where maintaining an equitable scheduling process across multiple schools is imperative. In addition, following a timeline each year reinforces the idea that the scheduling process should not be a copying over of the previous year's schedule. The scheduling process is a powerful yearly lever for designing impactful experiences for a unique set of students moving through a 10-month cycle of learning.

Timelines should be overstructured in the beginning. These frames act as guidance and reminders that will help the scheduling team develop a working system. The timeline never disappears but is refined and embedded into the school's way of existing and operating.

At the district level, imbalanced and/or misaligned scheduling timelines can impact staffing drastically. For example, if a school district is understaffed and/or finding it hard to staff positions, staffing inside of a district can be impacted by staffing outside of the district. If one district in a county has bargained staffing timelines that extend beyond what is standard in the county, that district could lose all student teacher and/or intern opportunities as placement has happened in other districts earlier. In addition, any temporary or probationary teachers who must reapply for their current jobs might choose to apply for jobs in a district where hiring timelines are earlier. Timelines must reinforce desired outcomes, not inhibit them.

It is also important to understand that staffing and budgeting timelines directly affect the school site's ability to complete/meet certain scheduling expectations. For example, many districts want their school sites to preview teacher and student schedules before the end of the school year. If a school site has any hope of making that happen, the district business and human resource divisions must release teacher allocations before winter break. In addition, requiring a preview of teacher and student schedules must be anchored in the understanding that this may never include the exact period courses are taught and/or the exact teacher preps as schools with high rates of course failure and/or student transiency may need the summer to finalize these specifics. Another timeline factor is who will be scheduling the students. If counselors are expected to schedule students in a

10-month contract cycle, they would not be able to adjust schedules unless they were paid over the summer or until they returned prior to the start of school. Timelines can become unmanageable if things like this are not carefully considered.

Finally, timelines must be leader-proof. They must support a scheduling culture that persists despite leadership and/or scheduling leadership changes. These timelines are scaffolding for the culture that is built when processes and systems align to site vision.

THE IMPORTANCE OF INPUT DURING TIMELINES

Many scheduling efforts can be thwarted by a lack of meaningful input from a variety of stakeholders. Architects of Equity build powerful timelines that establish the following:

1. **A clear definition of input.** Input is not "Do as I say." Input is allowing people to share their perspectives so that the Architects of Equity can synthesize this data to make sound decisions aligned to the school/district vision. It must be clear to all stakeholders that the principal has the right of assignment and will make the final decision when it comes to staffing decisions about the schedule. This does not mean that the principal works in secrecy or isolation, rather that the Architects of Equity make scheduling recommendations based on carefully collected input/feedback and the principal makes the final call.

2. **A well-defined cycle of input.** Soliciting input happens at multiple levels. The following opportunities should be considered when designing feedback loops:

    - Teacher Input: Meaningful teacher input can happen in many ways:

        ○ **Teacher Druthers Sheets:** Typically, druthers sheets are provided to each teacher so that they can share desires about classes they want to teach, clubs they want to sponsor, sports they would like to coach, preparatory periods they would like to have, and other features of their working assignment. A sample sheet is available in the appendices.

        ○ **Department Meetings:** It is typical for the Architects of Equity to get input from departments and/or department chairs. These meetings are important because they reveal the thinking of the department overall about how a particular discipline might be organized for the upcoming year. Information from a department, however, should not be used in a silo, as many times there are hierarchies in departments and some voices can be reduced in the larger group dynamics. These meetings should include specialty support staff like English learner and special education teachers.

- **Grade-Level Team Meetings:** If schools are organized by pathways, a powerful place to solicit feedback is at the interdisciplinary team level. This type of feedback is more specific to cross-disciplinary needs and the information provided can vary by grade level. These team meetings are very powerful when focused on what the administration can do to remove any boulders that might get in the way of student cohorts being successful.

- **Lived Experience Teams:** If the student community of a school is predominantly students of color (Latinx, African American, Native American, etc.), but the teaching staff is predominately white and/or Asian, it is always advisable to set up a committee of teachers who can look at decisions through a lived experience lens. For example, most staff at a school might want to adopt a bell schedule or add a support class but might not initially see the impacts of the decision through the lens of the people who will be experiencing it. Lived Experience Teams are an essential part of building a system of equity in schools.

- **Student Course Work Feedback:** Opportunities to make recommendations about student access to future-year course work is an important part of the feedback loop if it is done in partnership with other factors. The collection of teacher input by students in a spreadsheet should be accompanied by data associated with grit. Sites must try to identify opportunity youth—students who are ready for a challenge but have never been invited to AP, IB, and/or honors course work opportunities.

- **Formal and/or Mandated Teams:** Formal teacher teams would include union leadership teams, cross-department instructional leadership teams, governance teams, and so forth. It is critical to solicit feedback from these teams as they have been selected by their peers to speak from a specific lens about issues like scheduling.

- Counseling Input: Aside from making sure that a counselor is a member of the Architects of Equity, counselor voice can be a powerful equity lever when cast from a position of growth mindset. Counselors know in which classes, periods, and other realms students are thriving and/or struggling. Providing a safe place for counselors to provide input on scheduling decisions is an essential part of the feedback and/or input process.

- Student Input: Student input should extend well beyond the course selection card.

  - **Course Selection:** Many times, the course selection process is the only or main opportunity for student voice in the scheduling process. Typically, students will fill out a paper card and/or a Google survey to identify the courses they are interested in taking during the upcoming year. What this process does not typically include is a voice in the decisions about course offerings for the upcoming year.

Grade-Level Online Forums: Offer students the opportunities to provide feedback on the upcoming course of study through online forums by grade level. Provide students a link to a preview of the courses being considered in the upcoming year, other courses that are possibilities, and short-answer options where they can share additional course work opportunities that interest them. Let them rank course work by interest.

Clubs: An important place to check in with students about scheduling is in their clubs—and not just student government classes, which can be dominated by students who are very involved in the school. Architects of Equity seek out input from members of clubs who are composed of many students from the margins.

Surveys: Many sites will use survey data like Healthy Kids, Youth Truth, and others that seek to offer perspectives about school connectedness, engagement, and belonging. These data can be helpful in combination with other input data.

- Family Input: Families should be an integral part of an equity-driven input process. All communications (written and verbal) must be delivered in the home language if it is the primary language of the family.

    Course Selection: Many times, the course selection process is the only or main opportunity for family voice in the scheduling process. Typically, students will fill out a paper card and/or a Google survey to identify the courses they are interested in taking during the upcoming year. Parents and/or guardians will typically be asked to sign the form. What this process does not typically include is a voice in the decisions about course offerings for the upcoming year.

    Surveys: When surveys are provided to parents in their home language, they can be very powerful. Provide parents/guardians a link to preview the courses being considered in the upcoming year, other courses that are possibilities, and short-answer options where they can share additional course work opportunities that interest them. Let them rank course work by interest.

    Mandated Parent/Guardian Groups: Scheduling input should be garnered from board-mandated parent/guardian groups. These groups may include a District Advisory Committee, an English Learner Committee, a Special Education Committee, and so forth. Usually, there will be written guidelines for the frequency and manner by which data should be shared.

- Community Input: Community and/or industry input is especially important in schools implementing pathways. Input from colleges, internship providers, wrap-around service providers, and so on should be part of the scheduling process—especially when decisions about bell schedules are made.

All equity-driven timelines have carefully structured input/feedback loops that are carefully aligned to key decision-making points in the scheduling process. Architects of Equity make these opportunities transparent at the beginning of the process. While opportunities may be unique to the site context, all opportunities should address staff, student, family, and community feedback loops.

FINAL THOUGHTS

Architects of Equity are highly effective and overly structured vehicles for educational transformation. They use timelines to ensure that their work is transparent, authentic, and collaborative. These timelines are also aligned to efforts at the district level to ensure that the staffing and budgeting processes are meaningfully aligned to the site scheduling process. Establishing overall and job-specific timelines is an integral part of the work of the Architects of Equity.

TECHNICAL SELF-ASSESSMENT QUESTIONS	ADAPTIVE SELF-ASSESSMENT QUESTIONS
1. What site scheduling timelines currently exist? Do they need to be updated? Do they reflect alignment with district timelines?	1. Who should be part of the scheduling team? How will this determination be made? 2. How will scheduling team members share information with staff frequently, authentically and in a timely manner?

EPILOGUE

The secret of getting ahead is getting started.

—*Mark Twain*

Whether you are staring at a magnetic scheduling whiteboard in your office or sorting your way through a scheduling Excel file on your personal computer, stop wondering if the right time is now to do what you know is ethically and morally necessary. You have everything you need to get started. Don't wait for the perfect moment. There will always be a fire to put out, and no matter how much you work to clear your desk, every meeting you attend adds an inch to that pile. It doesn't matter if it is summer, winter, spring, or fall—get started. Do something to take that first step.

While issues of inequity and lack of access to the Equitable Core will not disappear with a perfect schedule, identifying and supporting the development of the Architects of Equity is an intentional and impactful step that will get things moving in the right direction. In a time when students and families are feeling less and less connected to schools, Architects of Equity can lead school teams to challenge the status QUO, get their mindSETs right, and organize equity-focused schedules that prepare all students for meaningful postsecondary success.

With so many competing priorities at stake—graduation requirements, budget cuts, traditional practices—it is imperative that scheduling teams maintain their focus on providing an equitable experience for all students. Architects of Equity must be empowered by school and district leadership to shift the paradigm so that scheduling is not seen as simply a logistical act, but rather a practice affecting the heart and soul of teaching and learning for all students (Chenowith, 2016). Teams must understand their great responsibility, one that requires courageous and grounded leadership to move forward. According to Clay et al. (2021), thoughtfully crafted and tightly structured schedules, those done with stakeholder feedback and joint decision making, are "living structures that reflect the culture, climate, expectations, vision, and priorities of the school" (p. 1). This idea must be forever present in the minds of those doing this difficult and necessary work.

Architects of Equity cannot underestimate their influence. These teams deeply understand the health of a school or system by examining the gaps between the current reality and the desired state—and they use the schedule to protect strategies to address these inequities. The crucial act of determining course sequencing and access within schools in relation to the inequitable postsecondary outcomes of underestimated youth must remain at the center of the conversation. Building scheduling teams within schools and systems that act with a sense of urgency and a growth mindset is one of the most impactful strategies in a leader's scheduling tool belt. Now that you and your team are fully prepared to be Architects of Equity, what are your next steps to ensure that your vision to support transformative schedule design becomes reality?

APPENDIX

Equitable Core Pathway Template	192
Equitable Core Standard Template	193
EL Pathway Template	201
Special Education and General Education Collaboration Pathway Model	202
Cohorting Tool Template	203
Pathway Selection Application Template	204
Course Selection Card Template	205
Course Tally Sheet (Blank)	206
Credit Check	207
Student Pipeline to Success: Academics and Agency Middle School Promotion Tracking Sheet	208
Multi-Option Freshman Course Selection Card Template	211
Site Schedule Timeline Roles and Responsibilities	212

online resources

Appendix content (including items discussed but not printed in the book) is also available for download from the site at
https://companion.corwin.com/courses/equitableschoolscheduling

Equitable Core Pathway Template

		Grade 9	Grade 10	Grade 11	Grade 12
CTE or VAPA Pathway	CTE or VAPA				
Academic Core Classes	ELA				
	Math				
	Science				
	Social Science				
	World Language				
	Visual and Perf. Arts				
	Mandates (EL, SpEd)				
	PE				
	Elective				

Board-Approved Graduation Requirements:
English: 4 years required
Mathematics: 3 years required
Science: 3 years required
Social Studies: 3 years required
Physical Education: 2 years required
World Language: 2 years required
Visual and Performing Arts: 1 year required

Note: All students must maintain an overall 2.0 grade point average.

Student: _____
Parent: _____
Counselor: _____
Date: _____

Equitable Core Standard Template

Academic Core Classes		Grade 9	Grade 10	Grade 11	Grade 12
	ELA				
	Math				
	Science				
	Social Science				
	World Language				
	Visual and Perf. Arts				
	Mandates (EL, SpEd)				
	PE				
	Elective				

Board-Approved Graduation Requirements:
English: 4 years required
Mathematics: 3 years required
Science: 3 years required
Social Studies: 3 years required
Physical Education: 2 years required
World Language: 2 years required
Visual and Performing Arts: 1 year required

Note: All students must maintain an overall 2.0 grade point average.
Student: _____
Parent: _____
Counselor: _____
Date: _____

APPENDIX 193

LINKED LEARNING HIGH SCHOOL SITE SCHEDULE EXPECTATIONS

In Linked Learning pathways students are cohorted together and have a set of shared experiences and courses that are part of their program of study. Linked Learning pathways include a set of 3–4 career technical education (CTE) classes that are linked with academic classes at each grade level for at least 50% or more of the school day. Pathway teachers need a common planning period to plan and collaborate. Below are some key areas related to site scheduling that are critical in a Linked Learning context. These should be used as a set of best practices that support Linked Learning. Each school and pathway should use this list to identify current strengths in their site schedule and potential areas for development or improvement.

Pathway Access

- All students are scheduled into the academic and technical core courses needed for graduation and college ready requirements (A–G in CA).
- CTE pathway courses are college preparatory or approved for UC A–G credit (CA).
- Grade level core course sequences are selected by pathway.
- Course selection cards are designed with pathway courses as the anchor.
- The number of pathways in a school is appropriate when compared with the number of students in the school. (at least 100 students per grade level per pathway)
- Student need is a priority over student course choice.

Common Planning Time Within the School Day

- Prep periods are scheduled to allow grade level team access to ongoing weekly planning opportunities.

Maximizing Instructional Time

- Bell schedule selection supports all student group access to the academic core, technical core, work-based learning, dual college and mandated support courses as defined by IEPs and ELPAC scores.
- Bell schedule selection supports academic and technical core teacher collaboration at each grade level.

Assigning Teacher Preps

- The union contract is followed when determining the number of preps a teacher is assigned.
- Teachers are assigned to grade level teams rather than courses.

Strategic Sequencing of VAPA Courses

- Visual and Performing Arts (VAPA) sequences are scheduled as pathways regardless of CTE courses/credentials.

Eliminate Tracking and Limit the Stratification of Courses

- Classes are not tracked. If possible, weighted credit is offered to all students through differentiated syllabi.
- If advanced, advanced placement, and regular courses must be offered separately only two bands are offered.

Strategic Supports

- Data-driven interventions are connected to tier I core coursework and cohorted at the grade level.
- Universal screeners are used to determine baseline student reading comprehension levels and algebra readiness levels for all students, including students with IEPs and English Learners.

AP, IB, and College Coursework

- All pathways offer at least one advanced studies program that all student groups may access.
- Pathways do not silo advanced studies programs, but allow full access to advanced studies options in each pathway.
- All students have access to early college credit opportunities before, during, or after school (as allowed by each college program.)
- If appropriate, advanced studies courses should be paired with appropriate supports that are cohorted at the grade level.
- Ideally, CTE courses are approved for college dual articulation opportunities.

English Learners and Students With IEPs

- English learners, students with IEPs, and general education students who struggle academically are given priority scheduling and access to expert teachers.
- All diploma bound students, including students with IEPs, are scheduled into regular education tier I coursework with core content teachers.
- English learner designated courses are cohorted with the grade level team.

Strategic Science Sequencing

- Sequencing of science courses in grades 9–11 includes biology, chemistry, and physics or an integrated science sequence. (Health pathways may use PBS in 9th grade in CA.)
- Science coursework is not selected to track based on mathematics performance.

Scheduling Incoming 9th Grade Students

- All incoming diploma bound 9th grade students are scheduled into general education tier I coursework.

Recovering Credits

- Courses used to ensure first time mastery are utilized more frequently than remediation and credit recovery, i.e., there are more prevention and acceleration courses than remediation or credit recovery courses.
- Opportunities for credit recovery are available within the school day/year.

Strategic Staffing

- The placement of teachers within the site schedule ensures that the students with the most needs have access to the most effective teachers.

Physical Classroom Assignments

- Classroom assignments should support the site's instructional program, structure, and teacher collaboration. A multi-year plan should be developed and implemented to ensure that classroom assignments are purposeful.

HIGH SCHOOL SCHEDULING EXPECTATIONS: *STUDENT-CENTERED AND EQUITY-DRIVEN*

Establishing an Equitable Core

- The Scheduling Team in partnership with the Instructional Leadership Team have approved a sequencing of courses that eliminates the possibility of tracking students, and limits the number of stratifying courses within the same subject area, in an effort to maintain overall school demographic heterogeneities within each course offering.

Postsecondary Access

- All students are scheduled into the courses needed for graduation and college ready requirements, i.e., the Equitable Core.

Maximizing Instructional Time

- The bell schedule is leveraged to support the instructional program by providing time for monitoring student learning. Alternative bell schedules such as a 4-by-4 block or a 7 period day provide students the opportunity to accelerate coursework, recover credits and engage in corequisite support within the school day. Schedules that include strong advisory and/or AVID programs provide opportunities for student goal setting, monitoring and mentoring, and the reinforcement and alignment of college/career readiness skills.

AP, IB, and College Coursework

- School staff are acutely aware of the diversity gap in Advanced Placement (AP) or International Baccalaureate (IB) courses offered on site, and the scheduling team has established goals and targeted scheduling strategies to increase the diversity of students accessing AP/IB courses offered.
- College coursework opportunities are strategically built into the schedule to expand offerings each year with the same awareness toward diversity gaps in student placement.

Embedded Supports

- Student performance and diagnostic data is reviewed and used to determine which students need corequisite support.
- School-wide diagnostic assessments for student reading comprehension levels and algebra readiness levels are used to identify all student needs beyond student labels such as ELL and IEP's.

Common Planning Time Within the School Day

- Preparation periods are strategically assigned to provide opportunities for teachers to collaborate during the school day. Common prep periods may be assigned by departments or grade-level interdisciplinary teams.

English Learners and Students With IEPs

- Diploma-bound priority consideration of course offerings are given to ensure on-time graduation requirements are met.
- Students are grouped strategically and placed with expert teachers certified to support English Learners.
- Support and services are pushed into the general education environment so that students can access tier I instruction.

Least Number of Teacher Preps as Possible

- Taking into consideration that strong instruction begins with thorough lesson planning and preparation, limiting the number of preps for teachers facilitates better planning and instruction.

Maximizing Enrollment in Elective and Physical Education Courses

- Scheduling ensures the adequate number of elective and physical education course offerings based on student enrollment and class size.
- Student choice and the variety within elective offerings does not supersede a student's academic needs.
- The Site Schedule Team in partnership with the Instructional Leadership has a clear vision of which courses will be offered to all students prior to course requests being collected.

Middle School Course Completions

- Student scheduling in 9th grade aligns to the course completions in 8th grade (e.g. world language, math, music, STEM courses, AVID) to properly schedule incoming students

Strategic Science Sequencing

- Sequencing of science courses in grades 9–11 include biology, chemistry and physics.
- Science coursework is not selected to track based on mathematics performance.

Strategic Sequencing of CTE/VAPA Courses

- CCTE and VAPA courses are an integral part of the instructional program and the students enrolled in these courses are interested in pursuing a multiple year sequence which includes foundational, intermediate and advanced courses.

Recovering Credits

- A thoughtful and strategic credit recovery plan which offers students a variety of methods for making up courses is developed and implemented. This plan includes viable and rigorous offerings within the school day, during extended days, online opportunities, and summer school offerings.

Strategic Staffing

- The placement of teachers within the site schedule ensures that the neediest students have access to the most effective teachers.

Physical Classroom Assignments

- Classroom assignments should support the site's instructional program, structure and teacher collaboration. A multi year plan should be developed and implemented to ensure that classroom assignments are purposeful.

MIDDLE SCHOOL SCHEDULING EXPECTATIONS: *STUDENT-CENTERED AND EQUITY-DRIVEN*

Postsecondary Access

- All students are scheduled into world language (or equivalent) and mathematics courses needed for graduation and college ready requirements.

Alternative Bell Schedules

- Consider alternative bell schedules such as a 4-by-4 block or a 7 period day to provide students and teachers the ability to collaborate in an interdisciplinary model.

Embedded Supports

- Student performance and diagnostic data is reviewed and used to determine which students need co-requisite support.
- School-wide diagnostic assessments for student reading comprehension levels and algebra readiness levels are used to identify all student needs beyond student labels such as ELL and IEPs.

Common Planning Time Within the School Day

- Preparation periods are strategically assigned to provide opportunities for teachers to collaborate during the school day. Common prep periods may be assigned by departments or grade-level interdisciplinary teams.

Establishing an Equitable Core

- The Scheduling Team in partnership with the Instructional Leadership Team, have approved a sequencing of courses that eliminates the possibility of tracking students and limits the number of stratifying courses within the same subject area, in an effort to maintain overall school demographic heterogeneities within each course offering.

English Learners and Students With IEPs

- Diploma-bound priority consideration of course offerings are given to ensure on-time graduation requirements are met.
- Students are grouped strategically and placed with expert teachers certified to support English Learners.
- Support and services are pushed into the general education environment so that students can access tier I instruction.

Least Number of Teacher Preps as Possible

- Taking into consideration that strong instruction begins with thorough lesson planning and preparation, limiting the number of preps for teachers facilitates better planning and instruction.

Maximizing Enrollment in Elective and Physical Education Courses

- Scheduling ensures the adequate number of elective and physical education course offerings based on student enrollment and class size.
- Student choice and the variety within elective offerings does not supersede a student's academic needs.
- The Scheduling Team in partnership with the Instructional Leadership Team has a clear vision of which courses will be offered to all students prior to course requests being collected.

Strategic Science Sequencing

- Science coursework in grades 6–8 are prioritized for NGSS preparation.

CCTE/VAPA Courses

- CCTE and VAPA courses that support the high school and cluster pathways are prioritized.

Strategic Staffing

- The placement of teachers within the schedule ensures that the students with the highest needs have priority access to the most effective teachers.

Physical Classroom Assignments

- Classroom assignments should support the site's instructional program, structure, and teacher collaboration. A multi-year plan should be developed and implemented to ensure that classroom assignments are purposeful.

EL Pathway Template

Prompt: Using your bell schedule, determine the multi-year course sequences of an incoming 9th-, 10th-, and 11th- grade student in a pathway-driven school.

	9th Grade	10th Grade	11th Grade	12th Grade	5th Year
Entering 9th					
Entering 10th					
Entering 11th					

Full examples of how to use this EL grid are available for download at https://companion.corwin.com/courses/equitableschoolscheduling

online resources

APPENDIX 201

SPECIAL EDUCATION AND GENERAL EDUCATION COLLABORATION PATHWAY MODEL

SPECIAL EDUCATION TEACHER	GENERAL EDUCATION TEACHER
Special Education teachers are assigned by pathway (not content area) and share a common prep with the pathway team. The Special Education teachers in each pathway act as the case managers for their pathway students. Weekly discussion about student progress takes place in the common prep meetings. Counselors attend weekly team meetings.	
Special Education and General Education Teachers use their common prep to plan lessons together. The General Education teacher is the content expert and the Special Education teacher is the accommodation expert.	
Student study teams, assessment teams, and IEP meetings are attended by the grade-level pathway team as a unit. While Special Education teachers write IEPs and plan IEP meetings, decisions about what is best for the student in relationship to mastery of the tier I content is determined by the team. The team shares a belief that the interdisciplinary model is the "intervention" and students remain in pathway courses like they were mandatory core course offerings.	
Special Education teachers attend core content professional learning with teammates and General Education teachers receive training in accommodations, methodologies, strategies, and so on from the Special Education teacher.	
When there are concerns about student progress in one class, several classes, or all classes, parent meetings are scheduled and attended by the team to address concerns. Teams address one another if grading practices do not reflect a competency-based approach.	
Implement IEP's within classes in which the case manager or paraprofessional is teaching. Monitor student progress quarterly in other classes unless concern is noted by general education staff.	Implement IEPs within classes in which the case manager or paraprofessional is not teaching.
If the team identifies a need, students are referred to the Psychologist to organize implementation of behavior support plans. Behavior support plans are implemented by the team. The team initiates transition services, if necessary.	
The team supports standardized testing.	
Attend professional learning with the co-teacher.	

SOURCE: Modified from a document developed in San Diego Unified School District.

Cohorting Tool Template

9th Grade 4x4 Schedule

Period	Fall Term	Spring Term
1		
2		
3		
4		

Period	Fall Term	Spring Term
1		
2		
3		
4		

Period	Fall Term	Spring Term
1		
2		
3		
4		

Period	Fall Term	Spring Term
1		
2		
3		
4		

9th Grade Six-Period Schedule

Period	Fall Term	Spring Term
1		
2		
3		
4		
5		
6		

Period	Fall Term	Spring Term
1		
2		
3		
4		
5		
6		

Period	Fall Term	Spring Term
1		
2		
3		
4		
5		
6		

APPENDIX

Pathway Selection Application Template

Please **PRINT** the following parent/student information. All sections MUST be completed for application to be accepted.

Grade Level _____ Name of school you are now attending. _____

Student Last Name _____ First Name _____ M. I. _____ Birth date _____ / _____ / _____ Sex: M   F
                                                                              Month   Day   Year

Parent/Guardian Name _____ (____) Home Phone _____ (____) Work Phone _____ (____) Cell Phone _____

Street Address _____ Apt. # _____ City _____ Zip Code _____

Please select your choice for acceptance into one of the four pathways at Equity High for the upcoming school year. Rank your selections 1–4, with "1" being your first choice.

_____ Media Arts   _____ International Business   _____ Environmental Science   _____ Engineering

I understand that every effort will be made to place me in the school of my first or second choice. I understand that once the school year begins, there will be no transferring between schools at Equity High.

_____ _____   _____ _____
Student Signature   Date   Parent/Guardian Signature   Date

Student Statement of Interest: (Please provide a statement that explains your reasons for wanting to be in a particular pathway. Describe what strengths you have that will help you succeed in that pathway. Please be detailed and thoughtful in your response.)

_____
_____
_____

Course Selection Card Template

English/Language Arts
☐ ELA 9
☐ ELA 9 Adv
☐ ELA 10
☐ ELA 10 Adv
☐ ELA 11
☐ ELA 11 Adv
☐ AP Lang
☐ ELA 12
☐ AP Lit
☐ ERWC

Social Studies
☐ World History
☐ Adv. World History
☐ AP Euro
☐ US History
☐ Honors US Hist
☐ AP US History
☐ Government
☐ Economics
☐ AP Gov
☐ AP Economics
☐ Psychology

Language other than English
☐ Spanish 1
☐ Spanish 2
☐ Spanish 3
☐ AP Spanish

Mathematics
☐ Algebra
☐ Adv Algebra
☐ Geometry
☐ Adv Geometry
☐ Algebra 2
☐ Adv Algebra 2
☐ Precalculus
☐ Honors Precalculus
☐ AP Calculus
☐ Statistics

CTE Course
☐ Intro to ED
☐ Principles of E
☐ CIMS
☐ CEA
☐ EDD
☐ Principles of BioMed
☐ Human Body S
☐ Medical Intervention
☐ Biomedical Innovations
☐ Intro Comp Sci
☐ CSP
☐ CSP A
☐ AP CS

Physical Education
☐ PE 9
☐ PE 10
☐ Athletics
☐ JROTC
☐ Health

Science
☐ Biology
☐ Adv Biology
☐ Chemistry
☐ Adv Chemistry
☐ Physics
☐ Adv Physics
☐ AP Physics
☐ AP Chemistry
☐ AP Bio

Art
☐ Orchestra
☐ Art
☐ Band
☐ Choir
☐ Dance
☐ ASB
☐ Yearbook
☐ Theater
☐ Journalism
☐ Ethnic Studies

Student Supports
☐ Designated ELD1
☐ Designated ELD2
☐ Designated ELD3
☐ Math Support
☐ Special Education Support

Course Tally Sheet (Blank)

Type	Number	Title	Total	# Sec.	Avg.	9th	10th	11th	12th

Credit Check

Student:_____ Class of:_____ Counselor:_____ Dates of Review:_____

Grade	A. History (6 credits required)	Grade Earned / In Progress
10	World History & Geography 1*	
10	World History & Geography 2*	
11	U. S. History 1*	
11	U. S. History 2*	
12	Government 1*	
12	Economics 1*	

Grade	B. English (8 credits required)	Grade Earned / In Progress
9	English 1*	
9	English 2*	
10	English 3*	
10	English 4*	
11	American Lit. 1*	
11	American Lit. 2*	
12	Senior Eng. 1*	
12	Senior Eng. 2*	

Grade	C. Math (6 credits required)	Grade Earned / In Progress
8	Integrated Math I A/B	
9	Integrated Math I or II A	
9	Integrated Math I or II B	
10	Integrated Math II or III A	
10	Integrated Math II or III B	
11	Integrated Math III A or Pre-Calculus	
11	Integrated Math III A or Pre-Calculus	
12	Pre-Calculus or AP Calculus	
12	Pre-Calculus or AP Calculus	

Grade	D. Science (6 credits required)	Grade Earned / In Progress
9	Physics 1*	
9	Physics 2*	
10	Biology 1*	
10	Biology 2*	
11	Chemistry 1*	
11	Chemistry 2*	

Grade	E. Language Other Than English (4 credits required)	Grade Earned / In Progress
7–12	World Language 1*	
7–12	World Language 2*	
7–12	World Language 3*	
7–12	World Language 4*	

Grade	F. Visual/ Performing Art (2 credits required)	Grade Earned / In Progress
9–12	VAPA 1*	
9–12	VAPA 2*	

Grade	G. College Prep Elective Can be Completed through 3rd year Science	See "D" Above

Grade	Physical Education (4 credits required)	Grade Earned / In Progress
9–12		
9–12		
9–12		
9–12		

*Can be UC "a-g" eligible if the course is on your school's UC "a-g" list at the time of enrollment. Some schools have site-adopted courses that meet these requirements.

Grade	Additional Elective Credits (8)	Grade Earned / In Progress
9–12		
9–12		
9–12		
9–12		
9–12		
9–12		
9–12		
9–12		

Courses needing remediation for graduation or UC/CSU Eligibility and/or to meet credit expectations	Date or Session	Grade Earned / In Progress

ADDITIONAL REQUIREMENTS:

Please Note: Additional requirements for diploma by June of graduation year:

___2.0 cumulative, weighted GPA in grades 9–12
___44 credits in grades 9–12

Student Signature:_____

Parent Signature:_____

APPENDIX

Student Pipeline to Success:
Academics and Agency Middle School Promotion Tracking Sheet

Grade	English (3 courses required)	Grade Earned
6	English 6th	S1: S2:
7	English 7th	S1: S2:
8	English 8th	S1: S2

Grade	Mathematics (3 courses required)	Grade Earned
6	Math 6th (4133) Accelerated Math 6	S1: S2:
7	Math 7th (4134) Accelerated Math 7th	S1: S2:
8	Math 8th Integrated Math I A Integrated Math I B	S1: S2:

Grade	Science (3 courses required)	Grade Earned
6	Science 6th	S1: S2
7	Science 7th	S1: S2:
8	Science 8th	S1: S2:

Grade	Social Science (3 courses required)	Grade Earned
6	Social Studies 6th	S1: S2
7	World History and Geography 7th	S1: S2
8	United States History and Geography 8th	S1: S2

Grade	Physical Education (3 courses required)	Grade Earned
6	Physical Education 6th	S1: S2
7	Physical Education 7th	S1: S2
8	Physical Education 8th	S1: S2

Grade	World Language	Grade Earned
7 or 8	Spanish* 1 or equivalent	S1:
	Spanish* 2 or equivalent	S2:
8	Spanish* 3 or equivalent	S1:
	Spanish* 4 or equivalent	S2:
7–8	I speak a language other than English so I took the LOTE test in 7th or 8th grade and passed. I know this counts for high school graduation or allows me to take a higher level of language.	

* or other World Language Course from the Course of Study

Grade	Agency	Level Met 6	Level Met 7	Level Met 8
6–8	I can read at or beyond my grade level as measured by a diagnostic assessment. (or I moved at least one grade level in reading each year.)			
6–8	I scored met or exceeded on the ELA standardized test.			
6–8	I scored met or exceeded on the Math standardized test.			
6–8	I reclassified from an English Learner within three years.			
6–8	If I have an IEP or a 504 Plan I know my goals.			
6–8	If I have an IEP or a 504 I know what accommodations I need for my learning. I ask for them if I need them.			
6–8	I took a strengths inventory and I understand my strengths, interests and values in relationship to my learning style and post secondary interests. I can communicate these needs to my teachers and counselor.			
6–8	I understand the middle school promotion expectations and monitored my progress towards meeting each goal each year			

	I have participated in a pathway (Engineering, medical, music, art or theater) and I know how my high school will continue to support these pathway interests
	
	Arts, Media, and Entertainment:
	    Explorations in Technical Theatre 1,2
	    Exploring Careers 6th–8th
	    Introduction to Video Production 6th–8th or
	    Photography 6th–8th
	
	Engineering:
	    Exploring Careers 6th–8th
	    Exploring Technology 6th–8th
	    Gateway to Technology			

6–8	I participated in at least one school club or school activity			
6–8	I took leadership of one school club, school event, community service opportunity, or collaborative project.			

Grade	Grades/GPA	Academic	Citizenship
6	2.0+ cumulative and term GPA semester 1	S1	
6	2.0+ cumulative and term GPA semester 1	S2	
7	2.0+ cumulative and term GPA semester 1	S1	
7	2.0+ cumulative and term GPA semester 1	S2	
8	2.0+ cumulative and term GPA semester 1	S1	
8	2.0+ cumulative and term GPA semester 1	S2	

Multi-Option Freshman Course Selection Card Template

Name:_____ Student ID#:_____ Date of Birth:_____

Option 1: Pathway Option

Step 1: Choose your theme. Rank your preference. 1 is the highest, 4 is the lowest. Students who choose the pathway option will take a foundation CTE course as their freshman elective.

Media Arts	Computer Science	Medical	Engineering
_____Rank 1–4	_____Rank 1–4	_____Rank 1–4	_____Rank 1–4
Design Mixed Media 1–2	Computer Science Essentials	Principles of Biomedical Science	Introduction to Engineering Design
10th: Design Mixed Media 3–4	10th: Computer Science Principles	10th: Human Body Systems	10th: Principles of Engineering
11th: Computerized Graphic Design 1–2	11th: Computer Science A	11th: Medical Interventions	11th: Civil Engineering and Architecture
12th: Computerized Graphic Design 3–4	12th: Cybersecurity	12th: Biomedical Innovations	12th: Engineering Design and Development

Step 2: Choose your core class preferences. English, Biology, Math, and PE are required for freshmen. Two years of a world language are required to graduate.

English/Biology	Mathematics	PE	Spanish
___English 1, 2 Biology 1, 2 ___English 1, 2 Adv. Biology 1, 2	___Int. Math I Int. Math I Adv. ___Int. Math II Int. Math II Adv.	___PE 1, 2 ___ROTC ___Drill Team PE ___Marching Band	___Spanish 1, 2 ___Spanish 3, 4 ___AP Spanish

Option 2: Non-Pathway Option

Step 1: Choose your course preferences to fill six periods.

English	Mathematics	Science
___English 1, 2 Adv. English 1, 2	___Int. Math I ___Int. Math I Adv. ___Int. Math II ___Int. Math II Adv.	___Biology 1, 2 Adv. Biology 1, 2

Physical Education	World Language	Elective
___PE 1, 2 ___ROTC ___Drill Team PE ___Marching Band	___Spanish 1, 2 ___Spanish 3, 4 ___AP Spanish	___Choir 1, 2 ___Orchestra 1, 2 ___Theater 1, 2 ___AVID 9 ___Yearbook 1, 2 ___Journalism 1, 2

Student Signature:_____ Guardian Signature:_____

SITE SCHEDULE TIMELINE ROLES AND RESPONSIBILITIES

ITEM	RESPONSIBLE	MONTH
Seat cost analysis of under enrolled sections in prior/current year		
Enrollment projections are provided		
Projected allocations are provided		
Budget is provided to the principal		
Budget is finalized and submitted by the principal		
SPSA goals are written and submitted		
Inter/intra district transfer opens		
Inter/intra district transfer closes		
Open enrollment begins		
Open enrollment ends		
Create and distribute teacher preference sheets		
Collect teacher preference sheets		
Engage the union representative		
Engage the instructional leadership team (ILT)		
Engage the School Site Council (SCC) and site ELAC teams		
Engage department chairs and/or pathway leads		
Engage the special education and English learner support staff		
Review the current credentials of staff		

SITE SCHEDULE TIMELINE ROLES AND RESPONSIBILITIES (CONTINUED)

ITEM	RESPONSIBLE	MONTH
Review any changes to labor contracts regarding staffing		
Teachers provide input on future student courses		
Teachers provide input on schedule frame without teacher names		
Schedule frame is vetted with all stakeholders prior to budget build		
Additional staffing requests are submitted		
Sites submit any teacher/staff reductions		
Post and bid/staffing descriptions are due		
Post and bid/hiring of staff ends		
Preview draft schedules/courses with students before summer		
Preview teaching lines with teachers before summer		
Make final staffing adjustments based on enrollment		
Rising/Future students are rolled over in SIS		
Data report of advanced studies outcomes and enrollment shared with staff (IB, AP, CTE and Dual enrollment)		
Summative data trends from last year and over multiple years are reviewed with staff		

(Continued)

APPENDIX 213

SITE SCHEDULE TIMELINE ROLES AND RESPONSIBILITIES (CONTINUED)

ITEM	RESPONSIBLE	MONTH
Course requests are loaded and evaluated against the schedule expectations analytics		
Counselors verify schedules in SIS		
Schedule is built in SIS		
Course requests are all submitted in the SIS		
The schedule is loaded		
Summer school grades are used to make course adjustments in the SIS		
The schedule is revised after the load		
The schedule "goes live"		
Before the courses are loaded, IT verifies that all students have 8 courses.		
Create and update special education and ELL mandated course sheets		
Use data to identify gaps and strategies to address		
Data analysis is used to justify fiscal and human expenses		
Distribute final schedules to students		
Distribute a final copy of the schedule to staff		
Course selections are reviewed and edited by the counselor		
Classes are balanced		
The cohorting tool is initially loaded		

SITE SCHEDULE TIMELINE ROLES AND RESPONSIBILITIES (CONTINUED)

ITEM	RESPONSIBLE	MONTH
Schedule frame is built (estimated)		
The course tally sheet is used to define cohorts and course names		
Student course selection ends		
Student course selection begins		
Counselor articulation and site visits begin		
8th grade course selection begins		
Development of course selection cards and catalog		
Approval of course selection cards and catalog		
Determine core course minimums by grade level		
Identify schedule team and roles/responsibilities		
Review schedule expectations		
Review schedule timeline		

GLOSSARY

Adaptive: An adaptive approach to scheduling takes into account the relationships and identities held by stakeholders in the scheduling process.

Architects of Equity: Scheduling teams that work to simultaneously address the relational and technical work to achieve an equitable schedule for all students. The team is comprised of four important roles, but not necessarily just four people: visionary, designer, builder, and agent.

Asset based: An asset-based approach focuses on strengths. It views diversity in thought, culture, and traits as positive assets. Teachers and students alike are valued for what they bring to the classroom rather than being characterized by what they may need to work on or lack.

Categorical funding: States provide base funding that is intended to cover the basic costs of education (teacher salaries, textbooks, materials, and more) as well as categorical funding, which is targeted to specific purposes (reducing class sizes, programs for English language learners, special education, and more).

Co-requisite: A co-requisite course is a support course that is typically taught by the core content teacher simultaneously to help a student succeed in the academic course. The support course curriculum is an extension of the learning in the core classroom. This is not a self-contained basics skills catch-up course. For example, a student may be assigned a math co-requisite to Algebra 1, to support passing the latter class.

Cohorting (verb): To cohort students is to create a schedule that purposefully groups students and assigns them to specific course sequences together.

Deficit thinking: Deficit thinking refers to the notion that students (particularly those of low-income and/or racial/ethnic minority background) fail in school because such students and their families have internal defects (deficits) that thwart the learning process, for example, limited educability, lack of motivation, inadequate family support, and so on.

English learners: Students whose primary language is not English and are limited in their proficiency in the English language. Across the country there are many different terms to denote these students, including English Language Learners, Emerging Bilingual Learners, Multi-Language Learners, etc.

Equitable Core: The Equitable Core is the standard set of required courses that any student can take to qualify for university acceptance. In the Equitable Core, courses are neither watered down nor given "fancy" names to make them appear more rigorous. The Equitable Core can be unique in each state, but whatever the state defines as the highest-level expectation for one is the highest-level expectation for all.

Full-time equivalent (FTE): An "FTE" represents a full-time equivalent teacher. Saying a person is a .4 FTE, for example, means they teach 40% of a full schedule. A teacher who is 1.0 FTE teaches the full contractual schedule.

Equity: Equity means the guarantee of fair treatment, access, opportunity, and advancement while at the same time aiming to identify and eliminate barriers that have prevented the full participation of some groups. Adhering to the principle of equity acknowledges that there are historically underserved and underrepresented populations, and that fairness regarding these unbalanced conditions is needed to assist equality in the provision of effective opportunities to all groups.

Logistical: A logistical approach to scheduling is an approach without strategy, but rather a school going through a process of isolated steps without making connections with students at the center of the decision making.

Meaningful graduation: A meaningful graduation from high school means students who earn their diplomas meet graduation requirements that ensure they are prepared to succeed in postsecondary education or the workforce.

Minoritized: Minoritized youth are those identified as members of an ethnic/racial group that is not White.

Opportunity youth: Opportunity youth in the workforce refers to young people aged 16 to 24 who are disconnected from school and work. In education this term also refers to students who have shown persistence and grit in regular coursework and should be enrolled in advanced coursework with appropriate supports.

Pathways: Pathways in high schools are created as a sequence of courses to expose students to academics and careers. They should allow students to explore their talents and interests while preparing them for postsecondary pursuits aligned to their skills and goals.

Push in/push out: Push in/push out refers to specialized support services for English learners, students receiving special education, and students who need additional academic support. A push in program has teachers pushing into general education classes to provide supports, whereas a push out program has the students leaving their general education classes to receive services.

Schedule: What was traditionally referred to as the "master schedule" is called the "site schedule" in this book, as the use of the word "master" is associated with oppression.

Strategic: A strategic approach to scheduling considers the interdependent nature of school processes and systems and leverages these to create a schedule that reflects the needs of all students.

Student cohort: A student cohort in a pathway model refers to a group of students who are assigned the same set of classes so they can be taught by a teaching team and learn collaboratively. Students typically form close relationships with one another as well as with their teachers over time.

Student information system: A student information system (SIS) is the software application used to manage student-related data in a school district.

Supplemental funding: The majority of school funding is provided through state and local governments. The federal government provides a small share of education funding through specific grant programs. These programs are designed to supplement funding for schools with at-risk youth, including students with disabilities or from low-income households.

Teaching team: A teaching team in a pathway model refers to a group of teachers that is assigned a cohort of students. These teachers use collaborative time to co-plan and collaborate for interdisciplinary experiences for the students.

Technical: A technical approach to scheduling focuses on changing processes, patterns, and structures in the schedules without considering the impact these changes have on the staff and students being scheduled.

Tier 1 instruction: Tier 1 instruction provides all students with high-quality, initial classroom instruction tied to a guaranteed and viable curriculum powered by research-backed strategies.

Tier 1 mainstream: Tier 1 mainstream—or the universal tier—is the curriculum, instruction, and assessment provided to all students in a grade level. This is the instruction and grade-level standards that are guaranteed for everyone.

Underestimated youth: Underestimated youth refers to school-age children who are typically underserved and approached as having "deficits," thus creating achievement gaps and unfulfilled potential for so many children.

REFERENCES

Alhadabi, A., & Li, J. (2020). Trajectories of academic achievement in high schools: Growth mixture model. *Journal of Educational Issues, 6*(1), 140–165.

Anaissie, T., Cary, V., Clifford, D., Malarkey, T., & Wise, S. (2024). *Liberatory design: Mindsets and modes to design for equity*. Jasso Plattner Institute of Design at Stanford University. https://dschool.stanford.edu/resources/liberatory-design-cards

Annie E. Casey Foundation. (2011). *Double jeopardy: How third-grade reading skills and poverty influence high school graduation*. https://eric.ed.gov/?id=ED518818

Annie E. Casey Foundation. (2014). *Embracing equity: 7 steps to advance and embed race equity and inclusion within your organization*. https://www.aecf.org/m/resourcedoc/AECF_EmbracingEquity7Steps-2014.pdf

Argys, L. M., Rees, D., & Brewer, D. (1996). Detracking America's schools: Equity at zero cost? *Journal of Policy Analysis and Management, 15*(4), 623–645.

Asia Society. (2023). *Understanding the world through math*. https://asiasociety.org/education/understanding-world-through-math

Bae, S. (2017). *It's about time: Organizing schools for teacher collaboration and learning*. Stanford Center for Opportunity Policy in Education.

Balfanz, R., DePaoli, J. L., Ingram, E. S., Bridgeland, J. M., & Fox, J. H. (2016). *A roadmap to postsecondary readiness and attainment*. Civic Enterprises.

Bastian, K. C., & Henry, G. T. (2015). The apprentice: Pathways to the principalship and student achievement. *Educational Administration Quarterly, 51*(4), 600–639.

Berwick, C. (2019, August 9). Is it time to detrack math? *Edutopia*. https://www.edutopia.org/article/it-time-detrack-math

Béteille, T., Kalogrides, D., & Loeb, S. (2012). Stepping stones: Principal career paths and school outcomes. *Social Science Research, 41*(4), 904–919.

Boaler, J. (2013). Ability and mathematics: The mindset revolution that is reshaping education. *FORUM, 55*(1), 143–152.

Boaler, J. (2016). *Mathematical mindsets: Unleashing students' potential through creative math, inspiring messages and innovative teaching*. Jossey-Bass.

Boaler, J., Schoenfeld, A., Daro, P., Asturias, H., Callahan, P., & Foster, D. (2018, October 9). Opinion: How one city got math right. *The Hechinger Report*. https://hechingerreport.org/opinion-how-one-city-got-math-right/

Bondie, R. S., Dahnke, C., & Zusho, A. (2019). How does changing "one-size-fits-all" to differentiated instruction affect teaching? *Review of Research in Education, 43*(1), 336–362.

Bottoms, G. (2022). How to transform high school? Let academics and career skills join forces. *Association for Supervision and Curriculum Development, 79*(8). https://www.ascd.org/el/articles/how-to-transform-high-school-let-academics-and-career-skills-join-forces

Bowles, S., & Gintis, H. (1976). *Schooling in capitalist America* (Vol. 57). Basic Books.

Bozick, R., & Ingels, S. J. (2008). *Mathematics coursetaking and achievement at the end of high school: Evidence from the education longitudinal study of 2002* (NCES 2008-319). U.S. Department of Education, National Center for Education Statistics.

Braddock, J. H., & Slavin, R. E. (1992). *Why ability grouping must end: Achieving excellence and equity in American education*. Center for Research on Effective Schooling for Disadvantaged Students.

Brown, B. (2018). *Dare to lead: Brave work, tough conversations, whole hearts*. Random House.

Bruno, P., Rabovsky, S., & Strunk, K. O. (2019). *Taking their first steps: The distribution of new teachers into school and classroom contexts and implications for teacher effectiveness and growth* (CALDER Working Paper No. 212-0119-1). Center for Analysis of Longitudinal Data in Education Research.

Bryk, A. S., Sebring, P. B., Allensworth, E., Easton, J. Q., & Luppescu, S. (2006). *The essential supports for school improvement*. University of Chicago Consortium on School Research.

Buczala, D. M. (2010). A comparative study of the Louisiana graduation exit exam science scores and student achievement based on block, *modified block, and traditional bell schedules* [Unpublished doctoral dissertation]. University of Louisiana at Monroe.

Burić, I., & Kim, L. E. (2020). Teacher self-efficacy, instructional quality, and student motivational beliefs: An analysis using multilevel structural equation modeling. *Learning and Instruction*, 66, 101302.

Burris, C. C., & Garrity, D. T. (2008). *Detracking for excellence and equity*. Association for Supervision and Curriculum Development.

Callahan, R. E. (1964). *Education and the cult of efficiency*. University of Chicago Press.

Carter, P. L., Welner, K. G., & Ladson-Billings, G. (2013). *Closing the opportunity gap: What America must do to give all children an even chance*. Oxford University Press.

Chenoweth, K. (2016). ESSA offers changes that can continue learning gains. *Phi Delta Kappan*, 97(8), 38–42.

Chetty, R., Friedman, J. N., & Rockoff, J. E. (2014). Measuring the impacts of teachers II: Teacher value-added and student outcomes in adulthood. *American Economic Review*, 104(9), 2633–2679.

City, E. A., Elmore, R., Fiarman, S., & Teitel, L. (2009). *Instructional rounds in education*. Harvard Educational Publishing Group.

Clay, A., Chu, E., Altieri, A., Deane, Y., Lis-Perli, A., Lizarraga, A., Monz, L., Muhammad, J., Recinos, D., Tache, J. A., & Wolters, M. (2021, May 4). *About time: Master scheduling and equity*. Center for Public Research and Leadership, Columbia Law School.

Coleman, J. S. (1966). *Equality of educational opportunity*. National Center for Educational Statistics, U.S. Department of Health, Education, and Welfare.

College & Career Alliance Support Network. (2018). *Master schedule guide*. https://casn.berkeley.edu/master-schedule-guide/

Daly, A. J. (2009). Rigid response in an age of accountability: The potential of leadership and trust. *Educational Administration Quarterly*, 45(2), 168–216.

Darling-Hammond, L. (2002). Research and rhetoric on teacher certification. *Education Policy Analysis Archives*, 10(36). https://epaa.asu.edu/index.php/epaa/article/view/315/441

Darling-Hammond, L., Ross, P., & Milliken, M. (2007). High school size, organization, and content: What matters for student success? *Brookings Papers on Educational Policy*, 163–203.

deGregory, A., & Sommer, C. (2021). *Improving equity through master scheduling* [Unpublished doctoral dissertation]. Lynn University.

DeMatthews, D. E. (2021, October 21). We're facing a looming crisis of principal burnout: School leaders are besieged by the pandemic and political battles. *Education Week*. https://www.edweek.org/leadership/opinion-were-facing-a-looming-crisis-of-principal-burnout/2021/10

Devilbiss, W. (1947). Criteria of a good master schedule. *NASSP Bulletin*, 31(149), 31–38.

Domina, T., McEachin, A., Hanselman, P., Agarwal, P., Hwang, N., & Lewis, R. (2016). *Beyond tracking and detracking: The dimensions of organizational differentiation in schools*. RAND Corporation.

Dweck, C. S. (2006). *Mindset: The new psychology of success*. Random House.

Education Commission of the States. (2005, October). *Prisoners of time*. https://www.ecs.org/clearinghouse/64/52/6452.pdf

Fullan, M. (2001). *Leading in a culture of change*. Jossey-Bass.

Fullan, M. (2014). *The principal: Three keys to maximizing impact*. Jossey-Bass.

Fullan, M. (2015). *The new meaning of educational change* (5th ed.). Routledge.

Futrell, M., & Gomez, J. (2008). How tracking creates a poverty of learning. *Educational Leadership*, 65(8), 74–78.

Goldhaber, D., Kasman, M., Quince, V., Theobald, R., & Wolff, M. (2023). *How did it get this way? Disentangling the sources of teacher quality gaps through agent-based modeling* (CALDER Working Paper No. 259-0223). Center for Analysis of Longitudinal Data in Education Research.

Grissom, J. A., Egalite, A. J., & Lindsay, C. A. (2021). How principals affect students and schools: A systematic synthesis of two decades of research. *The Wallace Foundation*. http://www.wallacefoundation.org/principalsynthesis

Grissom, J. A., Kalogrides, D., & Loeb, S. (2015). The micropolitics of educational inequality: The case of teacher–student assignments. *Peabody Journal of Education*, 90(5), 601–614.

Hahn, R. A., Knopf, J. A., Wilson, S. J., Truman, B. I., Milstein, B., Johnson, R. L., Fielding, J. E., Muntaner, C. J. M., Jones, C. P., Fullilove, M. T., Moss, R. D., Ueffing, E., & Hunt, P. C. (2015). Programs to increase high school completion. *American Journal of Preventive Medicine*, 48(5), 599–608.

Hammond, Z. (2015). *Culturally responsive teaching & the brain: Promoting authentic engagement and rigor among culturally and linguistically diverse students*. Corwin.

Hattie, J. (2008). *Visible learning*. Routledge.

Hibbeln, C. (2020, June 2). What transcripts reveal about our schools' values, priorities and inequities. *EdSurge News*. https://www.edsurge.com/news/2020-06-02-what-transcripts-reveal-about-our-schools-values-priorities-and-inequities

Higgins, M. (2019, Summer). Getting on the right track: How one school stopped tracking students. *Learning for Justice Magazine*, 62. https://www.learningforjustice.org/magazine/summer-2019/getting-on-the-right-track-how-one-school-stopped-tracking-students

Hilliard, A. (1991). Do we have the will to educate all children? *Educational Leadership*, 49(1), 31–36.

Intercultural Development Research Association. (2020, April 29). *Six goals of educational equity*. https://www.idra.org/equity-assistance-center/six-goals-of-education-equity/

Irizarry, Y. (2021, January 11). On track or derailed? Race, advanced math, and the transition to high school. *Sociological Research for a Dynamic World*. https://doi.org/10.1177/2378023120980293

Jones, C. (2024, April 19). More California high school students want career training: How the state is helping. CalMatters. https://calmatters.org/education/k-12-education/2024/04/career-pathways/

Kalogrides, D., & Loeb, S. (2013). Different teachers, different peers: The magnitude of student sorting within schools. *Educational Researcher*, 42(6), 304–316.

Kalogrides, D., Loeb, S., & Beteille, T. (2013). Systematic sorting: Teacher characteristics and class assignments. *Sociology of Education*, 86(2), 103–123.

Kanno, Y., & Kangas, S. E. N. (2014). "I'm not going to be, like, for the AP": English language learners' limited access to advanced college-preparatory courses in high school. *American Educational Research Journal*, 51(5), 848–878.

Kelly, A. M. (2013). Physics teachers' perspectives on factors that affect urban physics participation and accessibility. *Physical Review Physics Education Research*, 9(1), 010122. https://doi.org/10.1103/PhysRevSTPER.9.010122

Kelly, S., & Carbonaro, W. (2012). Curriculum tracking and teacher expectations: Evidence from discrepant course taking models. *Social Psychology of Education*, 15, 271–294.

Kettler, T., & Hurst, L. T. (2017). Advanced academic participation: A longitudinal analysis of ethnicity gaps in suburban schools. *Journal for the Education of the Gifted*, 40(1), 3–19.

Kezar, A., Holcombe, E., Vigil, D., & Mathias Dizon, J. P. (2021). *Shared equity leadership: Making equity everyone's work*. University of Southern California Pullias Center for Higher Education; American Council on Education.

Lafors, J., & McGlawn, T. (2013). Expanding access, creating options: How linked learning pathways can mitigate barriers to college and career access in schools and districts. *The Education Trust–West*.

Leithwood, K., Seashore Louis, K., Anderson, S., & Wahlstrom, K. (2004). *How leadership influences student learning*. The Wallace Foundation. https://wallacefoundation.org/sites/default/files/2023-07/How-Leadership-Influences-Student-Learning.pdf

Levitan, S., Holston, S., & Walsh, K. (2022). *Ensuring students' equitable access to qualified and effective teachers*. National Council on Teacher Quality.

Linderman, J. (1975). *Time pattern analysis in school scheduling* (Publication No. 0293980) [Doctoral dissertation, Massachusetts Institute of Technology]. ProQuest Dissertations and Theses Global.

Louis, K. S., & Marks, H. M. (1998). Does professional community affect the classroom? Teachers' work and student experiences in restructuring schools. *American Journal of Education*, 106(4), 532–575.

Lovely, S. D. (2020, October). Setting constructive rebellion in motion. *School Administrator*, 9(77), 40–43.

Luschei, T. F., & Jeong, D. W. (2019). Is teacher sorting a global phenomenon? Cross-national evidence on the nature and correlates of teacher quality opportunity gaps. *Educational Researcher*, 47, 556–576.

Mathis, W. J. (2013, May 13). *Research overwhelmingly counsels an end to tracking* [Press release]. National Education Policy Center. http://tinyurl.com/qa6cof3

McCoss-Yergian, T., & Krepps, L. (2010). Do teacher attitudes impact literacy strategy implementation in content area classrooms? *Journal of Instructional Pedagogies*, 4. https://www.aabri.com/manuscripts/10519.pdf

McFarland, J., Hussar, B., Wang, X., Zhang, J., Wang, K., Rathbun, A., Barmer, A., Forrest Cataldi, E., & Bullock Mann, F. (2018). *The condition of education* (NCES 2018-144). U.S. Department of Education, National Center for Education Statistics. https://nces.ed.gov/pubsearch/pubsinfo.asp?pubid=2018144

Mehta, J., & Fine, S. M. (2019). *In search of deeper learning: The quest to remake the American high school*. Harvard University Press.

Meyer, J. W. (1977). The effects of education as an institution. *American Journal of Sociology*, 83, 55–77.

National Association of Secondary School Principals. (2011). *The master schedule: A culture indicator*. https://www.escco.org/Downloads/Master%20Schedule%20as%20a%20Culture%20Indicator.pdf

National Council on Disability. (2018). *The segregation of students with disabilities*. https://www.ncd.gov/assets/uploads/docs/ncd-segregation-swd-508.pdf

National Equity Project. (2021). *Six circle model*. https://www.nationalequityproject.org/resources/frameworks

Nation's Report Card. (2024). *National achievement-level results*. https://www.nationsreportcard.gov/reading/nation/achievement/?grade=8.

Ngo, F., & Velasquez, D. (2020, March 3). Inside the math trap: Chronic math tracking from high school to community college. *Urban Education*, 58(8), 1629–1657.

Nord, C., Roey, S., Perkins, R., Lyons, M., Lemanski, N., Brown, J., & Schuknecht, J. (2011). *The nation's report card: America's high school graduates* (NCES 2011-462). U.S. Department of Education, National Center for Education Statistics. https://nces.ed.gov/nationsreportcard/pdf/studies/2011462.pdf

Oakes, J. (2005). *Keeping track: How schools structure inequality*. Yale University Press.

Oakes, J. (2008). Keeping track: Structuring equality and inequality in an era of accountability. *Teachers College Record*, 110(3), 700–712.

Ortiz, S. (2020, March 13). Underestimated youth in underestimated communities. *Micro Is the New Macro*. https://medium.com/micro-is-the-new-macro

Pisoni, A., & Conti, D. (2019, April 20). What does your school schedule say about equity? More than you think. *EdSurge*. https://www.edsurge.com/news/2019-04-20-what-does-your-school-schedule-say-about-equity-more-than-you-think

Ravitch, S., & Herzog, L. (2024). *Leadership mindsets for adaptive change: The flux 5*. Routledge.

Reardon, S. F., Weathers, E. S., Fahle, E. M., Jang, H., & Kalogrides, D. (2019). *Is separate still unequal: New evidence on school segregation and racial academic achievement gaps* (CEPA Working Paper No. 19–06). Stanford Center for Education Policy Analysis. https://cepa.stanford.edu/sites/default/files/wp19-06-v092021.pdf

Richardson, W., & Tavangar, H. (2021). *9 big questions schools must answer to avoid going "back to normal."* BIG Questions Institute. https://bigquestions.institute/9-questions/

Rickabaugh, J. (2016). *Tapping the power of personalized learning: A roadmap for school leaders*. Association for Supervision and Curriculum Development.

Rix, K. (2022, December 27). *The benefits of career and technical education programs for High schoolers*. U.S. News & World Report. https://www.usnews.com/education/k12/articles/the-benefits-of-career-and-technical-education-programs-for-high-schoolers

Sampson, C. (2019). *Stratification, tracking and course-taking patterns: An examination of the impact of mathematics course placement on achievement in a regional high school district* [Doctoral dissertation, Seton Hall University]. Dissertations and Theses, 2635. https://scholarship.shu.edu/dissertations/2635/

San Diego Unified School District. (2023). *San Diego enhanced mathematics*. https://sites.google.com/sandi.net/enhancedmath/home

Saunders, W. M., & Marcelletti, D. J. (2013). The gap that can't go away: The catch-22 of reclassification in monitoring the progress of English learners. *Educational Evaluation and Policy Analysis*, 35(2), 139–156.

Schiller, K. S., & Hunt, D. J. (2011). Secondary mathematics course trajectories: Understanding accumulated disadvantages in mathematics in grades 9–12. *Journal of School Leadership*, 21, 118–187.

Schiller, K. S., Schmidt, W. H., Muller, C., & Houang, R. (2010). Hidden disparities: How courses and curricula shape opportunities in mathematics during high school. *Equity & Excellence in Education*, 43(4), 414–433.

Shifrer, D., Callahan, R. M., & Muller, C. (2013). Equity or marginalization? The high school course-taking of students labeled with a learning disability. *American Educational Research Journal*, 50(4), 656–682.

Sof, E. (2018, July 22). *9 Navy SEAL quotes to improve your life*. https://special-ops.org/9-navy-seal-quotes-to-improve-your-life/

Sparacio, S. (1973). The master schedule—A pattern for schools. *Associated Public School Systems, APSS Know How*, 24(8), 1–5.

Spring, J. (2019). *American education* (19th ed.). Routledge.

Steenbergen-Hu, S., Makel, M. C., & Olszewski-Kubilius, P. (2016). What one hundred years of research says about the effects of ability grouping and acceleration on K–12 students' academic achievement: Findings of two second-order meta-analyses. *Review of Educational Research*, 86(4), 849–899.

Stern, D., Dayton, C., & Raby, M. (2010). *Career academies: A proven strategy to prepare high school students for college and careers*. University of California, Berkeley, Career Academy Support Network.

TNTP. (2018). *The opportunity myth: What students can show us about how school is letting them down—and how to fix it*. https://tntp.org/publication/the-opportunity-myth/

Travers, J. (2018). *What is resource equity?* https://files.eric.ed.gov/fulltext/ED593369.pdf

Tyack, D., & Cuban, L. (1995). *Tinkering toward utopia: A century of public school reform*. Harvard University Press.

U.S. Department of Education Office for Civil Rights. (2014, March). *Civil rights data collection: Data snapshot: College and career readiness* (Issue Brief No. 3). https://www2.ed.gov/about/offices/list/ocr/docs/crdc-college-and-career-readiness-snapshot.pdf

Villegas, L., & Ibarra, M. A. (2022, August 8). Former English learners outperform English-only peers on Texas' state assessments. *New America* [Blog post]. https://www.newamerica.org/education-policy/edcentral/former-english-learners-outperform-english-only-peers-on-texas-state-assessments/

Walqui, A. (2006). Scaffolding instruction for English language learners: A conceptual framework. *International Journal of Bilingual Education and Bilingualism*, 9(2), 159–180.

Wheatley, M. J. (2006). *Leadership and the new science: Discovering order in a chaotic world*. Berrett-Koehler.

Wheatley, M. J., & Dalmau, T. (1983). *Below the green line or the 6 circle model* [Unpublished manuscript].

Wilson, S. J., & Tanner-Smith, E. E. (2013). Dropout prevention and intervention programs for improving school completion among school-aged children and youth: A systematic review. *Journal of the Society for Social Work and Research*, 4(4), 357–372.

Yavuz, O. (2016). Educational leadership and comprehensive reform for improving equity and access for all. *International Journal of Education Policy & Leadership*, 11(10). http://journals.sfu.ca/ijepl/index.php/ijepl/article/view/684

Yonezawa, S., Wells, A. S., & Serna, I. (2002). Choosing tracks: "Freedom of choice" in detracking schools. *American Educational Research Journal*, 39(1), 37–67.

Yonezawa, S. S. (2000). Unpacking the black box of tracking decisions: Critical tales of families navigating the course placement process. In M. G. Sanders (Ed.), *Schooling students placed at risk: Research, policy, and practice in the education of poor and minority adolescents* (pp. 109–137). Lawrence Erlbaum.

Zajacova A., & Lawrence, E. M. (2018, April 1). The relationship between education and health: Reducing disparities through a contextual approach. *Annual Review of Public Health*, 39, 273–289.

INDEX

Act on equity, 53–56
Actualize equity, 36–37
Adjust for equity, 56–57
Advanced placement (AP), 15, 116
Advanced placement (AP) English Language and Composition, 59
Advancement via individual determination (AVID), 117
Agents, 8
  of compliance, 6–7
Allocational tool, 143–151
  acceleration, 150
  additional decisions, 150–151
  Architects of Equity, 144
  Equitable Core course work vs. additional strategies, 148
  Equity High School, 145, 145 (figure)–147 (figure)
  graduation requirement teacher minimums, 147–148, 147 (figure)
  student access to tier 1, 149
Anderson, S., 6
Architect of Equity, 6, 8, 17, 19, 21, 25, 30, 110, 113, 126, 144
Articulation process, 153 (figure)
  course selection process, 153
  course tally and verification process, 154
  section building, loading, and balancing, 154
  staffing assignments, 154
Asia Society, 66
Assess equity, 39–40

Being known well in school, 107–114
  common planning (prep) periods, 111–113, 112 (figure)
  competing priorities, 113–114, 114 (figure)
  teaching teams, 110, 111 (figure)

Bell schedules, 165–166
  cost of, 166–168
  mindset, 96–99
  selection considerations, 168
  traditional, 166
Boaler, Jo, 66
Builder, 7
Butts in seats, 5

Career technical education (CTE), 106
  course failure, 134
Climate changes, 2
Cohorting, 126–127, 128 (figure)
  definition of, 126
  graduation requirements, 129–130
  notice and note, 130–134
  schedule frame built, 130, 133 (figure)
  seven-period schedule cohorting model, 128–129, 129 (figure)
Collaborative learning experiences, 106
Collaborative teams, 110, 111 (figure)
Common planning (prep) periods, 111–113
  collaborative tasks, 111, 112 (figure)
  personalized learning, 111, 112 (figure)
  sacrosanct calendar, 111–112
  shared documents, 113
  standard agenda format, 112–113
Competing priorities, 113–117, 114 (figure)
  advanced course work options, 116
  built around programs, 117
  co-requisite supports, 117
  co-teaching, 117
  course mandates, 117
  critical elements of, 115, 116 (figure)
  pathway courses and students, 117
Confronting, 16–17
Conti, D., 25
Co-requisites, 69, 117
Co-teaching, 117

Counselor verification, 162–163
Course mandates, 117
Course of study assessments, 40–42
Course sequencing, 61
Course tally process, 157
  accurate enrollment counts, 163–164
  counselor verification, 162–163
  mandate verification, 163
  notice and note, 158–164
  organizing, 162 (figure)
  sample, 161 (figure)
  steps, 163 (figure)
Cuban, L., 13

Dalmau, T., 26
Deficit mindset, 86 (figure)
Designer, 7
Designing systems strategies, 74–77
Dual enrollment staffing, 96
Dweck, C., 22, 85, 85 (figure)

Educational services, 34
Enabling conditions, pathway design, 123–126, 123 (figure)
  broad pathway themes, 124
  designing teacher lines, 125
  integrating interests within courses/pathways, 124–125
  limiting pathway course sequences, 124
  matching teacher and student interests, 125
  organizing teacher teams, 125
  pathway enrollment, 123–124
  providing clarity on integration, 125
  student information system, 126
English language arts (ELA), 137
English Language Development (ELD), 81
English learners, 15, 86–91
Equitable core, 62, 68, 75, 117, 138
  designing systems strategies, 74–77
  equitable scheduling commitments, 72–74
  proactive monitoring, 77–78
  sorting talent, 60–62
  traditional sequencing, 63–72
Equitable scheduling
  commitments, 72–74
  considerations, 165 (figure)
Equity actualizing, 37–38
Equity by design, 175–187
  counseling activity timelines, 181

dual enrollment timelines, 178–181
input during timelines, 184–187
intentional structuring of time, 176–177
operating without timelines, 183–184
overall district and site scheduling timelines, 177–183
registrar timelines, 181–182
scheduling teams, guiding structures, 175–176
site tech/builder timelines, 182–183
Equity-driven schedule, 16

Fidelity, 107
Fullan, Michael, 10
Full-time equivalent (FTE), 96, 140
  teacher allocation, 141
Futrell, M., 61

Global Political Economic Decision Making (GLOPED), 93
Gomez, J., 61
Good intentions, 34–36
Grade-appropriate courses, 83
Graduation Procedure, 75
Graduation requirements, 129–130, 139–141, 139 (figure)
  staffing allocation, 140 (figure)
Growth mindset, 86 (figure)

High school scheduling expectations, 54–56, 196–199
Hilliard, Asa, 2

Individualized educational plans (IEPs), 35, 84
Inequitable outcomes, 34–36
Inequitable scheduling practices, 137–138
International baccalaureate (IB), 15, 116
Invisible hand of equity
  designing scheduling teams, 6–8
  focus maintaining, 10–11
  logistical scheduling vs. strategic scheduling, 8–10, 9 (figure)
  problems, 2–6
  scheduling mindsets, 1–2

Jeong, D. W., 8

K-12 school system, 63

Language other than English (LOTE), 72
Leaky pipeline assessments, 50–53

Leaky Pipeline to Graduation, 2, 3 (figure)
Leithwood, K., 6
Linked Learning
  AP, IB, and college coursework, 195
  assigning teacher preps, 194
  eliminate tracking and limit, 195
  English learners and students with IEPs, 195
  maximizing instructional time, 194
  pathway access, 194
  physical classroom assignments, 196
  planning time within the school day, 194
  recovering credits, 196
  scheduling incoming 9th grade students, 196
  strategic science sequencing, 196
  strategic sequencing of VAPA courses, 195
  strategic staffing, 196
  strategic supports, 195
Logistical scheduling, strategic scheduling vs., 8–10, 9 (figure)
Luschei, T. F., 8

Margins, scheduling
  barriers to, 99–101
  bell schedules and mindset, 96–99
  dual enrollment staffing, 96
  mindset, 83–96
  strategies for, 99
Mathis, W, 22
Math work, 118–123
  four pathways, 119, 120 (figure)
  potential pathway themes and sequences, 122–123
  pre-mapping Sunport High School, 118
  Sunport's current CTE offerings, 121–122
  three pathways, 119, 121 (figure)
Middle school scheduling expectations, 199–200
Mindset, 16, 83–96
Multiple four-year diploma, 83

National Association of Secondary School Principals, 4
National Center for Education Statistics, 68
Next Generation Science Standards (NGSS), 71
Ngo, F., 62

Opportunity sequence, 66
Own team discomfort, 19–21

Parallel courses, 83
Personalized learning, 111, 112 (figure)
Pisoni, A., 25
PK–12, 4
Postsecondary readiness data, 108
Prerequisites, 69
Proactive monitoring, 77–78
Professional learning communities (PLCs), 106
  time, 107
  transformative potential, 107

Racial unrest, 2
Resource equity, 137–174
  adjusted teacher minimums, 151–152
  aligning allocations connected to mandates, 152–153
  allocational tool, 143–151
  assigning teachers, 164–165
  avoiding misaligned course selection processes, 154–156
  avoiding singleton madness, 156–157
  bad build, 170
  bell schedule selection, 165–168
  building sections, 164
  course tally process, 157–164
  graduation requirements, 139–141
  schedule balance, 168–170
  site funding, 139–141
  standard model, 141
  student enrollment, 139–141
  supplemental services removed model, 142–143
  tools to monitor, 170–173
Right of assignment, 94
Road map, equitable core as
  designing systems strategies, 74–77
  equitable scheduling commitments, 72–74
  proactive monitoring, 77–78
  sorting talent, 60–62
  traditional sequencing, 63–72
Robotics, 105

Sacrosanct calendar, 111–112
Schedule assessments, 44–47
Schedule balance, 168–170
  course assignment balance, 170
  preparatory period balance, 169–170
  section and enrollment balance, 169–170
Scheduling mindsets, 1–2
Scheduling teams, 6–8, 109

credibility of, 113
guiding structures, 175–176
Scheduling theory of action, 6 (figure)
Scheduling whisperer
  act on equity, 53–56
  adjust for equity, 56–57
  assess equity, 39–40
  equity actualizing, 37–38
  good intentions, 34–36
  inequitable outcomes, 34–36
  leaky pipeline assessments, 50–53
  schedule assessments, 44–47
  self-assessment, four A's of, 36–37, 36 (figure)
  study assessments course, 40–44
  transcript assessments, 46–50
School leadership, 2
School personalization, 108
School shootings, 2
Science, technology, engineering, or math (STEM), 71
Seashore Louis, K., 6
Self-assessment, four A's of, 36–37, 36 (figure)
Seven-period schedule cohorting model, 128–129, 129 (figure)
Shared documents, 113
Shifting traditional scheduling mindsets, 15–16
Singleton, 156–157, 158 (figure)
Site funding, 139–141, 139 (figure)
Social justice movements, 2
Social media, 2
Social security number, 110
Sorting talent, 60–62
Staffing allocation
  graduation requirements, 140 (figure)
  total enrollment projections, 141
Status Quo
  changing practice, 29–30
  confronting, 16–17
  looking forward, 29–30
  own team discomfort, 19–21
  shifting traditional scheduling mindsets, 15–16
  strategically transforming, 25–26
  team mindset challenging, 22–25
  technical and adaptive changes, 27 (figure)–28 (figure)

uncover personal barriers, 19
Strategically transforming, 25–26
Strategic self-assessment, 34
Strategic structures, 105–135
  being known well in school, 107–114
  cohorting, 126–134
  competing priorities, 115–117
  CTE course failure, 134
  enabling conditions, 123–126
  math work, 118–123
  pathway balance, 134
  pathway failure, 134
  pathway size, 134
  wall-to-wall pathways, 107, 108 (figure)
Student enrollment, 139–141, 139 (figure)
Student information system (SIS), 7, 118, 126
Study assessments course, 40–44

Teaching teams, 110, 111 (figure)
Team mindset challenging, 22–25
Technical and adaptive changes, 27 (figure)–28 (figure)
Theory of action, 3 (figure)
Traditional conversations, 2
Traditional school scheduling priorities, 114
Traditional sequencing, 63–72
Transcript assessments, 46–50
Travers, J., 138
Tyack, D., 13

Uncover personal barriers, 19
Under-enrollment, 137
University of California Curriculum Institute, 124
U.S. Navy SEAL, 20

Vacant seat analysis tool, 173 (figure)
Velasquez, D., 62
Visionary, 7

Wahlstrom, K, 6
Wheatley, M. J., 26
World language (WL), 98

ZIP Code, 110

CORWIN
A Sage Publishing Company

Helping educators make the greatest impact

CORWIN HAS ONE MISSION: to enhance education through intentional professional learning. We build long-term relationships with our authors, educators, clients, and associations who partner with us to develop and continuously improve the best evidence-based practices that establish and support lifelong learning.

Equity in Education
Is every student in your school thriving?

Street Data
Shane Safir
Jamila Dugan

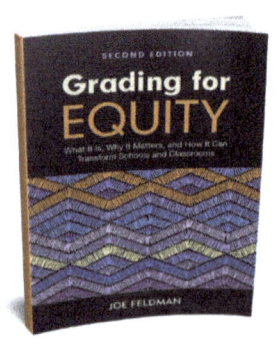

Grading for Equity
Second Edition
Joe Feldman

Culturally Responsive Teaching & the Brain
Zaretta Hammond

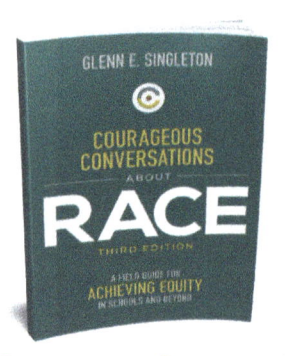

Courageous Conversations About Race
Third Edition
Glenn E. Singleton

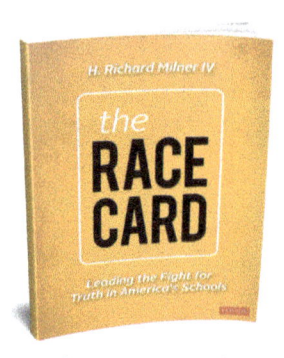

The Race Card
H. Richard Milner IV

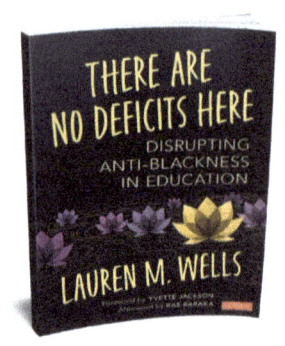

There Are No Deficits Here
Lauren M. Wells

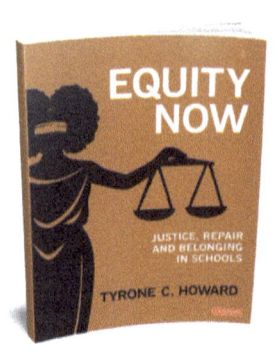

Equity Now
Tyrone C. Howard

Start With Radical Love
Crystal Belle

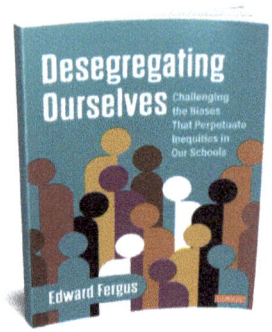

Desegregating Ourselves
Edward Fergus

To find these and other best-selling books, visit **corwin.com/EquityBooks**

GP241067104

Free Professional Development

WEBINARS
Listen and interact with education experts for an hour of professional learning to gain practical tools and evidence-based strategies—and maybe win some free books!

LEADERS COACHING LEADERS PODCAST
Join Peter M. DeWitt, Michael Nelson, and their guests as they discuss evidence-based approaches for tackling pressing topics that all education leaders face.

CORWIN CONNECT
Read and engage with us on our blog about the latest in education and professional development.

SAMPLE CONTENT
Did you know you can download sample content from almost every Corwin book on our website? Go to corwin.com/resources for tools you and your staff can use right away!

SOCIAL JUSTICE RESEARCH
Takeaways for K–12 from the latest research on advancing educational equity and justice.

corwin.com/resources

CORWIN